JOB INTERVIEW

This book includes:

GUIDE TO A WINNING INTERVIEW

HOW TO ANSWER QUESTIONS

PREPARATION

QUESTIONS AND ANSWERS

JIM HUNTING

Table of Contents

GUIDE TO A WINNING INTERVIEW

HOW TO ANSWER INTERVIEW QUESTIONS

INTERVIEW PREPARATION

JOB INTERVIEW QUESTIONS AND ANSWERS

GUIDE TO A WINNING INTERVIEW

Questions and Answers for Job Interview Success. How to Be More Confident, Be Yourself and Answer Interview Questions.

Jim Hunting

Introduction

Whether you are a fresh college graduate or someone who is looking to kick start a new career, one of the things that you should be fully cognizant of is the dynamics of the job-hunting process including of course the often-dreaded interview portion.

While there is no right way to do an interview, there are a couple of pointers that you should take note and be mindful of to make sure that your interview goes well and hopefully helps you land your target job.

However, even before embarking on a job-hunting adventure, it is essential that you develop a deep sense of self-awareness. Knowing who you are, what your values and competencies are, as well as what your goals are will help you in coming up with a clearer vision of your future self.

Know what you do best.

Applying for a job should always be preceded by identifying the things that you are capable of doing well. A longstanding problem in the labor market is the apparent mismatch of jobs available and the skill set of the labor pool. If you want to have a job that you are competent and fully comfortable in, you should look for positions that cater to your abilities and strengths.

Find your market.

If you are looking for a job in the finance industry, it makes sense that you look for one in a financial district. If you are looking for an arts-related profession, you need to factor in the available art venues and spaces in a particular place. On some occasions, this might mean that you have to step out of your comfort zone and move in to an entirely new area.

Know how much you are worth.

Since applying for a job is essentially a way of showcasing your knowledge and experience in a particular field, then it goes without saying that you should have a clear idea of how much you should be worth. Don't be afraid to aim for the best.

Improve on your skills, if you must.

Some jobs require specialized skills, experience or educational attainment. If you are keen on earning such kind of job, then you should take the time and effort to meet the basic criteria.

Have realistic and reasonable expectations.

Your excitement and enthusiasm over the prospect of getting a job you like should be guarded by reason and logic. This doesn't mean that you should sport a pessimistic outlook, either. Basically, you should have a way of gauging your abilities and your performance in the exercise of such abilities. You should be honest enough to admit if there's any weakness you should work on or conversely, highlight the strengths that you can use as leverage in the future.

Find the right motivation.

There is nothing more powerful than being motivated to reach your goals. But motivation comes in different forms for different people. Some see money as a powerful motivating factor. In choosing jobs, they go for openings with a relatively higher pay.

Meanwhile, other people lean more toward job opportunities that provide a profound sense of satisfaction and boost their sense of self-worth. When picking jobs, these people look at the culture of the workplace and gauge it based on how being part of this particular organization can make them better.

Ideal worker mindset

But no matter the motivation, an inarguably essential factor to take into account is the importance of developing an ideal worker mindset. You must come across as a perfect fit to the job opening that you are aiming for. Your skills, attitude and character must match the requirements of this particular employment opportunity.

A good way of making yourself better prepared for the challenges of job hunting is by making yourself familiar with the dynamics of the labor market, as well as the history and background of the specific organization that you want to be a part of including the working environment.

Chapter 1: Crafting Your Cover Letter

Now that you understand what a cover letter is and its importance, it is time to learn how to craft your own well-written letter, also known as a CV.

While there are many dos and don'ts in writing a cover letter, thankfully, there is a basic pattern that every professional cover letter should follow.

You can use this guideline with your own information to ensure that your CV is always the correct format.

A basic no-fuss cover letter should consist of:

- Your Name
- Phone number
- Email address
- Date
- Addressed to the name and professional title of the hiring manager
- Name of the company you are applying for a position at

This is the most basic of cover letter guidelines, as you can see, it doesn't even contain much information on the individual. This is because while the standard guideline above is needed, the rest of the letter can be highly personalized.

Along with the above guideline, you also must add other information. This can include a variety of components, depending upon the person. Some options include:

- The address of your professional website

- Your professional title

- Your home address

- Links to your LinkedIn or Twitter

- City of Residence

While you want to illustrate your personality in your cover letter, it is important to do so in a professional manner.

For instance, you want to use an email address that illustrates professionalism. Such as [your name]@gmail.com or email@[your website].com.

You never want to include unprofessional email addresses on your cover letter or resume, as this can be a deal breaker. If your email is something such as SexyTiger135@gmail.com or

CottonCandyFTW@yahoo.com you will want to create a new email address for professional purposes.

Ideally, you want to stick with either Gmail or an email created with your own website domain, as these are seen as the most professional options.

Similarly, you should avoid using an email address that contains your current work information.

If your professional email address contains your current company or position, it is disrespectful to both your previous company and the new company to use this address.

Lastly, ensure that your contact information is consistent across the board. You want your resume, cover letter, and social media to all use the same information.

You now understand the basic format of your cover letter and the most important information to include in each and every CV. However, these are only the bare bones of a cover letter.

You still need to include information that will make the employer want to hire you. For that, follow the tips below to get a customized and successful letter.

Use the Proper Format

The cover letter, while it can show your personality, needs to remain professional.

For this reason, use the same formal format that you would for any professional or business matter.

For this, you want to use either Times New Roman, Calibri, or Arial fonts in size twelve or ten point.

When writing your name, contact information, and date align them along the top of the letter. Lastly, keep the cover letter to a single page with three or four short paragraphs.

Address the Hiring Manager

Some people may address this cover letter's to "whom it may concern," but this is bad practice.

This will make it appear that you either have not done enough research on the company or that you are mass producing this CV to send out to multiple companies.

Instead, you want to directly address your letter to the person who will be hiring you. This person's name may be written in the job posting.

However, if it is not, then try calling the main phone number for the company and asking for both the name and position of the hiring manager.

This may seem like an unnecessary step; however, it will leave a big impression on the hiring manager and increase your likelihood of getting hired.

This will also give you the opportunity to learn more about the company in general.

If you have any personal connections to the company and would-be colleges then feel free to subtly mention these connections.

By doing this, it gives the hiring manager the opportunity to ask the people who know you their opinion of your work ethic and capability.

Use Keywords

Often times, employers don't simply read through every cover letter they receive. Instead, they may run it through a filtering software that is meant to scan for keywords in resumes.

This software allows an employer to wade through resumes and cover letters, only reading those that match their preferred keywords of desired skills and experience.

In order to get your cover letter read, you need to naturally and conversationally incorporate key phrases and words that fit the job's description.

You can do this by mentioning how many years of experience you have, degree type, developed skills, communication and organization abilities, and any history you have in project management.

Some examples of keywords to use include:

- Skill Keywords:

- Planned, wrote, analyzed, designed, quantified, programmed, trained, taught, surveyed, organized, critiqued, inspected, assembled, solved, engineered, maintained, operated, administered, appraised, audited, budgeted, calculated, projected, researched, directed, developed, performed, acted, established, fashioned, illustrated, founded, programmed, coached, communicated, instructed, enabled, encouraged, guided, informed, built.

- Result-Oriented Keywords:

- Implemented, planned, managed, upgraded, assessed, strengthened, persuaded, initiated, adapted, oversaw, lead, redesigned, helped, launched, began, adopted, boosted, headed, operated, increased, trained, educated, reformulated, expanded, acquired, generated, produced, initiated.

- Self-Descriptive Keywords:

- Independent, creative, unique, attentive, dependable, responsible, ambitious, analytical, sensitive, reliable, enthusiastic, adaptable, logical, initiative, efficient, experienced, effective, sincere, productive, personable, instrumental, honest, adept, loyal, diplomatic, insightful.

Keep the First Paragraph Strong

At the beginning of your letter, you should start with a strong and personal greeting directly to the hiring manager.

But, don't slack off after this greeting.

It is vital to have a strong opening paragraph that catches their attention and draws them into reading your entire letter and your resume.

This means that you absolutely must avoid any misspellings or typos.

You also need to include something interesting about yourself that sets you apart from the crowd.

While the entire cover letter is important, the most important areas to strengthen are the beginning and then end.

After all, it is vital to make a good first impression and leave off with a good impression.

Highlight Relevant Details

In your cover letter, you are able to go into more detail on how and why you are a perfect fit for a job.

While a resume simply highlights your experience, the cover letter explains why this experience makes you an ideal fit.

Therefore, when highlighting your experiences, be sure to stick with experiences and reasoning that fits the specific job.

For instance, if you were a waiter and are now applying to a job in another field, it may not at first appear that it is a relevant experience. Yet, the cover letter allows you to explain why this experience actually makes you the best fit. You can take the time to explain that your interactions with customers, managing disputes, and working as a team will enable you to better do the new job, if you are hired. If possible, try to use data and numbers to explain your strengths, as employers like to see hard numbers.

Tie Yourself to the Company

Whenever possible, speak of yourself in relation to the company.

This will show the hiring manager that you have knowledge of the company and convey enthusiasm.

You can do this by mentioning how much you care about the company's vision or mission.

If you have followed the company or used their products/services of years, you can mention how much they have beneficially impacted your life.

Similarly, you want to speak within the letter as if you have already been hired.

For instance, imagine that you are speaking to a manager after being hired and they ask why you chose the company.

You can answer with your interest in the company and enthusiasm about working for them.

For instance: "When I discovered DreamCloud Animation was hiring, I simply knew I must apply. I had been searching for a company that truly makes a difference, where I could make an impact. I was inspired by the company and their mission to consistently produce high-quality animation that tells a story to warm people hearts and increase the appreciation of the seemingly mundane. I believe in the mission of DreamCloud Animation, and I wanted to work with you so that I too can make a difference."

Name the Position Title

It may seem simple, but it is important to add in the name of the job title you are applying for.

This helps the employer to know that you are knowledgeable and understand what you are applying for.

This can be done easily, as you can say something to the effect of "Regarding the Graphic Design position," *or* "I am writing to apply for Floor Manager position [company name] recently advertised."

Illustrate How You Can Solve a Specific Problem

Are you a problem-solver? While stating this in a cover letter may seem beneficial, it actually has little impact on the hiring manager.

After all, what problems can you solve? By simply stating you are a problem-solver you might as well be saying you know how to "solve" the problem of not knowing what to eat for breakfast when the pantry is nearly bare.

Instead of telling the hiring manager that you are great at solving problems, detail exactly what problems you can help them solve.

How can you use your skills to help the company better and solve their problems? Take time to consider exactly what you can do for the company and then detail it.

Share a Story

You want your cover letter to be captivating, interesting, and informative.

One of the most successful ways in which you can do this is by sharing a story or anecdote about yourself.

This can allow the employer to get a better idea of your personality, work style, and skills. Although, it is important to share the right story while keeping it short and sweet.

How do you know if a story is right for your cover letter?

You can start by looking at the job description and researching the company.

Once you understand the position and company well, you can compare your skills, talents, and experience compared to what they are looking for in an employee.

For instance, the company might be looking for a team player, someone with communication skills, and a person who is able to resolve conflicts, and a person who is able to train those under them.

Keeping these aspects in mind, you can consider your past and think of an anecdote that contains as many of these traits as possible.

For instance, you might have volunteered at a place in which you managed a team, kept everyone on good terms while resolving conflicts, trained newcomers, and communicated the needs of the day to those working with you.

You can share this anecdote, while specifically mentioning these skills and traits you made use of.

By being able to hear a story of how you specifically have used your skills and traits in the past a company can get a better idea of how you will work on the job.

Stay Honest

The worst mistake you can make in your cover letter is being dishonest.

Not only does this have moral implications, but it will also come back to bite you.

If you tell the company that you have an experience, talent, or skill that you don't actually have, then they will find out in the future.

They will soon learn that you are unable to do what you stated, and it will get you into trouble.

Instead, stay honest while putting your best foot forward and highlighting your actual skills and traits in the most positive light possible.

Be You, Stay Unique

The cover letter is created to set you apart from the crowd, which your resume alone is unable to do.

Yet, many people fail to capture any of their unique qualities into their CV, leaving the hiring manager unimpressed and on their way to the next candidate.

This all too often happens when a person uses phrases such as "Hello, I am John/Jane Smith. I am a hard-working, multi-tasking, and detail-oriented person. I was born to be a leader and believe I could help your company."

A hiring manager or employer isn't going to be interested in a basic cover letter template that sounds as if it could be created by anyone. Highlight how you are unique and stand out from the crowd.

You can do this by switching out common words. For instance, instead of saying you are a *"natural-born leader"* you might say *"I excel when leading a team."*

This helps your cover letter to sound different, catching a person's eye better.

However, the best way you can stay unique is to share your stories and personality.

Work these into the letter by sharing with the hiring manager stories and examples of how you can best help the company, excel in the position, and make use of your strengths.

Illustrate Your Goals, Passions, and Dreams

An employer doesn't only want to know your strengths and why you are qualified for a position, they also want to know why you care and the career path you envision.

After all, they know that the more passionate a person is about their work the more motivated they are to do a job well done.

If you are passionate about the career, express this. If you dream about becoming a manager and leading a team, let them know.

If your goal is to advance in your field, don't hesitate to add that.

An example: "Graphic design and integrating it into advertisements has been my passion for many years, which is why I pursued my degree in graphic design at New York University. Not only do I dream of working in this field, but I believe my skills will help me to excel. My enthusiasm, passion, and work ethic will push me forward to new heights, making me a wonderful candidate for the position of Graphic Designer at Think! Advertisements."

End on a High Note

When concluding your cover letter in the last paragraph, be sure to use one or two sentences to reiterate why you are the perfect candidate for the job.

As most people will read the resume directly after the cover letter, you want to use this final paragraph to highlight anything important that you want the manager to notice following in your resume.

After you have reiterated anything important, you want to mention that you have attached your resume and that you are looking forward to hearing back from them.

You might even give them a date by which you will contact them if you don't hear back.

For instance: "Thank you for taking the time to consider me for the position of Graphic Designer. I hope my resume, which I have included, proves to be helpful. I look forward to hearing back from you in the near future. I will stay in touch, making a phone call in one week, unless I hear back from you in the meantime."

Unique Visual Format

Humans naturally remember something when it stands out from the crowd. For this reason, instead of simply typing out and printing your cover letter, it is a good idea to give it a unique visual format.

However, this must be done carefully. You don't want to use bright and flashy gimmicks that will turn off the reader or make it more difficult to focus on the contents of the letter. This means that you want to avoid brightly colored paper, unusual fonts, more than two types of fonts, or colored fonts for the letter contents.

The cover letter must remain professional and easy to read.

If you do choose to play around with the visual format, look at some of our examples below to get an idea of what works.

While you want the body text of the letter to use black ink, you might decide to use a dark blue or green ink for the heading text.

Adding a picture of yourself doesn't hurt, as long as it doesn't take up too much of the page space.

Try to arrange your text on the page so that it is visually appealing, rather than appearing in one big difficult to read block.

While you shouldn't use brightly colored paper, you can use a high-quality white or off-white paper.

Chapter 2: Sell yourself like a pro

The job market today is more competitive than ever. Think of it this way:

It's easy to advertise a product when there are fewer competitors. All you need to do is to show the product to the consumer (example: show potential consumers an image of a bath soap and they'll buy it because they know what it's for.) However, if there are several similar products on the market, showing the consumers an image of the product is not enough to convince consumers to buy it. You have to remind them what it's for, how it will make their lives easier/better, and all the other reasons why they should buy it (this is when you start using commercial models, the perfect script, perfect background music, perfect packaging, etc.) More importantly, you have to show potential consumers why your product is better than all the others. It's for this reason why TV and printed ads strive to be more colorful, more interesting, and more unique.

And with the number of job-seekers out there, this is exactly how you should sell yourself as well.

What makes a great salesman great? It's when he's able to take control of the situation while making the clients believe that they're the ones in control. An experienced salesman will discuss the needs and concerns of the clients while persuading the customers that what he's selling is the answer to their problems.

A job interview is no different. View the interview as an opportunity to make a sale. You take control and then subtly guide the interviewer into making you a job offer. Your main goal during the interview is to transform yourself in the eyes of the interviewer from a total stranger to someone that his company must buy.

Listen actively

One of the greatest misconceptions about interviews is that it is the interviewee's moment in the spotlight where he can speak as much as he wants to about himself. On the contrary, active listening is twice as important as speaking in interviews. While a chatty candidate's enthusiasm to please the employer may seem amusing, it doesn't always result to a productive interview. Simply put, it's not about how much you say but how much value your words contain.

Listen closely to what the interviewer says about his business/organization. Your responses must be based according to his company's needs. This way, you turn from being a job applicant to a partner who's eager to share ideas and solutions.

Be on the lookout for conversation builders

From time to time, the interviewer will say some things that you can use to build an interesting conversation.

Example:

Interviewer: "The low inventory turnover is one of our biggest problems."

Applicant: "I understand completely. I've had experience in finding solutions for low inventory turnover in my previous position. Exactly what type of problems are you facing at the moment?"

Mirror

When you listen, don't just sit there like a cold marble statue. This would embarrass or offend your interviewer. Worse, it might send the message that you're not that interested in the job after all. Respond through your body language. Nod in agreement from time to time. That said, don't exaggerate your responses by agreeing to every single thing that the interviewer says. You must have your own opinions. Even so, restrain yourself and put your opinions on hold long enough to hear the interviewer out. You may not 100% agree with what the interviewer is saying, but play your cards right by finding a common ground and taking it from there.

Example:

Interviewer: "I think _____ is highly important. To accomplish this, we must use Approach A or Approach C."

Applicant: "I certainly agree that _____ is of primary importance. And I also favor approach C. While I can see the advantages of using Approach A, have you considered trying Approach B?"

Interviewer: "Why?"

Applicant: "Well, based from my experience, one of the greatest advantages of Approach B is..."

Lean forward slightly or sit at the edge of your seat to communicate to the interviewer that you find the exchange stimulating. Practice the art of mirroring the interviewer's message. This means that you match his/her tone. When he's excited about something, reflect his enthusiasm. When he adopts a serious tone while discussing a certain topic, reflect his seriousness.

Important: Limit your use of mirroring techniques, especially when it comes to mimicking your interviewer's body language.

It's true that mimicry may serve as a social glue that can assist in the promotion of rapport between human beings. In fact, years of research has proved that generally, subtly mirroring another person's tone, vocabulary, words, posture, and gestures can make you seem more likable to that individual. However, more than one recent study by psychological researchers reveal that when it comes to job interviews, mimicry must be kept to a minimum, especially when there is more than one interviewer.

In an experiment done by scientists from University of California, San Diego, several mock interviews were recorded. In the interviews, some of the participants mimicked the interviewers' gestures while others did not. After this, the scientists asked judges to watch the videos and measure the interviewees' level of competence, likeability, and credibility. The result? The judges found the candidates who kept mirroring to a minimum to be more competent, credible, and likeable.

A similar study was conducted by a team of experts at Texas Tech and Drew Universities. According to the study, mirroring can have negative effects on an applicant's success. This is because humans mimic not only positive gestures but also negative gestures as well. In other words, if your interviewer happens to find you less likable or if he's just having a bad day, mirroring his gestures, his facial expression, or his tone of voice will only cause you to send a negative message to his subconscious. You become a living mirror of his negative emotions. Seeing you reflect how he's feeling inside will only serve to reinforce his negative perception of you.

Therefore, use mirroring strategies sparingly. Instead, concentrate on using body language to convey confidence and enthusiasm. You already have a lot on your mind during an interview and this is one less thing that you should worry about.

Repeat and rephrase

Rephrasing is one way to prove to the interviewer that you've been listening to him attentively. Like mirroring, rephrasing must be kept to a minimum. Make sure you restate only the most important points to the interviewer.

Example:

"If I understand you correctly..."
"From what I understand, you're saying that..."

Remind the interviewer why you're there in the first place

This may seem a bit frustrating, but in case the interviewer comes unprepared, his rambling thoughts may lead the conversation into an unpredictable path that will hinder you from selling yourself most effectively. At this point, your job is to give him a little nudge back to the right direction.

Example: "I just can't tell you how excited I am to be here. I believe that what I have to offer could be of use to this company."

With a statement like this, you're placing the focus back on the reasons why you're the right person for the job.

You might come across an interviewer who likes to monopolize the conversation. Should you butt in? Definitely. How else would you be able to have the opportunity to sell yourself?

But how do you interrupt a talkative interviewer's monologue without seeming rude?

First, absorb what you can from the interviewer's words. What you're actually listening in for are conversation builders and opportunities to highlight your selling points. Once it comes out of your interviewer's non-stop mouth, pounce on it.

Example:

INTERVIEWER: "As I was saying, one of the biggest challenges in this business is to guarantee sufficient cash flow--"

APPLICANT: "Allow me to interrupt you for a second. What you're saying is just too interesting. Management of cash flow is actually one of my main areas of interest. I have a couple of fresh ideas which you might be interested in hearing and I can't wait to hear your thoughts on them..."

Another type of interviewer you might come across is the stressed out, overworked type. He/she may be distracted during the whole interview. He/she may even cut you short to answer phone calls. Instead of feeling indignant, express your sympathy. Then, use it as a way to bring up the value that you can add to the company.

Example:

"Wow, you really are very busy during this time of the year. I know what it's like and I can totally see why the company could use someone with my skills and experience."

This will direct the interviewer's attention back to you.

Remember: There are times when the job interviewing task falls on a chiefly technical person. When this happens, you get an interviewer who will lead the conversation into a discussion of technical matters. While it's important to demonstrate your technical know-how, it is also necessary to remember that this isn't all that your interviewer wants to know about you. Naturally, he'll also want to know what you would be like as an employee. Chances are, he may be having a hard time communicating what he really wants to ask you. The solution? Look for a way to connect your technical skills with your transferrable skills. Provide examples of situations where you used *both.*

Keep in mind the lessons that your high school teacher taught you

Whoever said that high school subjects have no practical application in real life wasn't familiar with the rules of successful interviews. Remember when your grammar school teacher kept hounding you about using a substantial topic sentence, an engaging introduction, and a powerful conclusion in your essays? Well, you have to follow the same rules when answering interview questions.

Open with your topic sentence. Then, proceed with statements that support the topic sentence. Finally, end with a conclusion that summarizes your point.

Example:

"I understand that it's my job to find out and cater to our potential clients' needs, which will, in turn, enable me to INCREASE *the company's sales.* This is why I made it my business to help the company to *earn* _____ dollars in sales last quarter. I was able to *persuade* former clienteles such as _____ and _____ to *purchase* the company's most recent products. I also *secured* new clients such as _____ and _____. Moreover, I *collaborated* with _____ and _____ departments to help

draw more attention to the company's flagship product, which is _____, and thus, maximizing its visibility to potential consumers. *Within one year of being in the company, I increased the company's sales by ____ % through diligence, social skills, salesmanship abilities, and by being a team player.*"

Phrases that Keep the Ball Rolling
Using the following magic phrases will aid in maintaining the momentum of the conversation:

"I agree..."
"I can certainly relate..."
"That's interesting..."
"We should talk about..."
"Tell me more..."
"We should pursue that further..."
"That's also one of my biggest concerns..."
There are also phrases that could stop a conversation dead in its tracks. Here are a few examples of what you must avoid:

"Definitely not..."
"I absolutely disagree..."
"There is no way..."
"It's impossible..."
"It's final..."
"That's not how it should be done..."

Be on the lookout for 'Buy Signals'

You'll know an interviewer is interested in you when he starts using phrases such as the following:

"Sounds great."

"Interesting."

"I like that!"

Buy signals like these are signs that you've successfully caught your employer with your hook. Now it's time for you to reel him in, proverbially speaking. You do this by expounding on the idea that captured his interest. That said, unless they're really, really impressed, interviewers are rarely expressive. Often, their buy signals come in the form of a request for you to elaborate further on the topic.

Example:

"Can you tell me more about..."

"I'd like to hear more about..."

"Let's go back to..."

"Would you care to be more specific about..."

Now, most interviewees would dread the idea of being asked to speak more about a certain topic. Since you're reading this book, you shouldn't be feeling this way any longer! This is an indicator that you've hit the right button. But what is the correct way of expounding on an idea?

In marketing, a product's *features* refer to the characteristics of the product (ex: portable, compact, etc.) If you're a product, then your features are your skills (ex: great managerial skills, reliable, trustworthy, etc.) On the other hand, a product's *benefits* refer to the positive things that it can do for the user (ex: portable, compact materials can be used while on the go and are easy to store.)

It's your *features* that will catch the interviewer's attention. To draw him in, you now have to present your *benefits*. In other words: *How can your skills make the employer's business/life more profitable/better?*

Example:

"I believe that the most important part of my position as an assistant manager is to *provide you* with more *time* to pursue higher responsibilities. My goal is to support you in the management of the store so you can have more valuable time in your hands."

Make a closing statement that closes the sale
You're playing the part of a salesman. This means you're not leaving the interview room without urging the employer to seal the deal.

Wrong: "So, did I get the job?"/"Did I do okay?"
This comes across as overly presumptuous, pathetic, and perhaps worst of all, needy. You're likely to end up with

the standard dismissive response: "Don't call us. We'll call you."

Correct:

"Based on all that I've told you, don't you think I would be a great fit for the company?"

This part can be quite tricky. You need to make use of a closing statement that will actually extract a positive answer from the employer. To use or not to use closing statements like this will depend on how well you've established rapport with your interviewer and how effectively you were able to answer the interview questions. If you have a good feeling about the interview, proceed to prompt the employer into action. If not, follow a different route:

"Thank you so much for your time, Mr./Mrs./Ms. _____. It has been great pleasure and I do believe I have a great deal to offer to this institution. But please, if there's anything that I wasn't able to discuss to your satisfaction, do let me know. What could I tell you to encourage you to make a proposal?"

Keep in mind that it's not about pressuring the employer to make a decision on the spot. This is about increasing your chances of urging the employer to commit to you positively. Closing statements like these suggest a hint of urgency without the sense of impatience or desperation. It simply reminds the interviewer of your value.

Chapter 3: Experience Related Questions

What would your boss say is an area you could improve on?

Question Type:

Background and Personality

Question Analysis:

The interviewer will use this question to assess how well the candidate embraces critical feedback. No matter how strong a performance review might be, most managers will offer up at least one area for improvement. The interviewer is looking for the candidate to be candid about an area for improvement and discuss how they are taking action. Ideally, your response would discuss an area you are new to and investing time to improve.

What to Avoid:

You should avoid criticizing your boss's judgement. A response such as "my boss told me I need to pay better attention to detail but I disagree with her assessment" will not go over well with the interviewer. It will portray you as someone who is not receptive to critical feedback from superiors. You should also avoid saying something such as "my boss has never suggested an area for improvement." Remember that this question is a hypothetical. If your boss has not provided critical feedback, then you can still come up with your own area for self-improvement. Finally, you should avoid discussing areas that would be concerning to the interviewer. If you are interviewing for a sales position and you mention that you need to become better at communicating with customers, you will create a cause for concern.

Example Response:

My boss would say I could get better at recognizing when my work load is at full capacity and delegating work. I recently moved into a supervisor role, but I still put too much on my own plate which causes me unnecessary stress. When tasks and projects come up I tend to gravitate toward taking full ownership over them instead of working with my team to find out who is in the best position to do the work.

I recently implemented weekly update meetings with my team so that we can run through everyone's workload and availability. These meetings have helped me identify opportunities to delegate project work throughout our team to create a better balance for everyone.

Why is there a gap in your employment history? (if applicable)

Question Type:

Background and Personality

Question Analysis:

If the interviewer asks this question they are looking for an upfront and honest response. The best way to approach this question largely depends on the reason for the gap. If you were laid off, you should provide some details of the situation and discuss why the company decided to reduce headcount. If you took a leave of absence, you can explain the situation from a high level but there is no need to go into too many personal details. For example, "I had a health scare I needed to resolve" or "a family member became ill and needed my full attention" is enough detail. You should try to incorporate positive items in your employment history before and after the gap. It is also beneficial if you can discuss your ambitious intentions during the gap period.

What to Avoid:

You should avoid getting defensive with your response. Your answer should not be centered around any excuses with past employment. Whether it was a result of a prior job or a personal reason that resulted in the gap, you should avoid going into too many unnecessary details.

Example Response:

When I previously worked at XYZ Company, they unexpectedly lost their largest customer and needed to take drastic action to stay in business. 25% of the sales force was laid off including most members on my team. It felt like a punch in the gut, but I understood the Company did not have much of a choice.

As I considered my next steps, I decided that it was important not to jump at the first opportunity but instead take the time to find the right fit for my career. I treated the job search like a full-time position, spending most of my days making new connections and setting up coffee or lunch meetings with business contacts in the area. I also made time to take a two-week online sales training course I had been interested in for over a year. After 4 months of networking and consideration, I decided to accept a position for a territory sales manager at XYZ Company.

What are three skills all professionals in this field should possess?

Question Type:

Industry and Company Specific

Question Analysis:

The interviewer will likely ask this question using the name of the profession such as "What are three skills all accountants should possess?" You should be prepared to discuss skills that are highly relevant to your profession and align closely with the job description. The interviewer is typically looking for the candidate to hone in on certain skill sets that are a must for the profession (i.e. excellent verbal communication skills for a nurse). The following skills are highly relevant to nearly all professions: Effective communicator, attention to detail, excellent planner, and strong time management.

What to Avoid:

Your answer should avoid overly generic skills that are presumed for all professionals such as "hard worker." Your answer should also not be a laundry list of skills. Be sure to discuss how each skill benefits the professional in their respective field.

Example Response:

(Example response is for accountants)

Successful accountants focus on attention to detail to ensure their work is complete and accurate. We work in a profession where small mistakes can have profound consequences. Attention to detail in this profession means fully understanding the scope of the work and expectations before completing it. It also means critical self-reviews before finalizing our work.

Accountants should also be excellent at planning their work at a micro and macro level. Time management is essential to staying on track and meeting deadlines.

Finally, all successful accountants should be effective communicators. Whether it is meeting with a boss, collaborating with team members, or discussing an issue with a client, accountants need to have strong written and verbal communication skills.

What was something you did not like about your previous (or current) position?

Question Type:

Background and Personality

Question Analysis:

This can be a tricky question because candidates are often tempted to heavily criticize their previous job or employer, but this can reflect poorly on the candidate's own personality and professionalism. You should discuss why you did not prefer a certain management style, a team dynamic, or a job limitation from a professional perspective.

What to Avoid:

Unless something drastic happened (such as fraud or harassment), it is important to stay away from character attacks or interoffice drama because the interviewer may associate it with your own personality. It is also wise to avoid criticism of common challenges that occur in most work environments such as "too much stress," "long hours," or "a demanding boss." These answers may lead to the interviewer questioning whether the candidate can handle adversity which will come up often in most positions.

Example Response:

Overall, I was really satisfied with my previous position. I worked with a great team and grew as a professional. I do wish I would have had more leadership opportunities in my previous role. The company was traditional in the sense that most project work was initiated and micro managed by the company's leadership. I thrive in an environment that offers leadership opportunities for all employees.

Question Type:

Behavioral

Question Analysis:

The interviewer will use this question to assess the candidate's team working capabilities. They want to know that the candidate possesses sufficient emotional intelligence to successfully adapt to the various personalities of co-workers. You should discuss an example that shows your ability to effectively communicate with a differing personality to achieve the desired results.

What to Avoid:

You should avoid criticizing a team member's personality. You should also avoid examples of working around another team member or excluding them from the work. The interviewer wants to see that you are able to adapt to various situations to find positive ways to work together with other team members.

Example Response:

S/T: Last year I lead a system implementation project with four other team members. I scheduled weekly update meetings to discuss the status of the project and to encourage collaboration on technical issues we were encountering. I noticed that one of our team members was extremely quiet during our team meetings, but he would often email me afterwards with excellent insight and ideas about the issues we had just discussed in the team setting. Not hearing his ideas until after our meetings was hurting our team collaboration. It was also inefficient for me to communicate his ideas back to the team versus all of us discussing them during the meetings.

A: I looked into his experience and employment history and noted that he had just graduated from college and joined the company one month prior. Instead of talking with him about the issue during the next team meeting, I decided to schedule a one-on-one meeting. I explained to him that I was a bit nervous and shy when I first started with the company and that it was completely normal. I also tried to boost his confidence by explaining how valuable his follow up ideas had been toward the project. I explained the benefits of speaking up during team meetings but made sure not to make him feel too much pressure.

R: Over the course of the next few weeks we all started to observe him grow more comfortable with sharing his input during the team meetings. While he may be disposed to a more reserved personality, the ability to acknowledge that and work with him enabled us to use his talents to add more value to our team.

Do you prefer working in a team setting or independently?

Question Type:

Background and Personality

Question Analysis:

This question can be tricky to some candidates because it sounds as if the interviewer is asking them to take up a definitive preference for one setting over the other. However, most positions require candidates to work both independently and within a group. Unless the job description explicitly calls for working independently or in a team setting at all times, the best response is to explain that you are comfortable working in both environments.

What to Avoid:

It is okay if you prefer working independently over working with a team or vice versa but you should avoid making a bold preference in your answer. The interviewer may view your strong preference as a sign that you are weak in the other area.

Example Response:

It largely depends on the situation. Some projects and tasks are best accomplished through team work and collaboration while others are more effectively completed through independent work. I have a do-whatever-it-takes mindset and feel comfortable as a team player collaborating in a group setting but can also buckle down and work independently when needed.

Did you get along with your prior boss?

Question Type:

Background and Personality

Question Analysis:

The interviewer will use this question to get a better sense of the candidate's ability to work well with superiors. The interviewer wants to know whether you create or burn bridges. You will usually only hurt yourself by heavily criticizing your previous or current boss. Unless your boss did something highly unethical or illegal, you should focus on a positive answer.

What to Avoid:

You should avoid personal insults and character attacks when describing your previous boss. If your answer is strongly critical of your boss, the interviewer will likely view you as someone who does not respect superiors or get along well with co-workers.

Example Response:

I enjoyed working for my former boss. She never let her team get bored with their work. I was always presented with new challenges and learning opportunities. She also placed a strong emphasis on team communication and had an open-door policy for new ideas. Her management style helped me grow as a professional.

What type of salary are you seeking?

Question Type:

Background and Personality

Question Analysis:

Unlike question #69, you should not offer up a dollar amount in your response to this question. Instead, focus your answer on your enthusiasm for the position and desire to receive a competitive offer. Effective salary negotiators typically avoid being the first one to throw out a figure.

What to Avoid:

You should avoid discussing a specific desired salary figure in your response.

Example Response:____

I am excited about the opportunities that come with this position but have not focused on a specific salary figure. If you were to offer me the job, I would hope to get an offer that is competitive with the salary range for this position while taking into consideration my experience and skillset.

Tell me about a time you had to deal with a difficult co-worker. What was the outcome?

Question Type:

Behavioral

Question Analysis:

The interviewer will ask this question to assess the candidate's ability to manage conflict in the work setting. They want to know that the candidate will not ignite a conflict but will also not run away from it. Your answer should demonstrate that you are able to work through a disagreement in a professional manner and find resolution toward a common goal.

What to Avoid:

When discussing why a co-worker was difficult to work with you should avoid insulting them or getting into too many personal details about their character. Your answer should focus more on the resolution than the individual. You should also avoid discussing tedious or irrelevant conflicts such as "she always eats my lunch from the refrigerator."

Example Response:___

S/T: In my prior role as a financial analyst, I was tasked with testing our key financial reports when updates were made to our ERP system. After a significant update, I noted that one of our accounts receivable reports was broken. The data it produced was critical to our quarterly reporting package which was due in three days. The systems analyst who managed the technical side of the financial reports was not responsive to my emails or phone calls and when I stopped by his desk to let him know the importance of fixing the report, he blew me off.

A: I was frustrated with his response and lack of interest in helping our team get the report fixed. However, I remained calm and requested a meeting with him to sit down for fifteen minutes to help clear the air. He apologized for not being attentive to our request and explained that he had five different projects going on and was working thirteen-hour days to keep up. We both decided it was best to schedule a meeting with him and his manager to explain our team's urgent situation and help prioritize his time.

R: After meeting with his manager, she was able to shuffle around some of his project work to ensure our report was fixed on time. They were both appreciative that I took the time to sit down with them to explain the situation and find a solution that worked well for everyone.

Chapter 4: Education Questions

The more recent your graduation, the more intense the interest will be in your education. Because your work experience may be limited, expect to be quizzed for clues to your interests and motivation. For example, how you chose your college and your major (or why you switched), what your extracurricular activities were, any internships you had, and any future career plans (or why you didn't graduate or attend college). Of course, the more your college days recede into the distant past, the less interest there will be in your education. The interviewer can then focus his or her eagle eyes on your work experience.

Why did you choose your major and minor?

These courses were relevant to my chosen career and provided a solid foundation for it.

What the interviewer is asking/looking for: The interviewer wants a sense of your thinking process and interests, and this seems like a good place to start.

Good answer: Give a reasonable reason why. In many jobs, such as computer programming or engineering, it's expected that you majored in computer science or engineering. In other jobs, a wide variety of majors is found in employees. Or perhaps you are passionately interested in the subject, even if it's not "practical." Even if you majored in the Greek and Roman classics, philosophy, or Far East studies, and are interviewing for a job where this is not remotely relevant, be prepared to defend your choice without being defensive. But regardless, be ready to discuss the skills you learned, whether it's researching, writing, communication, or analytical skills.

Bad answer: An answer that shows lack of thought, laziness, or lack of direction. "Because I had to choose something," "It was cool" or "an easy A," or because your parents insisted, your friends were majoring in it, or the workload was lighter than other majors.

What extracurricular activities did you take part in?

I was on my college debate team, arguing topics from ethical to economic issues—and it was a good preparation for my business career.

What the interviewer is asking/looking for: The interviewer wants more of a sense of your interests and how you occupy your leisure time. They hope that you are a well-rounded person who devotes energy and time to something besides your studies.

Good answer: Show that you were interested and involved in things outside school hours—the more these are job-related or show traits the job requires, the better.

Perhaps you worked on your college newspaper or yearbook as a prelude to your career in public relations or magazine, newspaper, or book publishing. Or your college basketball games taught you the importance of teamwork and listening to your coach. If you were busy working to pay for college or family bills, with little or no time for clubs or sports, don't be afraid to admit this, noting how you got a jump start on the work world and responsibility over your peers.

Bad answer: Anything that smacks of being a couch potato who simply watched TV or goofed off with your frat buddies after (or instead of) your classes.

Did you have an internship or a cooperative work-study program? If so, what did you learn?

My work-study program taught me a great deal about the field and valuable skills like working with others or research skills, which tie into the job I am seeking.

What the interviewer is asking/looking for: An internship (paid or unpaid) or cooperative work-study program is an excellent way to demonstrate work experience while still in college, differentiate yourself from your peers, and show seriousness of intent.

Good answer: Even if yours was of the coffee-fetching, photocopying, ho-hum variety, highlight the good points, like the chance to actually see and hear how the work was done and network with colleagues.

Bad answer: Bad-mouthing your internship or work-study program, having one in an utterly unrelated field (which makes the interviewer wonder about your real interest in this job), or acting like a smug know-it-all because of your experience.

An internship or cooperative work-study program isn't just a great way to land work experience that looks good on your resume—it may lead to a job. Employers hired 38 percent of their interns and almost 51 percent of their work-study students, a survey of 360 employers by NACE found.

Why are you looking for a job in a field other than in your major?

I enjoyed a volunteer work in this field so much I wanted to switch.

What the interviewer is asking/looking for: The interviewer wants to know your thinking behind your change of direction. Changes of direction are common among young job-seekers—and many older ones as well—but he or she wants to be convinced this job in this field is right for you, now.

Good answer: Make a case on how you looked more carefully at your career goals and the job you are interviewing for is more suitable for various reasons. Perhaps it's a fast-growing field with more opportunity - and jobs for medieval French literature majors were limited. Focus squarely on this job, and relate the skills you developed in your major and any work experience to it as much as possible.

Bad answer: A vague response that reveals you haven't given much thought to your change of direction, and perhaps are taking a scattershot approach to your career planning.

Name an accomplishment during your college years that you are proud of...

I captained the debate team and led it to victory.

What the interviewer is asking/looking for: The interviewer is looking for evidence that you devoted time and energy to setting a positive goal and achieving it, and demonstrated traits or skills which hopefully you will carry over to your career.

Good answer: Anything from an extracurricular activity (at college or outside of college) to a job or volunteer work that shows traits or skills in demand in the work world, such as leadership, initiative, or communication skills. Perhaps you started a campus business making T-shirts, sponsored a child overseas with your parents, or were a candy striper at the local hospital.

Bad answer: Stunned silence, a fumbled response, or anything that tempts the interviewer to think your college years were one long spring break (or that the movie Animal House was modeled after your college experience).

Be sure to dress appropriately and act professionally during the interview, even if the company has lots of young, casually dressed employees. Young job-seekers often are casually dressed in T-shirts, flip-flops, and shorts; answer their cell phones; and pepper interviews with words like "cool," "awesome," "you know," and "like," hiring managers complain.

If you had it to do over, what college courses would you take?

Marketing and public speaking.

What the interviewer is asking/looking for: The interviewer hopes your answer will show your understanding of what the job will require, and include a relevant course or two.

Good answer: Naming courses relevant to the job at hand, in terms of knowledge or skills. For example, marketing, statistics, journalism, or public speaking courses are good answers, if you can make a case the job requires this subject matter or skills.

Bad answer: Anything that shows a complete change of direction from the major you chose, or courses irrelevant to the job at hand, like Chinese art history or philosophy.

Why did you choose your college?

Because it offered a particularly strong program in my field of interest.

What the interviewer is asking/looking for: He or she wants to see anything that shows seriousness of purpose and solid decision-malting ability.

Good answer: Perhaps your school features outstanding professors with time for their students.

Bad answer: Anything that confirms the interviewer's worst fears that you chose your school for the chance to party nonstop without your parents around, because it was the only school that accepted you, or you were forced into it because your father or mother went there.

How do you keep learning? (Or: How do you stay informed?)

I read a local newspaper and at least one business publication, such as The New York Times every day.

What the interviewer is asking/looking for: The interviewer wants to know if you are a professional with an inquiring, curious mind who strives to keep up with information and update your skills. Continuing education has never been more important than today, since technology and globalization have changed every industry.

Good answer: You regularly read trade publications in your field to keep on top of what's happening in your industry. Perhaps you also belong to a professional association, attend its conferences, meetings, or workshops and read its newsletter, take a class to learn a new skill or even a graduate degree like an MBA at night, or teach a class or speak at conferences in your field.

Bad answer: Anything that implies you stopped learning when you finished school, perhaps have not cracked a book open since then, have closed your mind to new things, and get all your information from TV.

Why didn't you finish college? (Or: Why didn't you go to college?)

I had to drop out due to lack of money but I'm willing to finish it within a few years.

What the interviewer is asking/looking for: The interviewer hopes you had a solid reason, as opposed to lack of interest in learning or discipline.

Good answer: If there was any extenuating circumstance, like needing to support your family, or health problems, by all means say so. If you are currently completing your college degree, or plan to, admit it, since this shows you realize its importance. Many people who didn't finish college, stopped after a while, or didn't attend right after high school go later in life when the timing is better, and sometimes go on to earn graduate degrees, including law and medicine.

Bad answer: An answer that shows insufficient interest in learning, displays the inability to focus or discipline yourself for very long, or leads the interviewer to wonder if you knew why then or even now.

Why did you leave college and return later?

I chose to work full-time for a while to gain solid work experience and money to complete my degree.

What the interviewer is asking/looking for: The interviewer hopes to hear any good explanation for your stop-out.

Good answer: Perhaps you traveled, which you found an invaluable learning experience, devoted time to caring for your family, or simply needed to explore your interests and focus your goals more clearly.

Bad answer: You can't articulate a reason for either why you left or why you returned, or say you simply wanted to party a lot.

Summary

You've learned your college days can reveal a lot about you, so treat them as you would your work experience. Be ready to give examples of how you demonstrated communication skills, leadership, a strong work ethic, and other things that employers value highly. Don't be surprised if your employer wants to know how you keep learning, even now.

• Tie in subjects you studied, your accomplishments, and extracurricular activities to the job at hand as much as you can.

• Talk about what you learned from internships and part-time, summer, and work-study jobs.

• Dress, speak, and act professionally in the interview.

• Give a good reason for bad grades or leaving/ not attending college, if that's the case.

Chapter 5: What You Will Bring to The Position

Once they have gotten what a sense of your personality is like, they will then start to try and investigate why they should pick you over all the other candidates. You made it past the point of being a qualified person on an individual level through your own character and experiences. This is your chance to shine and set yourself apart from all other candidates.

Remember to not simply memorize the answers that we are giving you. This only makes it harder on you in the actual interview. The point of the example answer is just so you can get a sense of a realistic and solid response. Keep it personalized to you, because setting yourself apart from the rest is of utmost importance!

"Tell me where you see yourself in the future (six months/five years/ten years from now)."

This is a common question that interviewers might even ask right at the beginning of the interview. This is a question that will be inclusive of all aspects of your life. Where do you see yourself in your career? What about your family life? In your personal goals? They don't just want to hear, "Hopefully working here!" They want to know that you are thinking about your future and that you have a plan. They want to see if they will fit into your plan. You might consider saying something like this when that question is asked:

"In six months, I hope that I am settled into a position and in a place where I can focus on really improving my skills. At the same time, I want to ensure that I'm doing my best to also consistently check in with my personal goals. Eventually, I hope to achieve a position of employment where I'm making a comfortable amount of money. I know the future is always changing so I'm also excited to see what surprises the future might bring me!"

"Why should we hire YOU?"

Every job will have several people applying for the position. All of the questions asked so far likely helped them to realize whether or not they want to hire you based on your experience and so on, but other candidates have probably fit the criteria they have too. Why should they hire you and not someone else? What stands out about you that will make you the best candidate? This is going to be specific to you. Perhaps you have a valuable skill that's hard to come by. Maybe it's something in your history that makes you unique. What are the qualities that really set you apart from the competition?

"I believe I'm the right pick because of my set of skills and experiences that I have had. I not only do what I'm asked, but I make sure to go above and beyond and deliver something greater than what I was asked. I take pride in my work, even if it is not a task I am particularly passionate about at the moment. I will always deliver work with exceptional detail and attention to the things that matter the most."

"What about this position makes you want to work here? Why do you want to get hired?"

The "Why do you want to work here" question is always going to be in the interview. It's not a trick question! Your interviewer will legitimately want to know why it is that you chose them. The obvious answer is, "Because I need a job and I saw you were hiring. I want money." This is usually the first thing that we will consider when applying to a job. While this might be the truth, try to honestly remember why it is that you want this position and not another. Have your reason prepared before even making your way into the interview. When you can give substantial answers based directly on their mission statement, then that will give you a big advantage.

"I want to work here because I have always been a lifelong supporter of this company. I have frequented the stores and I understand what the clientele is like. Not only do I think this will help me to be more passionate and dedicated to my work, but I think it helps because I will be more knowledgeable about what the business actually stands for. When I have this connection to the workplace, it is easier to go above and beyond because I have the confidence to know what my talents are and how the company will benefit from them."

"What do you know about us? How would you describe our company?"

This is a question that will require a lot of research! Make sure you Google your company before the interview. Don't just go to their site either. Read reviews if it is a service-based place or a retail location. If it is a huge company, look up news articles that might focus on them. Go on forums and see if anyone else has worked there and what their stories are like. The more you know about them, the easier this will be. Make sure that you list out what their services are, what their employees do, and what their mission statement is. This is a specific question, so make sure that your answer is based specifically on the company that you are interviewing for!

"What unique skills do you have that only apply to this specific position?"

This is another specific one that will apply only to the position that you are interviewing for. If you are looking to get hired as a front desk clerk, then you would want skills involving talking to people, handling requests, taking messages, making appointments, and other clerical work. If you are applying to be a construction worker, then you'll need to make sure that you can lift heavy things, operate heavy machinery, and have basic construction knowledge.

Whenever you are applying for a job, they'll usually have a list of objectives in their job description. Make sure that you study these. They will give you the exact insight needed to understand what unique skills that you have specifically for this job. They might have a job description that says things like:

Must be proficient in Word

Have excellent communication skills

Punctual and reliable

And so on.

Remember them, and when you get to your interview, you will be able to state them in your own way. Discuss your technical skills on the computer. Talk about how you can communicate. Give examples of how you are reliable. When you bring up keywords that they're looking for, they're going to be more likely to keep you in the back of their mind when making the final decision.

"What are you hoping to accomplish in this position?"

This is a seemingly obvious question, but it can actually catch a lot of people off guard. It seems to be one of the most obvious questions that can actually reveal a deeper truth about someone who might be applying for the job. There are a few ways that you can answer this. You can discuss how you would like to move up to a higher position if that is something you believe to be an option. Alternatively, you can discuss how you hope to gain valuable skills if it is not a position that offers a lot of growth.

"I hope while I'm working here, if hired, of course, that I can discover new skills that I may have and improve on things I need to work on while also helping the business thrive. I know the things that I need to improve on, and I have goals for myself. I think this company's goals and the goals I have for myself line up well together so that we can both mutually benefit from what I might experience here."

"How many responsibilities do you feel comfortable having at a time?"

This is a good question to help them to determine whether or not you are a multi-tasker. Some people are comfortable handling just one thing at a time, while others can handle several different things at once. Do your best to answer honestly because even if you struggle to do several things at once, that doesn't mean you're not a good employee! We all have a different pace for completing tasks so ensure that you are being honest with them. Can you handle several projects, or are you someone that works at a slower pace on one thing at a time? While you can easily lie and say that you can take on a bunch of things at once, you are just setting yourself up to make things more challenging later on. Be honest!

"I am pretty good with time management, so I don't mind taking on a few things at once. I will always try to complete tasks much faster than I say I will so that I can go above and beyond. I don't take on too much at once because I know my limits and do my best to avoid feeling overwhelmed or burnt out."

"Can you adjust quickly to a rapidly changing environment? Would you be able to change your plans if something unexpected happened?"

There may be a time when your employer has to send you to a different location, or perhaps they need you to work in a different department, depending on your skills and the versatility of management. It is up to you, then, to make sure that you know how to adapt should a situation like this occur. Be honest with them and let them know if you are going to be able to quickly adapt to situations like this if that's what you have to do later on.

"I have no problem trying new things. I appreciate having a set schedule so that I know what needs to be done, but when things change, it can just make work feel more exciting, making going to work more enjoyable. I'm not concerned about my abilities to adapt should there be a situation when I need to quickly adjust to change."

"What strong organizational skills do you have?"

Being organized is incredibly important. They can simply ask, do you have this skill, or this skill, or this skill, and so on, but instead, they are leaving this question for you to fill in the blanks. Rather than blatantly stating that you are detail oriented, punctual, and so on, put an emphasis on sharing your actual steps to become organized so that they can have a better sense of whether or not you are really someone with a great set of organization skills.

"I think organization is incredibly important in order to avoid any issues that might arise during any given project. To get organized, I first make a list of all the tasks that I need to do. From there, I will prioritize them by importance and separate them by how much time they will take and look at ways that I might be able to complete two tasks simultaneously. From there, I do my best to adhere to timelines, always giving myself a little extra time to account for any incidents that might occur!"

"If you were part of a group project, and you started to feel as though other members weren't pulling their weight, how would you handle this situation?"

This can be a frustrating feeling. Maybe there's a group project that includes five people, but there's that one guy who is not pulling his weight. Alternatively, perhaps everyone else is doing all the work and not letting you have the chance to thrive. Your interviewer wants to know how you would handle it if you found yourself in either of these scenarios.

"First, I would address whether there are issues within myself. Am I not delegating tasks properly? Is there a lack of communication? I would ensure I was doing everything I could on my part, and then address issues within the group. I would do it one on one and pull people aside to have personal conversations about the project. If I felt like I wasn't having the opportunity to pull my weight and others were too controlling or were doing the work for me, I would take the same steps."

"What is a strong value that you have that is only related to a working environment?"

When we think of values, we might first think of religion, politics, or philosophy. You won't need to think of this for a question about your working values, however. They want to know what is important to you. How would you describe your work ethic? What is something that you always remind yourself when the going gets tough at work? This is another question specific to you, and there are a few ways you can answer. Here is one of them:

"One value that's important to me is persistence. Sometimes things don't go as planned, and you might have moments of failure, but I always remind myself to try again. If something consistently is not working, then I'll look for a different way to solve the problem. The more I focus on getting back on my feet and continuing the fight, the easier it is to achieve my goals. Even if I fail nine times, the 10th time might be the time I succeed, so it's always important for me to continue on."

"What traits do you think an employee in this specific position should have?"

This is an important question because it will be specific to the employees and what you know about the company already. It shows them what you really think that you will be doing in the position if hired. The question is not just about you, it's about the position. You should put yourself in the perspective of the person conducting the interview, making it easier to see what they might be looking for. When you can do this, it becomes easier to know what a good answer would be. You might base this on a job description that you saw, or it could simply be something that you gathered as you discussed different things throughout the interview. Your response might be something like this:

"I think that it's important for an employee in this position to be reliable. There are several people depending on them, and it seems as though there will be some high-pressure scenarios. If they can't be trusted professionally and personally, then that can put a wedge in the working environment."

"Can you sell me the chair that you are sitting on at the moment?"

This is a question that might be specific to those who are interviewing for a sales position. Even if you won't be working with sales, numbers, or customers at all, it can still be a question that pops up. It is one that will show how well you can try and persuade someone. Are you a good schmoozer? Do you have a creative mindset that helps you to see the benefits even in something as mundane as a chair? They will ask questions like this especially if you are in sales, but the question might differ in how it is presented. They might say something like,

"Sell me this pencil", or ask you to sell another object that's around. Your sales pitch might look like this:

"This chair is great for anyone who is looking to sit down. We all could use a break, and when we do decide to get that moment of rest, then this chair is going to be your top choice. It has a cushioned top that makes it comfortable for your bottom, especially for those sitting for long periods of time. It has features where you can adjust the height of the chair, so anyone can benefit from it. Not only does it have great comfort features, but it's aesthetically pleasing as well. Why don't you give it a try for yourself?"

"Is it more important for people to like you in a managerial position, or for people to fear you?"

This is a common question, especially if you are going to be interviewing for a managerial position. It's a frequent discussion of whether or not a manager is supposed to be feared or if they should be liked. Do you want to be the boss that's popular with everyone or is it more important that they become obedient and respect your authority? The best way to answer this is that you should be right in the middle of both.

Chapter 6: Questions on Salary, Promotion and Benefits

How much was your last salary?

Most times, this question is hardly asked during job interviews. However, it is exclusively for people whose curriculum vitae show that they have been working. This is why this question is not asked to job seekers whose application packages show that they are fresh or new in the labor market. If the above question is asked, it is expected that the job you applied for should have higher and better prospects than the past ones. This means that the salary of the prospective job should be higher than your past salaries. If the difference is too wide, you may be considered under qualified for the job. You will be considered overqualified for the job if the salary of your past job is also higher than that of the job you applied for. But the exact difference, most likely, will be unknown to you since you know of the past salary alone. If you had/have a job with a good salary, mention the amount. Do not exaggerate or inflate your past salary because you may not have sufficient evidence, especially bank documents, to defend your false claim, if it is requested. Besides, some employers confirm their applicants' claims on salary prior to making a job offer. However, if your last salary is far below your salary expectation from the prospective job, politely appeal to the interviewer to wave the question aside.

Sample Answers

I am a fresh graduate. So, I have not been on salary as an employee.

I will crave your indulgence to wave this question aside because I am more concerned about the future than the past.

About how much do you expect to be paid as salary?

Try as much as you can to find the salary the organization is will be willing to pay if you are offered an appointment. Your ability to achieve this will help you not to overprice or underprice when you are asked this question. If, however, you were unable to find the salary structure of the organization and the amount the organization will be willing to pay if you are offered the appointment, you should apply caution in answering this question. The first caution to apply is to avoid mentioning anything about compensation or remuneration, before the question is asked. If salary-related issue should arise, let it be raised by the interviewer. Do not be in a haste in responding to this question. You should not give a specific answer to this question because the amount you mention may be too high or too low. In other words, you may overprice or underprice. You may not be considered for the job if the amount you mention is too high, as the employer may be afraid that you cannot be at home with the organization with the amount it can afford to pay. You may also be rejected on the ground that your standard is below that of the company, if the amount you mention is too low. One of the best approaches to answering this question is to give an open and unspecific answer. Another approach is to tell the interviewer that you have insufficient information to estimate your salary. If, however, you belong to a professional body that has a standard for the remuneration of different categories of its members, you can cite their recommendation/standard. The sample answers below reflect these categories of answers.

Sample Answers

I believe the salaries of your employees are determined by your corporate policy, and accepting your policy is a requisite for being an employee of your organization.

All other things equal, I know that the salary of an employee is determined by a variety of factors. This includes the value/worth of the employee, the status of the organization and the responsibilities and challenges of the job. I do not have enough information to comment on the salary, as I know of the first factor only - my value.

I am a member of the Institute of Chartered Accountants. The institute specifies that members who have my qualifications should be paid a minimum of Nabc,000 per annum. I expect that my salary should be within that range.

Is salary among the factors that determine the satisfaction you derive from a job?
Sample Answer

Though my salary has a role to play in making me happy in a job, it is not the most important thing to me about work. I am more interested in the career prospects of the job and its impact on my personal development.

How often do you expect increase in your salary?

Sample Answer

I believe this would be determined by a number of factors. This includes the policy of the company, my productivity in the organization and the overall success of the company.

How would you justify your salary?

Sample Answer

I expect to be paid from the money I make for the company, and I know that the organization will remain in existence only when the employees generate more money than they are paid. I will justify my income by ensuring that my services to the company surpass my remuneration.

What are your expectations if you are hired?

This question is not as simple as it appears to be. Just as you (should) have some expectations from the job you applied for and your prospective employer, the organization also has its expectations from you. However, you should choose a job because of your expectations from it but justify your interest in the job by emphasising the interest and expectations of the prospective employer. The expectations organizations are delighted with are employees' contributions to their success. Hence, do not say, "I expect the company to be prompt in the payment of salary". Also do not say, "I hope the company will soon increase my salary". You should also avoid saying, "I expect to be promoted very soon". Also avoid saying, "I hope the company will sponsor my vacations". No organization will offer you an appointment because of your expectations from it. Every prospective employer's interest in a job seeker is determined by its expectations - the value the job seeker will add to its organization. This is the area your answer should focus.

Sample Answers

I expect to be an invaluable asset to your organization if I am offered an appointment.

I hope to assist the company to the best of my ability in achieving her organizational goals.

If the interviewer insists on knowing your expectations from the job which will profit you, you should tell him about what you hope to profit from the job if you get the appointment. The expectation should have long term significance. Such question may be, **"Do you have other expectations from this job?"**

Sample Answer

I hope this job will afford me the opportunity to advance my career, if I get the appointment.

How soon do you hope to be promoted?

Sample Answer

I believe that my promotion will be determined by the policy of the company. I also know that my performance also has a role to play in earning my promotion because I will not be qualified for promotion until I am overqualified for the position I occupy.

Has your salary been delayed before?

Sample Answer

My past employers were very prompt in payment.

Has your salary ever been reduced?

Sample Answer

I am yet to have that experience in a place of work.

What would you do if your salary is delayed for any reason?

Sample Answer

It depends on the factor that is responsible for the delay. As an accountant, I will always know when the company is making profit and when it is having financial challenges. I am confident that the organization cannot afford to risk her reputation by owing the employees at a time it is making profit, and I also know that this organization has a reputation for accelerated growth.

Will you leave us if you get a better offer?

"How soon would you join us if you are employed?" Both questions are related, likewise their answers. Your answers to both questions should cohere. In the book, it was advised that you should be very careful with your answer because the prospective employer will not expect you to (promise to) start the new job immediately if you claimed to be working with an organization. It was also remarked that it is wrong to resign from a job without prior notification in order to join a new organization. In addition, it was noted that the interviewer may be afraid that you are not saying the truth or that you will frustrate their organizational activities with an abrupt resignation if you get a better job while with them, if you promise to start immediately. While answering the question, "**Will you leave us if you get a better offer?**", do not be in a haste with denying that you will not accept a better offer if it comes your way in the future. Remember, you aspire for progress, and one of the ways of achieving that is getting a job that is better than the one you applied for, even if you are offered appointment. You should be mindful of the fact that the interviewer is not ignorant of this. Consequently, exercise diplomacy and caution in answering this question.

Sample Answer

I desire progress in life. I also desire to advance my career. I know that I may not achieve that without getting a better job. However, I do not consider a job as a better one just because it has a higher remuneration. There are other conditions like job security and future prospects which are more important to me. However, I will not be in a haste to leave your organization so that I will not frustrate your activities. Since I will likely not spend the rest of my working years in your organization, I will respect your policy whenever I am about to resign.

Chapter 7: Managing Third-Party Recruiters

If you have not applied for jobs in a while, or if you are relatively new to the job market, then you need to pay close attention to this chapter.

Who Are Third-Party Recruiters?

Third-party recruiters (also known as headhunters, external recruiters, staffing or talent acquisition specialists, talent agents, among other titles) are professionals who companies hire to help them find candidates for open positions. The recruiters can either work for small or larger organizations or they can be independent contractors.

Regardless of where they work, it is important to understand that third-party recruiters work for the **companies they are helping**, not you. They have a financial interest in placing you, therefore, all of their advice to you must be taken with this in mind.

Well, one of the work-arounds for companies (other than ATS) is to have these external recruiters take care of this part of the process for them, so they don't have to comb through piles of résumés. Recruiters will do the initial screening of candidates and then present companies with several options, so the process is more manageable and efficient.

There are both positives and negatives with having third-party recruiters as part of your job search. Let's discuss both.

The Positives

1. If you connect with a recruiter and he or she winds up sending your résumé to a company, then you are substantially increasing your chances of your résumé being seen and then getting called for an interview.

2. A lot of times these recruiters have established relationships with the companies they represent which also means they have a good idea of what a particular hiring manager is looking for and what types of questions you can expect during the interview. This is incredibly valuable information.

3. Recruiters will help negotiate your salary and other benefits on your behalf so you do not need to speak with the company directly about any of those topics.

4. If you do not get an interview or an offer, and you enjoyed working with the recruiter, then you now have a new contact for possible future opportunities.

The Negatives

1. Recruiters only get paid (or earn a decent portion of their compensation) when you agree to a company's offer. In other words, they work on commission. Therefore, they may try to justify a weak dollar offer or a company's unwillingness to give you an extra week of vacation in the hopes that you'll sign your offer letter so they can get paid. Only <u>you</u> know what's really best for you.

2. Low barrier to entry. In today's world, almost anyone can be a recruiter and the market is, therefore, saturated with them. It can be a very cut-throat business when there are so many players which is why it's important to understand the potential pitfalls.

3. Some recruiters will use under-handed tactics to try and extract information from you that they can potentially use for their own purposes. More on this in a minute.

Over the years, I have heard (and personally experienced) many stories about questionable, rude, and/or unethical behavior toward job seekers by external recruiters. Recruiters who behave in this way are not worth your time. Only spend time working with the true professionals.

How to Connect with Recruiters

You can connect with recruiters in two ways: they reach out to you (usually via LinkedIn or your email) or you actively seek them out. Let's take each scenario separately.

They Reach out to You

This is common especially when your LinkedIn profile is updated. They are looking for potential candidates who may be willing to entertain the idea of switching companies.

If you are contacted by a recruiter, first make sure they want to discuss a **specific** position and you get the job description from them in writing before sending your résumé along. The reason this is important is because there are some recruiters out there who will "fish" for professionals to add into their databases and will lie about having an open position just to get your résumé and other details.

Story: Here is an actual email exchange to illustrate what I mean:

A recruiter sent an email with a brief, generic job description for a position in a job seeker's general geographic location. The company and location were not revealed.

Job Seeker: Thank you for the email. Can you tell me who the company is and the location?
No response from the recruiter. Job Seeker follows up with another email three days later.

Recruiter: This is a semi-confidential search in that we are disclosing the company once we have had a pre-qualification discussion via phone.

Job Seeker: I understand. I'd like to learn more. When is a good time to chat?

Recruiter: Are you actively looking?

Job Seeker: I'm keeping my options open. I'm free Thursday morning. Will that work?
No response from the recruiter.

No decent recruiter is going to drag his feet when there is an interested candidate for an open position. This exchange was highly suspect from the radio silence the recruiter gave the job seeker after the recruiter initially reached out. Fortunately for the job seeker, no real time was wasted and the recruiter only got the fact that the job seeker was interested. It doesn't matter because that recruiter has already proven not to be worth the job seeker's time.

Look out for nonsense like this.

There are right ways to build relationships and there are many wrong ways to go about it. Just be diligent and aware like you would when someone you don't know reaches out and starts asking for sensitive information.

You Reach out to Them

If you find you are having trouble searching on your own, either because of time or other constraints, then you can proactively reach out to recruiters as they may be able to help you.

There are also independent recruiters who are easily found on LinkedIn.

If they're smart, they will take your call and if they're professional, they'll be honest with you regarding whether they can ultimately help you then or in the future. In these cases, you will send them your résumé so they can get a clear understanding of your background and what you're looking to do next.

Note: In either case, never hand over your résumé unless you first have their agreement, in writing, that they will not send your résumé to any company without your written permission. Any good recruiter will understand this.

What's the big deal if they send out my résumé? It can't hurt, right?

Wrong.

The reason this clarification is necessary is because there are some recruiters who will send your résumé to companies without you even knowing! The problem with this is the company receiving your résumé does not know that you did not give consent, and then you can potentially look bad (without you even knowing), especially if a recruiter is over the line or aggressive with the company.

Don't let someone else tarnish your reputation with unprofessionalism. Guard your résumé closely and only give it out directly to companies or recruiters whom you trust and/or are comfortable with.

Speaking with Recruiters

Once recruiters have your résumé, you will most likely have a call with them so they can learn a little more about you and what you're looking to do next. This is very common and should be an easy conversation. The initial phone call should be casual but professional and fairly brief. You should not be surprised by any questions or made to feel uncomfortable in any way.

Be cognizant of how the conversation is going. A good recruiter will want to know your work history, where you are looking to go next in your career, how far you would be willing to commute, and possibly what your salary requirements would be.

Questions to Watch out for

Unfortunately, this is not always the case. All of the below questions (among others), including the many variations, are red flags. All of these questions are meant to work against you as negotiating leverage for a company; or are just plain nosy and rude.

Do not answer any of these and, if more than one comes up during a conversation, don't continue to engage with this particular recruiter. They are not worth your time.

Note: The same goes for company employees. They should not be asking you these types of questions either.

• What is your current salary?

• What is your salary history?

• What is the lowest salary that you'll accept?

• Do you have a family/kids?

- Do you own a home?

- How old are you?

- What year did you graduate college?

- Where are you from originally?

While some of these questions may come across as a recruiter innocently wanting to get to know you better, the fact is that all of these questions are offensive and none of his business.

If you reached out to a recruiter, then you will discuss what you are looking to do next as well as whether there are any current openings that might be a potential fit. And, if you are speaking to him about a specific role, then you will talk about your work history, your salary requirements, and also work to learn as much about the new role as he can tell you. That's it.

All of those other questions are totally irrelevant and, in some cases, illegal.

Recruiters are not your career counselor, friend, or mentor. They are **agents for a company** and are trying to earn a commission by placing you. Your relationship with a recruiter is also a *business relationship*. You don't need to answer offensive questions to be seriously considered for open positions, so don't allow them to make you feel small in any way. You are in total control of these interactions.

Finally, like with many of the topics in this book, use your gut. If recruiters (or anyone else you connect with) are making any types of disparaging or negative comments about you or your work history, you don't have to tolerate it. Your work history is what it is and you have nothing to apologize for. Don't get involved with someone who doesn't take the time to understand who you are and what you are looking to do next. Do not get drawn into a bad relationship. If it doesn't feel right, walk away and cut off all communication. There are plenty of good recruiters out there with whom you can work.

Knowledge Is Power

This book, especially this chapter, is meant to empower you on your journey to your next job. The more information you have about all of these moving parts, the more powerful you will be which will quickly translate into confidence.

Confidence impacts everything we do and everyone we meet in a positive way. Having confidence in yourself is the keystone to becoming a strong and successful job seeker, and this confidence will serve you best during the most important part of the process, the interview.

Chapter 8: The Negotiation_

When this time of talking about salary and wages comes up, you will likely encounter some negotiation. Negotiation is something that many people are afraid of. People are afraid that if they ask for too much, they will offend the employer. People are also afraid that if they do not ask for enough, they will get offered lower than they would have if they would have just waited for the employer to offer first. Negotiating is still extremely important. Negotiation is the way that you can get what you want and the way that you can get what you deserve. It is the way to get the best possible salary and wage the company can offer you. Negotiation is a way to stand up for yourself and to show what you are truly worth it. In this chapter, we are going to look into negotiation and how to do it successfully.

Negotiating successfully

First, let's look into what you need to know about negotiation. Negotiation is not about arguing over wages; it's about knowing your worth. One of the things that you need to do to negotiate well is to know what you are worth before going into an interview. Decide what you would want to make, and stick to it. You know that you are a great worker and that you are worth more than what some jobs are offering. You need to know the salary that you are comfortable with and the salary that you are looking for. If you do not, you will likely get a wage that you are not happy with. This may possibly be the cause of you not having the ability to be happy in your dream job. It can be the cause of stress in your life.

You may not always get what you negotiate for, but at least you know you tried. If you negotiate, you know that you are getting the best the company can offer you. If you do not negotiate, you may not be getting the best. This is because companies will usually offer you a lower amount of money that they are planning to pay first. The company will offer you a lower amount to see if you take it. This is not meant to be offensive toward you or to any other employees; it is just simply meant to save the company some money. The company likely knows they are starting out with the lowest possible wage, and they probably know the highest amount they can go to as well. For this, they usually expect there to be some type of negotiation involved in the hiring process.

Since companies are expecting a negotiation, it is not something that you need to be afraid of. When you negotiate, it actually shows companies you are confident and that you know your worth. Even though it causes companies to pay you more money and lowers their profit, many companies may actually be happy about the fact that you want to negotiate. It shows you can stand up for yourself, that you are serious about the position, and that you care about how you feel in the position as well. If you do not negotiate, the company may feel as though you are not as serious about the position as other applicants. For this, you might as well always at least try to negotiate salary during a job offer.

Another thing to think about when negotiating during a job offer is that you do not lose anything if they say no. It is not like they're going to lower their wage that they previously offered you. If you asked to make more money and you'll get it, great. Then your negotiations were worth it. If you ask for more money and you do not get it, okay. More than likely, the company will not be upset with you at all, and you will still be at the same wage you were before you asked. For this, it is easy to see that negotiation does not hurt you in any way. It can be uncomfortable at first, but maybe either leads to a better result or the same result, never worse.

When you are going to a job interview, you should know that negotiations could happen either during that interview or afterward during the job offer. You should never bring up wages during a job interview. If wages are brought up, they will be brought up by the person who is conducting the interview. If the person conducting the interview brings up wages, you can feel free to negotiate.

This is because if the person who is conducting the interview starts talking about wages, it is likely that they are interested in hiring you. If you talk to them about negotiation during this time, it can save you from coming back for another trip if the salary is too low for what you need. If you ignore the chance to negotiate, you may not have a chance to negotiate later on.

Sometimes, wages are not brought up in interviews at all. If wages are not brought up in your interview, do not mention them on your own. If you get a job offer, they will be offered then. It is possible that the job is not interested in hiring you and why they're not talking about wages, or it could be that their policy is to wait to discuss wages until the job offer happens. Either way, you should wait until the company brings the wage issue up first.

If the wage is brought up during your job offer, then this is a completely appropriate time to negotiate. If you get a job offer, they will likely tell you how much you will make. You can decide if you want to take the job or leave it with this number. If you do not like the number they give you, you can negotiate it and see if they can give you more. Either you will end up making more money, or you will end up making the same amount you were going to make before you asked for the possibility of the salary to change. You will never make less money just from asking a question. For this, if we just brought up during a job offer, you might as well try to negotiate it.

As an example, you could say, " I am focusing on jobs in the variety of $70,000 per year". If you say this, the job will know exactly how much you were looking to make each year.

Again, it is important to have this number picked out before you go to the interview or before you get the call for the job offer. This is because you want to have the number ready in your mind before you have to say it. You want to think this number over to make sure that you are getting as much as possible while still being reasonable. For this, you probably want to choose the number when you have some time to think about it and not during an interview or job offer.

When you get this number in your head, stick to it. Do not lower it just because you want to take a position. Do not lower it just because you do not feel like negotiating. You know what you are worth and you need to stick to that. You should make what you feel you deserve. If you do not, you could resent your job later on with it.

When you are negotiating, remember to be confident. For this, if you are their top choice for the job opening, you will likely get more money than what they are offering. They could always go with someone who did not want to make as much money, but then they would be sacrificing the quality of the candidates that they were hiring. Most companies will not do this, so you do not need to worry about it.

When you tell the employer how much you want to make, they may offer you a lower amount. If they do this, consider negotiating. Try to meet in the middle. If the company can only offer you so much, there are other ways that you can get up to the salary that you want. To give an example, if you ask for $70,000 per year, but they can only offer you $65,000 per year due to their budget size, you could ask them for a $5,000 sign on bonus to reach your annual wage. You could tell them that this will get you up to the wage that you need for this year, and you will talk about next year when that time comes.

Another way that you can negotiate is their benefits. If a job can't pay you how much you want, consider asking them for extra vacation time. Most people are willing to work for less money if it means they can have more time off of work. As an example, if you took a $5,000 per year pay cut, you could get an extra week or two of vacation time to make up for it. This would give you more time to do things that you love to do, like to stay home with your family or travel. This extra time may possibly be worth the pay cut. If it is, consider negotiating with benefits if the job can't give you the wage that you were looking for. This may help you to feel better about making less money because you know you are still getting something out of it. It will also help you to know that the company is doing everything they can to give you what you need, even if they can't pay you the wage that you want to make.

When you are negotiating, things may not always go well. There may be times when you have to tell a job no when they offer you a number you cannot afford to take. If a job offers you a lower amount than you are willing to accept, and they're not in a position to negotiate with you, do not feel bad about turning them down. This not only means you need to fight for what you are worth, but it also means you need to walk away sometimes when a company is unwilling to give it to you. If you cannot negotiate a deal that you are happy with, consider moving on. If the company does not see what you are worth, they simply do not deserve you. This can be hard at first because you can see a company that seems like it would be your dream workplace, and then you find out that they cannot pay you as much as you want to make. However, another company will always come up sooner or later that sees your worth. A company will come up that actually deserves you. You just need to be patient and wait for it to happen.

When you are negotiating, remember to have a number in place before you go into the conversation. Otherwise, save this number for the job offer. You can discuss it and negotiate about it at that time. Also, remember it is okay to negotiate. They will not get mad at you for doing so, and you will not lose anything. You will either come out making more money or the same amount of money that you were before you talked about it. You will never make less money after negotiations. Remember when negotiating, you can likely meet in the middle. If the company cannot give you the amount you need, consider asking for a bonus or for additional benefits to make up for it. Also, remember that if your negotiations do not work, feel free to move on. You will find a company that knows your worth and that treats you the way you deserve.

Negotiation can feel scary, but it doesn't have to be.

Chapter 9: How to Handle Closing Questions

"If you were hired, what would you seek to accomplish in the first three months in the new job?"

Employers ask this question to gauge how you think about ramping up on your new role, how fast you are going to complete the onboarding process, and the types of standards and goals you have set for yourself, especially it being a new environment.

Remember that this time is also when you will be learning a lot about your responsibilities, your leaders, as well as the workplace etiquette. You will be adjusting and learning how to fit into the larger organization.

A part of your own interview preparation should be understanding what the particular job responsibilities and company structure will be like and to align it with your goals in order to ace this question.

Clearly, the longer it would take you to contribute significantly to the organization, the less admirable you would be. Therefore, avoid being vague or showing how you will probably still be adapting to the new environment. Employers today are interested in the fast-paced, innovative, and easily adaptable personnel.

A good answer would be, for instance, "Besides getting to know the team and fully tuning to the role, there is a lot more I'd like to accomplish in the first three months. In the first month, I want to learn the design of our marketing projects. After two months, I want to redesign and launch a project by tuning the efforts of the team, and after three months, I want to be able to track the growth of our marketing efforts."

"What questions haven't I asked you?"

Employers make this inquiry to assess your interest in the field and your enthusiasm and commitment to improving yourself as a worker in the industry. It offers a chance to showcase your ability to decipher information and establish anything you feel is important that they have not touched. Pointing out such a thing is what sets you apart and shows that you know what brought you here, how different you are, and your planned contributions.

Naturally, a person to be considered will be the one who seems truly invested in the industry and their personal development.

Be sure to emphasize your stage of career development, how you want to develop yourself professionally, and your long-term goals.

Avoid arrogance like showing you are the pinnacle of development with nothing extra to learn. Do not emphasize your idealized salary and fun job.

You could say, for instance, "My main focus is to continue developing my leadership and organizational skills, and I believe in constantly challenging myself to achieve more. My vision is around the big picture, and I want to exploit that ability the best possible way."

"What questions do you have for me?"

As the interview comes to a close, the interviewer is most likely to ask if you have any questions for them. It may feel as if you have covered everything in the course of your interview, but it is paramount to respond to this question rather than decline.

Your response should be guided by the knowledge of with whom you are interviewing. If it is your potential manager, then you can ask questions about the responsibilities of the position. If it is human resource personnel, however, you can ask questions generally about the organization.

You should prepare a list of various questions to ask during this phase in case some of them are addressed during the interview. Your response to this question will tell how keen you were during the conversation.

About the company you can ask:

- Can you talk a bit about the company culture?

- What are the goals of the company for the upcoming year?

About the role you can ask:

- Could you please share more about the daily routine responsibilities of the job?

- What is the major indicator of accomplishment in this job, from your perspective?

Avoid questions on topics such as off-work activities, interviewer's personal life, minor things you could answer yourself, as well as salary and benefits.

"Why should we hire you?"

By posing this question, employers are really asking to hear what you have to offer them and what other candidates may not. You should take this opportunity to reinstate your skills and prowess in doing some of the tasks you believe you can do best. Remember that the reason they need to hire someone is for them to solve a particular problem. Hence, your goal should be to show that you are the best person to solve their problem.

To prepare for this question, match your qualifications with the job requirements. Then, use anecdotes to illustrate your qualifications. Anyone can say that they have strong communication skills, but few can tell a story about how they have used those skills to negotiate a deal and successfully complete a major project.

Be sure to focus on your uniqueness to make yourself stand out among other applicants. Also, identify skills that may add extra value, including volunteer experiences that could have provided you with a unique outlook.

However, avoid bragging and assuming that you are the summit of progress. Present your response politely.

A typical answer would be:

"I feel that my experience in this industry and my ability to utilize a unique and work-related capability makes me a good match for this role."

Then explain how in a recent role you used this ability.

"When can you start working?"

This question also comes in the form of, "How much notice do you need to give to your current employer?" which especially applies to candidates who are currently working in another company.

This question can feel exciting and promising, but do not take it as the guarantee of a job offer. This question is not necessarily an indication that you will be offered this job.

The first thing to avoid is sounding desperate or like you are too eager, since this behavior may make employers suspicious of your motives for the job.

Even if they have selected you already but they do not tell you when they need you to start, some flexibility is allowed in determining a date that is good for you. If they give a date, inform them whether you are okay with it and avoid making a commitment you cannot keep.

If you are currently employed, the answer depends on the amount of notice that you need to give your current boss, or any other plans you may have. An appropriate answer would be, "My employer requires me to give one-month notice before I leave, so I would be able to start on [insert date]."

If you are not employed, you may want to begin working immediately to settle your bills. But do not underestimate the time you might need to gracefully tune yourself into the work mood. An appropriate answer would be, "I would greatly appreciate a few days, say a week or two, to clear the decks before I begin, but I can be flexible if you need me a little earlier."

"Would you work holidays and weekends?"

Simple as it looks, this question can effectively set aside individuals to be hired and those to be rejected. Some industries require workers to be flexible and be able to juggle work and other commitments because of frequent projects or long hours of operation needed at times.

Some tips when answering this question include being realistic about your time, but give your response a positive spin. For instance, you can say, "I have no problem working on weekends or holidays as long as I can schedule myself as early as possible."

Also, know your limits. Employers need confidence in a candidate who can keep time commitments. For instance, you can say, "Due to family commitments, I cannot commit to working every weekend and every holiday, but I can certainly give some of the days if need be."

You do not want to say a flat no and give your interviewer the impression that you cannot give up some of your free time for work purposes. Industries such as hospitality require this element.

Ideally, show some flexibility in your schedule, indicate that you have time management skills, and be confident and tactful. Avoid committing to a schedule that you cannot keep, and do not disclose more information about your schedule than necessary.

"How would you fire someone?"

This counter-intuitive question is raised especially when you are looking for a management position. The recruiter wants to assess if you have really got what it takes. Are you able to deliberate and fire an employee when necessary or just ignore the problem? Also, they are concerned that you will fire someone in a way that upholds the rights of the company and confidentiality of the employee when firing them.

Take this opportunity to demonstrate your management style and re-emphasize the leadership skills (such as emotional intelligence) you expressed in earlier parts of the interview. Show that you would never take firing someone lightly.

Avoid being mean when role-playing, as it is not the time to channel your perceived inner strength. Rather, respectfully show that you are firm and ready to make reasons for firing clear.

A reasonable way to fire is to say something like, "I'd first of all try to see if there is anything I can do to prevent having to fire the individual, such as constant communication and performance review. If it comes to the point that I have to terminate their contract, I'd engage with them privately without the knowledge of any other employee and explain the reason for termination."

Chapter 10: Bonus Questions

You really can never be too prepared in an interview. While you don't want to over-practice and make yourself nervous, it's still a good idea to keep up with potential questions and focus on thinking of all the loose ends that need to be tied up before the interview.

It's encouraged to come up with your own ideas of questions that the person conducting the interview would potentially ask. When you can put yourself in their shoes, you will be able to easily see the kinds of things that they might believe are the most important.

"How do you manage your stress levels?"

Stress is something that everyone feels. Even when we try our best to manage it, stress can still creep into our lives in seemingly small ways. The answer to this question is not about trying to deny that you get stressed. Instead, give a realistic method that you use in order to alleviate some of the symptoms. Here is a good answer:

"I make sure that I am managing my time first and foremost. When I can prepare and prevent it helps to keep the stress from creeping up in the first place. I do know my limits, however, so when I am feeling stressed I will do my best to take a break so I can come back with a clear mind, better ready to focus."

"How do you prioritize your tasks?"

We talked a lot about prioritization, and how you will need to do it first when you are organizing anything. But how exactly might you prioritize tasks? This helps the person conducting the interview to determine what's important to you and how you will gauge whether or not something needs your attention. Here's an example of what you might consider saying:

"I prioritize tasks first by how important they are. Then, I will number them and try to base what I'll do around this list. I also look to see if there are any tasks that I can quickly do to get out of the way. Sometimes it makes it easier to focus on the most important things if some of the smaller fluff is out of the way. I always ensure that I am focused on managing my time above all else."

"What steps do you take if someone you don't like in the office is really bothering you?"

We have all had that one coworker who seems to get really annoying. Maybe they chew their gum loudly every day, or perhaps they like to glance at your computer screen over your shoulder. Whatever it might be, you don't have to mention what they do that's annoying! What they will be looking for is how you might be able to handle this situation. Here's something you could say:

"I would first make sure that I am showing patience to them. It is easier to be annoyed with things on bad days, maybe if I were stressed about something outside of work. I would do my best to be patient and not let the little things bother or distract me. If I had a close relationship with them and felt comfortable, I might say something, like 'Would you mind not chewing your gum so loudly?' If not, then I would avoid the situation, and maybe wear headphones if permitted."

"What did you do to prepare for this interview?"

This is a good question that kind of breaks the awkward wall that was created surrounding this interaction. We don't always talk about how this can be a stressful time that we have to do our best to prepare for! This is a time when you will want to be honest above all else. Here's a good thing to say:

"I started my morning making sure I got enough rest before heading here so I could be relaxed. I got ready, got dressed in what I picked out this morning, and had a nice breakfast. The night before I made sure to go over my resume once more and freshen up on what questions I might be asked. On the way here, I listened to some relaxing music to reduce stress so that I would be able to relax and give honest answers throughout!"

"What are you hardest on yourself about?"

This is a good question to ask because it allows the person conducting the interview to get an idea of the kind of things you might personally struggle with. They will want to ensure that whatever you are saying is not something that will affect your job, but they also want to hear some personal honesty from you. Here's something that you might consider telling them:

"I feel as though I never do enough. Even when I have a fully productive day, I feel like there was more I could do. I think this is just because I understand how precious time can be and I want to make the most of my life, but that sometimes can cause me to be stressed and feel like I always need to be doing more!"

"What TV or movie character do you most relate to?"

This is a great question. It lets people understand first what it is that you enjoy. Which movies or shows do you like? What books do you read? After that, it can help them relate your personality to someone that they might know. When you answer this question, you will be able to give them a familiar idea of the type of personality that you might have. Here's an example, but make sure to pick something specific to you as well:

"I would have to say that I am like Ariel from The Little Mermaid. I am curious about learning more about the world, I enjoy swimming, and I have a diverse group of friends!"

"What is the last object that you fixed?"

This is a good question because it shows that you are a problem-solver. Even if you will never have to fix anything in the position that you are applying for, it still lets them know that you do have some handy skills and that you know how to get yourself out of certain situations. Answer this honestly, but here's an example of something you might wish to say:

"The last thing that I fixed was my garbage disposal. For about a week it wasn't working, and I was too afraid to stick my hand down in there in case that would be the moment it started working! Finally, I turned off the power and got a heavy-duty glove to help resolve the issue! My hand came out safe and the disposal is working better than ever!"

"When is the last time you lost something? Did you find it?"

This is a question to show your level of responsibility. It's easy to say that we hold onto all sorts of responsibility, but at the same time, practical questions like this actually help to show what your level of accountability is. Try and think of what the last thing you actually lost was and find a way to relate it to this job. Here's an answer that you might choose to say:

"The last thing that I lost were my house keys. I went to grab them and realized that they weren't in their usual spot. Then I retraced my steps and realized I had left them in the pocket of my pants which was in the dryer! They weren't lost for more than a few minutes, but I was able to remember everything I did so I could easily find them."

"Can you describe to me how you would make a PB and J sandwich?"

This question is not because the person conducting the interview is legitimately curious about how to make a PB and J sandwich. They might slip an easy question like this in there just to see what you thought process is. Where do you start? Are you going to begin by telling them to spread the peanut butter on the bread and then the jelly? Always start at the very beginning of the process and make sure you thoroughly explain all the steps so that they can really see what your thought pattern is. Here's a great way to answer this:

"First, I would start by gathering my ingredients, and making sure they're there in the first place. I'd place out a plate with two slices of bread, a knife for the peanut butter and then a spoon for the jelly. I'd consider who would be eating this as well. If it were me, I'd go heavy on the PB and light on the jelly. If it were for someone like my little sister, on the other hand, I'd cut the crusts off and make sure to put a scoop of extra jelly. I'd spread the ingredients on the bread and put the two pieces together. I'd serve the sandwich and then clean my utensils, putting my supplies away."

Chapter 11: Follow-Up

After your interview, send a thank you note to the interviewer. My recommendation here is that you send an actual thank you card (something plain) that you purchase at a local store. Ensure that your name and contact information is clearly printed on the inside of the card. If you have more than a few sentences to say, then it would be appropriate to send a personal letter instead of a card (or included with the card). For your thank you card to have any impact on your interview results, you need to send it immediately. If you wait a few days, the employer may have already made a decision before he/she receives your thank you card.

Your thank you card should be just that. Begin by noting how much you enjoyed meeting the interviewer and then thank him/her for considering you for the job.

If you decide to send a letter instead of a card, then you could add statements such as "I left with a better understanding of the role of ... at your company." You might also say things like "I believe this position would be a good match for me (and you might state one or two of your best strengths that match the company's needs).

End your letter with a simple statement along the lines of "I look forward to hearing from you further."

If you have a letter of reference that you have not yet shared with the employer, you could insert it into your thank you letter.

It is also appropriate to send your thank you by email, although I would allow a few hours or even half a day to pass before you do this. Keep in mind though that emails tend to get deleted (almost immediately) whereas an actual hard copy thank you note tends to stay on the person's desk (often for a few days).

A question I am constantly asked by job seekers is "Should I call the employer if I haven't heard back within a few days?"

In response to this question, at the end of your interview you should have asked about the next step (and timelines) in the interview process. This information is one of your clues to deciding when to contact an employer after your interview. I would recommend you wait a few days after the deadline that the employer gave to you before calling. Some career experts would even say to wait a week, but I wouldn't go beyond this.

When you call the employer, you could begin the conversation by stating that you believed a decision related to the job was going to be made by such and such date. As this date has now passed, you were wondering if the timeline has been extended or whether a decision has been made.

If you are told that a decision has been made and you were not successful, be genuine in your thanks to the employer for considering you and taking the time to interview you. It would also be beneficial for you to end the conversation by stating your continued interest in working at the company if some other related job should become available.

There is one final note I should mention about what you should be doing after a job interview. Once the interview is over and you have sent your thank you card, then it is important to resume your job search. I have seen people sit around and do nothing for weeks after a job interview, only to find out they didn't get the job. Not only have they lost the job they were interviewed for, but they have potentially lost some other possible jobs that might have been available while they stopped their job search. Until you have received a definite job offer, persist in your job search.

The reality is that in some job interviews, you will be asked what you expect your salary to be. It is therefore important to research the salary range that could be expected for the position that you are applying for, along with a solid understanding of your own financial needs.

The following page provides some tips on salary negotiations.

SALARY NEGOTIATION TIPS

1. Don't bring up the topic of salary during your first interview unless it is mentioned by the interviewer.

2. Before a job interview, know how much money you need to make (what is your bottom line in order to meet your living expenses?).

3. Research the salary range for the job you are applying for. If you are asked what salary you are expecting, give an amount that falls within this range, or you could even state the range and say that you would be willing to start at a salary that fell within this range. It could be to your benefit to appear to have some flexibility.

4. If you plan on stating a starting salary that is near the top of the range that you researched, then be prepared to explain why you are worth this salary.

5. When salary is being discussed, it is important for you to be aware of any benefits such as health insurance, pension, etc. It would also be useful to gain an understanding of opportunities to increase your base

salary such as commissions, incentives, bonuses, or overtime.

6. It is important for you to clearly understand exactly what is expected of you in our job position before you settle on a salary amount.

7. Emphasize your value by talking about how you can help a company to be more profitable.

8. Avoid talking about your needs. It doesn't help to tell the employer about your car payments, or mortgage, student loans, or any other form of personal financial information.

9. Be open to options. Perhaps, there are some creative incentives for meeting specific objectives or goals that could increase your base salary.

Be realistic. If your training and previous job experience doesn't warrant that you should be placed in the top salary range, don't demand it. Whenever you are uncertain about a salary offer, ask for a day or two to think things over.

Chapter 12: Common Mistakes Made During An Interview

Having inappropriate or questionable content in social networking sites.

Remember, organizations do a background check before recruiting any one. About 70% managers in the recruiting department of different organizations have said that candidates make a grave mistake of uploading and posting compromising content in different social networking sites. Through the content, managers get to learn about writing skills and other insights of candidates.

Asking few questions.

This portrays that the concerning person is not interested in the job. The key is to ask not vital but smart questions. This way, you will not come across as a clueless or disinterested person.

Being overconfidence

This is mostly made by the younger generation. It is because they are conditioned and trained to have a strong sense of self-esteem, which most of the time, develops as overconfidence. They often make the interview process, only about them.

Turning Up Late

This should not happen in the first place which is why you don't need to take the chance. Set off very early. Its irritating how, only on the day of your interview that traffic and everything else seems to work against you. If it happens, you had better have such a reasonable excuse that it cannot be ignored. And at every opportunity, call in and let the interviewer know.

Fidgeting with Unnecessary Props

Please! Please! Please! Find a very diplomatic way of hiding your nerves and fears. Don't fidget with the pen, the books, folders, mobile phone, nails, your thigh or beard - don't do it. It sends too many wrong messages. For example, that you may be lying about something, or that you are not confident you can settle in the role, *etc.*

Unclear Answering and Rambling

If you don't know the answer to a question, say so and with a "sorry," but don't rant something totally off track. It isn't really the time to fool your way out. It can make the interviewer feel his/her intelligence is being insulted. And don't mumble. If the interviewer(s) has to ask what you just said more than three times, then you will start to lose it all on their score-sheet.

Speaking Negatively About Your Current Employer

If you don't have anything good to say about your former employer(s), please don't say anything. It won't go well for you if you do. The potential employer is likely to see himself in the same position when you finally leave their employment.

Discussing Money or Time Off

Unless it is put on the table by the interviewer, avoid as far as possible talking about salary packages, sick and holiday leave, or welfare policies. It soon becomes obvious you are not attending the interview for anything other than for money and people with that kind of dispensation hardly add any value to any role – they simply take!

Not Following Up

This is something not many candidates do after an interview – so the few that do it get an extra advantage. Even if you think your performance at the interview wasn't that great, you should still send the potential employer a short email message to say thank you for the opportunity and that you are still very enthusiastic about getting the job. Don't leave it days after the interview – do it the same day of the interview. The little extra effort only goes to show that you are a cut more serious about the role than all the others.

Assuming an Interview is an Interrogation

Too many interviewees assume that an interview is a process of the interviewer asking a series of questions and the interviewee finding responses to those questions. This is simply not the case. An interview is a two-way process. The employer is as much on trial in an interview as the interviewee. Be prepared to probe the interviewer for information and keep on with follow up questions until you are satisfied with your answers. Remember - this is your career that we're talking about! You don't want to wind up at a company who files for bankruptcy six months after you join, the signs of their impending doom having been painfully obvious to see had you just been a bit more assertive in your line of questioning.

Responding to a question without thinking

Sometimes in an interview we can lose focus. When this happens we either lose track of what we are saying or don't know how to respond to a question. The worst thing to do in this instance is to panic and blurt out the first thing that comes to mind. If you find yourself in this situation, choose a more constructive approach. Win yourself some time by repeating the question out loud to help you to refocus or ask the interviewer to repeat it. If you've forgotten what you are saying, admit as much to the interviewer and ask him/her to repeat the question.

Never try to muddle through without having a focus on a question as it will only confuse you and the interviewer.

Not doing your pre-interview homework

Failing to make time to do your research on the employer, or planning how you can emphasize the qualities on your resume, or what questions you should ask the employer when prompted then you'll be doing yourself a huge injustice. The better prepared you are to answer questions about yourself, your career and your personality then the more likely you are to impress the interviewer and land that job.

Being Arrogant

Knowing within yourself that you have answers to all the questions being asked and being happy with it should not make you come across as arrogant. Don't start speaking or behaving like you've already got the job – you might be unpleasantly surprised. It will be far more profitable to your chances if you keep calm throughout the interview. If you know something that a panelist or interviewer doesn't know, control yourself. Don't let it show on the large screen of your ego. Nothing puts off a potential employer than an arrogant candidate – from the point it is first exhibited, most interviewers simply shut down from listening to you any further.

Turning the Weakness Question into A Positive

When interviewers ask about your weaknesses, they know we all have a few, so it's quite insulting of their intelligence if you try to paint yourself as someone without any. Instead, I suggest to think about a weakness that can be improved, but which does not impact on any of the core requirements of the job you are applying for.

Get caught lying.

A definite guarantee that you will not get the job is to lie during the job interview. If you are going to make a bold claim or state something that is not true, seriously think about your chances of getting away with it. Companies run background checks on potential hires. Whether it is about your credentials, accomplishments or your work history, honesty will usually be the best policy. It's tempting I know, but honestly what would it prove? If you lie about qualifications the employer will find out. If you lie about your career history the employer will find out. If you lie about your knowledge and experience you could end up getting into a very embarrassing situation in the interview itself!

Inappropriate humor.

Be confident, but avoid cracking jokes unnecessarily or saying things probably best left unsaid. A little touch of humor could work in your favor, provided that it is appropriate to the context of the interview. You do not need to be funny, especially when it is at the expense of appropriateness and formality. The last thing you want is for the hiring manager to think you are not serious about the job opportunity.

Getting personal.

A job interview is a formal meeting to assess if you are the right fit for a job. Everything in your personal life, your subjective opinions and how you are feeling should be left outside the door, and not be brought up during the interview.

Not appearing attentive.

It goes without saying that you should give 101% of your attention to the interviewer and respond to questions accordingly. Not smiling, playing with something on the table, bad posture, no eye contact, and fidgeting too much are behaviors indicating you are not paying attention. Additionally, checking your phone or answering calls are almost definitely job interview deal breakers.

Ask when the interview will end.

Nothing says "I don't care about this job and I am just wasting your time" like asking the interviewer how long the interview will be, or when will it end. You will also be doing just as much damage by constantly looking at your watch. When you are called in for a job interview, you are expected to make time for it, if you really want to get the job.

Bad-mouthing previous companies

It does not reflect well on you to talk negatively about companies on your resume. It's natural to have a few bad experiences, but be sure to paint them in the right light. If you talk negatively about a previous company, it implies that you will talk negatively about the company you're interviewing for now in the future. I've seen CEO's reject candidates at the last minute because of this.

Don't come under-dressed

This is a sensitive one. It's hard to know exactly what to wear. Overdressing typically means wearing a suit. Use your judgment, of course but always lean toward overdressing. 75% interviewers have said that most candidates turn up dressed shabbily or inappropriately for an interview. Follow the above attire checklist for creating a great impression.

Cursing

Please watch your language. Cursing implies that you don't communicate professionally in the workplace.

Conclusion

I believe the content of this book is very insightful. It has enlightened you on uncommon truths that are helpful in getting a job. Numerous people across the globe who have been unemployed for many years after graduating from tertiary institutions would have been enjoying better, happier and more prosperous lives as employees if they had access to the information in this book while they were fresh graduates. Numerous fresh graduates would unarguably get good jobs (even faster than they think) if they digest the content of this book and allow it to guide their job search activities.

You are very fortunate if you came across this book as a fresh graduate, as long as you will apply the principles it recommends in your job search activities. This book will save you years you would have wasted searching for jobs. It will also help you to make the best out of job opportunities you will come across, some of which you would have wasted. You are also very fortunate if you come across this book as a worker (and you are willing to be guided by its content) because it can help you get a better job, if you desire such. This book simplifies how to get a job. It enlightens the reader on what employers want from job seekers. It is a very reliable and authoritative manual for job seekers.

In competing for limited job opportunities, I am very confident that the job seeker who has undergone training in recruitment education has higher chances of getting a job than his competitors, even those who are more intelligent than he is, but lack recruitment education. The ideas that were exposed in this book have no place in the school curriculum (from the least to the highest level). As a matter of fact, I am very fanatical about the limitations of the educational system in its present form. The type of education that is offered to students in conventional schools does not adequately prepare them for real life challenges (after graduation).

This is one of the reasons most graduates have difficulties meeting real life challenges after numerous years of leaving school. This is why I recommend Supplementary Education to every graduate. Ideally, supplementary education ought to have a place in the school curriculum to assist students to be more focused and productive when school days are over. Most unfortunately, it does not. This shows that much of what students are taught in school are things they do not need to succeed in real life. By this token, most of what students need to survive in the real life are not taught in the school. I once argued that

"An uncommon truth among most graduates is that most of what they need to know in order to achieve a bright future are things that are not taught in school. This, however, is not a way of discrediting the value of education. The society cannot do without school. The school system produces professionals the society cannot do without. Your years in school should not be considered a waste of time and resources. The point being made is that what you learnt in school is inadequate for your success. The deficiencies of the school system make room for Supplementary Education. Supplementary Education is complementary, auxiliary and ancillary education. You will have no meaningful success in the future, even as a graduate, if you lack this type of education, no matter your course of study, your grade or the school you attended."

As noted above, it is impossible to have any meaningful success in the real life (i.e. life after school) in the absence of supplementary education. The major factor that underlies the failure of most graduates in real life is the absence of supplementary education. This highlights the necessity of this type of education. As seen above, one of the reasons many graduates remain unemployed after years of leaving school, despite being exceptionally intelligent, is that they lack Recruitment Education. They are ignorant of what employers want from job seekers. They are ignorant of what they need to know in order to be able to convince prospective employers that they are the best candidates for the positions they applied for.

This book in your hand is aimed at providing you with one of the supplementary education you need. This is, perhaps, the first type of supplementary education you need to succeed in the real life. It is called Recruitment Education. It is an education that prepares you for getting a job, if not for getting your dream job. This is the aspect of life's challenges it is geared towards addressing. There are other types supplementary education which are geared towards addressing the challenges in other areas/aspects of life. Since success is essentially concerned with striving for balance in all areas of life, this supplementary education is inevitable for everyone, even non graduates, who sincerely and conscientiously desires to achieve a meaningful and successful life.

HOW TO ANSWER INTERVIEW QUESTIONS

Guide to a Winning Interview with Amazing Interview Answers. How to Use Emotional Intelligence to be More Confident in your Job Interview.

Jim Hunting

Introduction

When attending an interview, you need to show your assertiveness, you have to practice being confident. Often, confidence starts with the mindset that you can accomplish all things on your agenda. Being more assertive starts with being proactive about your own life. When you think about what you want to do, then you can set a goal and do it faithfully. That means practicing what you preach. You have to try to do your best at what you do, because then you can be confident. It all starts with being excellent at what you do. However, even then, you can develop confidence when your skill is not the best.

Begin by getting good at what you do

One thing that you have to do is be good at what you do. That will be the first step to a successful interview process. You cannot succeed in securing a good job if you're not good at what you do. Even if you do succeed at the interview, you won't last long, if you're not skilled at the job that you want to do. Therefore, it is crucial that you find ways of developing your talent and tailoring your skills to your job. Then, you can have the qualifications necessary to get the job that you want.

Get qualified and get the education you need

The next step is getting qualified. Go and get that certificate. Get the credentials that you need to confidently submit your resume to the place where you want to work. You will need these things, because when you talk about your experience, then you can bring them up at the interview. Get as many qualifications as you can, because these will enable you to get the interview, and you'll be able to support your candidacy. The more qualified you are, the more confident you will be.

Emphasize your strong points but don't gloss over your weaknesses

Now that you are qualified, you should try to emphasize the strong points in your life that you have. Write down all your strengths on a piece of paper, and expand on each of them. Consider them deeply and think about what makes you great at what you do. Then, you can talk about your weaknesses. For every weak point that you have, try to come up with ways that you are handling these weaknesses. Think of ways you're improving yourself or finding ways to get more training and support to help you along the way. It will show some humility and the fact that you want to continually advance in your life.

Do some breathing exercises

Another thing that you should do is some deep breathing. Try to take in as much oxygen as possible before and during the interview. It is important that you are breathing a lot, because that will help you feel better. Also, if you can focus on one thing, it should be breathing in a healthy way. Try doing this, and you should notice how your nerves simply melt away.

Be positive

Believe that you deserve and are meant to be at the place where you're going to. You should show confidence, and by being positive and having a good mindset, then you'll be ready to show that you know your stuff in the interview. The important thing is to keep your chin up and keep going, even when your body is fighting and making it difficult to function while you're in the interview.

Don't fidget during the interview

Avoid making fidgety movements during the interview, which could show that you are very nervous and could make it more difficult for you. Try to remain as stationary as possible in your seat so you don't make any involuntary movements. Be conscious of your posture at all times, and keep your feet planted in front of you.

Press the pause button

Another thing that you need to do is press the pause button when you feel like you're going to veer off course. Let's say you're answering a question, and you have to talk about your previous job experience and how it was. You don't want to go off endlessly in the wrong direction about it. If you hit the pause button, then you can stop yourself from answering a question in too much detail. To answer a question succinctly and fully, you should try to say what is needed without including any additional information. Stop yourself from going any further.

Chapter 1: Before the Interview

1. Research the Backgrounds of the Interviewers*

The company you are interviewing with will typically send over the interview schedule in advance. If there are multiple rounds of interviews, you may only interview with one person the first round and then with multiple people in subsequent rounds.

It is essential to know some background details about each person who interviews you. Each interview usually begins with small talk to break the ice. Having knowledge of the interviewer's professional background goes a long way in building rapport early on. It is also an excellent way to develop relevant questions for the interviewer at the end of the session (See tip #2 for more detail).

I recommend starting your research with the company's website. If it is a small to mid-size company, you will usually come across profiles of the leadership team. Larger companies do not always publish leadership profiles. If you are unable to find the profile of your interviewer on the company's site, LinkedIn will be an excellent resource. Within each LinkedIn profile, you will find "Experience," "Skills & Endorsements," and "Activity" which will include articles or posts made by that individual to their network. There is also an "Interests" section which will show which companies and organizations that person is connected to. Reviewing the interests section is a great way to find clues about which causes and charities they focus on outside of work. I do not recommend making a "Connect" request to your interviewers on LinkedIn before the interview. They may not recognize who you are beforehand, and it is a much more natural progression to make the request after meeting them during the interview.

You can also conduct a Google search to look for articles and information on your interviewer. You will often find local news articles about business leaders getting involved in community and charitable events.

As you are conducting research on your interviewers, jot down bullet points of relevant information that you can leverage during your interview. Here is an example of what your notes might look like:

Jim Vandenberg, Director of Procurement

- Attended University of Michigan (From the dates, I'm noting that he attended when they won the 1997 national championship in football).

- Manages a team of 21 professionals responsible for sourcing raw materials, warehousing, suppliers, and logistics.
- Started career in corporate finance.
- Interested in St. Jude's Children hospital.

Possessing this background information on Jim gives you a huge advantage for the interview! The key is not to lead with any of this information but to naturally incorporate it into your conversation and leverage it to ask excellent questions. For example, you would never want to say something like:

"I saw that you were attending Michigan in 1997, did you attend any games the year the football team won the championship?"

Or

"I noted that you follow St. Jude's Hospital. What other charitable organizations interest you?"

These questions would be coming out of left field and scream to the interviewer that you investigated them. Instead, use this information during the natural progression of the conversation. For example, the interviewer will typically tell you some of their background information in the beginning. If the interview is still in the "small talk" phase and Jim stated that he attended the University of Michigan, you can say something like:

"I'm always thrilled when fall comes along and it's time for college football season. Michigan has such a rich history in football. Did they have good teams while you attended?"

You can be assured that 99 out of 100 times, Jim is going to light up like a Christmas tree and tell you about being on campus when they won the national championship. This will get him excited to discuss it with you and the interview starts out in a positive direction. If football (or whatever background information you found on the interviewer) is not your thing, do not sweat it. You certainly do not want to use the above example if you have no interest in football. However, you should be able to find something else in their background that you can relate to and bring it up when the time is right.

At the end of the interview Jim is going to ask if you have any questions. Since you researched his background information, you can ask him some excellent questions you come up with in advance such as:

"As the director of procurement, how do you take steps to mitigate the risk of large or unexpected price movements in raw materials?"

"Does XYZ Company offer employees the opportunity to get exposure working with multiple departments?"

"Does XYZ Company encourage employees to give back through charitable causes?"

Notice how each question is driven by background information from the notes above? They are also highly relevant questions that Jim will be eager to discuss.

You can certainly come to the interview with relevant questions that are not rooted in an interviewer's background information, but most candidates struggle to come up with two or three strong questions for each interviewer. Leveraging their background information is an excellent way to formulate them.

2. Develop Questions for Each Interviewer*

One of the most critical parts of the interview is towards the end when the interviewer will ask you if you have any questions for them. Not only do they expect you to ask questions, they also expect the questions to show that you did your research on the company and are genuinely excited about the position.

Candidates should be ready to ask each interviewer a minimum of 2 questions, but I always recommend having 3 questions prepared. When coming up with your questions, be sure to avoid any question that can be answered with a simple "yes" or "no" response. For example:

"Does XYZ Company offer paid leave for new fathers?"

Even though this question will probably not result in the interviewer providing a simple "yes" or "no," it is possible to be answered with a one-word response and is usually not relevant to the interview. In fact, the interviewer may not even know the answer to this question which would disrupt the flow of the conversation. This type of question should be saved for your HR contact after they offer you the job.

Your questions should be broad enough to get the interviewer thinking but specific enough to their background and role that they are enthusiastic about answering them. This is too broad of a question:

"What do employees enjoy about working at XYZ Company?"

Instead be more specific to the interviewer's role and show you did some research with this question:

"As someone who works closely with a wide range of customers in the consumer products industry, where do you look for opportunities to bring added value to your customers?"

The best way to develop highly relevant questions for each interviewer is to research their background and experience (see tip 1). Below are a couple more examples of taking notes on your research to create high quality questions.

Nicole Bennet, Accounting Manager

- Attended University of Utah, was in Beta Alpha Psi (accounting group).
- Spent time in public accounting at a Big Four Firm (PwC).
- Is responsible for overseeing quarterly and annual financial reporting with SEC and coordination of audit with independent accounting firm.
- Interested in hiking and outdoors groups.

Question 1: "What role does technology have on the challenges and opportunities facing the financial reporting profession as it relates to SEC reporting?"

Question 2: "How do you leverage student organizations on college campuses in your recruiting efforts?"

Question 3: "How does XYZ Company encourage employees to be active and participate in fitness activities?"

Kelvin Smith, Regional Sales Manager Software company

- Lives in Chicago, responsible for all Midwest sales.
- Previously was a recruiter for sales positions.
- Oversees large sales team with customers primarily in automotive manufacturing.
- Interested in Veteran Affairs and supporting VA hospitals.

Question 1: "How does your team leverage CRM (customer relationship management) technology to bring value to your customers?"

Question 2: "With software and technology changing so rapidly, how does your sales team work with the operations and technology teams to leverage customer feedback and interaction?"

Question 3: "How does XYZ Company and its employees give back to charities, veterans causes, and the local community?"

It can be challenging to remember all of your questions if you will be interviewing with multiple people. Be sure to jot them down under the name of each interviewer and bring them with you. You will typically have a brief break between interviews which will afford you the time to review them. You should usually avoid glancing down at them during the interview but just having them there will aid your confidence.

3. Ask the Interview Contact What Type of Interview to Expect

The style of the interview is dependent on the company's preference. Most companies prefer a traditional style interview where the candidate meets individually with the interviewers in separate sessions. However, some companies will conduct other types of interviews including:

*Panel interviews where multiple people observe the interview session and take turns asking the candidate questions.

*Presentation interviews where the candidate is expected to put together a presentation and present it to a group of interviewers.

*Brain teasers or test type interviews where the candidate has a fixed amount of time to complete a competency test to assess knowledge and critical thinking skills.

Some interviews are set up as a combination of the types listed above. For example, the candidate may be asked to complete a 30-minute competency test before commencing a more traditional one-on-one interview session. Regardless of the type of interview coming your way, you can be fully prepared to succeed. However, it is essential to know what type of interview to prepare for as soon as possible.

The type of interview can usually be determined by the schedule or itinerary sent over. If the company does expect you to give a presentation, they will let you know up-front. If the schedule shows you meeting with various individuals in interview sessions, you can expect to have a more traditional style interview. If your schedule only shows the beginning and end times of the interview, be sure to reach out to your contact and ask them what to expect. Being mentally prepared for one-on-one interview sessions is much different than interviewing in front of a multi-person panel. When asking what to expect, be sure not to phrase it in a way that insinuates you are looking for tips or inside information about the process. Instead, emphasize that you would like to know what to expect to help you prepare for the interview. Here is an example email you could use to send to your HR contact:

"Hi (first name),

I am looking forward to interviewing with XYZ Company on mm/dd (date). As I am starting to prepare for the interview, I wanted to reach out to you with a few questions that came up.

Should I expect the interview to be conducted in multiple sessions or will I be interviewing in front of a panel of people?

If possible, could you please provide me with the names of the people who will be included in the interview process?

Should I bring a calculator or pencils for any testing procedures?

Once again, I greatly appreciate the opportunity to interview with XYZ.

Thank you,

(your first name)

4. Take Note of the Company's "About Us" Information

Companies will almost always have a section on their website that discusses their values, culture, mission statement, history, and objectives. By absorbing this information, you will have a great sense of what they tend to look for in candidates. Many studies show that companies place a higher emphasis on cultural fit than any other trait when deciding whether to hire a candidate.

It is not uncommon for an interviewer to test a candidate on their knowledge of the company's values. They may ask the candidate which values they look for in an employer to see how well they align with the company's values. You can use the information obtained in your research to emphasize key values of your own that match up well with those of the company.

I do want to emphasize that you should not waste time memorizing everything on the company's "about us" section. It is more important to take bullet point notes of their values, mission, and culture. You can use that information to think of ways to emphasize your own values and interests that closely align with those of the company. If a company's values include the following terms:

*Integrity

*Accountability

*Diversity

*Quality

You should find ways to integrate some of these values into your answers to the interview questions. For example, if the interviewer asks you to provide them with an example of a time you faced a tight deadline on a project and in part of your answer you say, "I always place a high emphasis on quality, no matter what type of pressure I face," you have successfully aligned your answer with one of the company's values and the interviewer will usually make that connection.

5. Use Twitter/Facebook/LinkedIn to Research the Company's Personality

Social media is an excellent way to learn about the culture and atmosphere within a company. Companies will usually post news articles, press releases, updates, and engage with their audience on their social media page. Reviewing this activity on social media will give you a strong sense of their culture and tone. Is the tone they use on their social media pages very professional or is it more laid back and casual? Do they only self-promote on their pages or do they find other ways to engage with their audience? What positive news and information are they sharing with their audience?

Within a few minutes of reviewing their social media activity, you will get a strong sense of the company's culture and personality. This will usually be an indicator of the style of the interview. It may be serious and professional or more laid back and casual. You will not know for sure until the interview takes place but their activity on social media will provide a lot of clues. If any exciting updates or news articles shared by the company catch your attention, be sure to take note of them and you can bring them up during the small talk phase of the interview or even turn them into a question for the interviewer.

Chapter 2: The Power of The First Handshake

Never underestimate the power of a handshake. Handshakes are a symbol of goodwill and agreement, but it can also be used to send a strong subliminal message of authority.

There are three kinds of handshakes.

The dominant handshake that uses the palm-facing downwards to create an impression of authority. Use the dominant handshake in meetings that have a crucial agenda where the decision will either benefit or damage your firm.

While, the submissive handshake delivers the opposite message with the palm faced upward. It is never recommended to use the submissive handshake because you need to lead people and not the other way around.

And the standard handshake creates a sense of equality between two people by making both hands hold in the same manner. Make a standard handshake when you meet customers and clients to imply that you are both in the same level. This also helps make you appear approachable to people. After sealing a deal, use the standard handshake again to send a message of satisfaction.

Make your handshakes firm and warm. A firm handshake is a sign of confidence and power. In the US, women shake their hands only by holding the edge of the fingers. However, women in business don't. They still prefer the classic business shake. Holding on to the edge of the hand will make people think that their hands are dirty or you don't like them at all.

Time the handshakes well. Simply hold and pump the hands three times in an up-down motion. You can further reinforce friendship by using the other hand to slightly hold the shoulder, elbow or forearm of your partner. Finally, while you shake hands, make it sincere by brightly smiling at them. Although handshakes are a small gesture that happens only in 5 seconds, it creates positive energy both at the beginning and ending of meetings.

Establish authority with non-verbal communication

In the business world, not only do we need to create trust, we also need to build authority. Our behavior during a meeting speaks a lot about how credible and confident we are. A good show of body language can affect your sales and even job position.

Your posture and height are the one of the few things that people notice. People who are tall and stand straight are associated as being confident. This is highly important in business especially when dealing with clients. Posture creates positive energy that you are not burdened with problems. Straight posture can further add authority if your chin is slightly pointing upward and your chest is projected outward.

People get influenced easily if you speak to them while looking in their eyes. This conveys an image of seriousness and adds credibility to your message. Be mindful that you should look in a person's eyes only 60% of the time. Any more than this will intimidate your client. Use the other 40% looking at random areas beside the eye to ease tension.

While walking exude confidence and authority by swinging your arms in a firm manner. Make every action precise. Eloquence while moving make it appear that you don't make mistakes and that you calculate every movement.

Previously, we discussed the Merkel Rhombus, which is a hand gesture created by holding your hands together and forming a triangle, and then slightly moving the thumbs toward you to make a rhombus shape. The Merkel Rhombus is a new gesture that symbolizes a calm but serious behavior. Using this body language will make you approachable at the same time respected.

The Merkel Rhombus goes well with a firm and soft voice. People tend to listen more closely to a soft but audible voice rather than a loud one. A slow rhythm will make every person cling on to your every word. Just be careful not to speak too slowly because people might lose interest in you.

While standing up, take note of your feet. You might be appearing confident from the waist up, but if your legs won't lose their nerves, they'll make it obvious. Counter this by slightly opening your legs and creating a 45 degree angle between them. Refrain from moving because it might bring back your anxiety and soon you'll be shaking again.

Contrary to popular belief, putting your hands on your waist is not a sign of felinity. In fact, male executives do this gesture more than women, for you make it appear that you are calm and relaxed in the face of stressful activities.

Combining these non-verbal authoritative cues to gestures that establish rapport will help you become an effective businessman. Non-verbal communication greatly increases your charisma that persuades people to agree to you.

Chapter 3: Questions About Your History

After they get a good sense of who you are inherently, they are going to start to pull information from you to determine what experience you have. If you are a good person with a good head on your shoulders and have a good sense of responsibility, then of course, you've already passed the first part of the interview. The thing is, just being a good person doesn't mean you are always the right candidate for the job.

These types of questions will help them to see your history, what kind of educational experiences that you have, and what skills and lessons from your last job you will bring into this one. These are questions that will give the person conducting the interview the greatest sense of the type of employee that you would be.

"Why did you leave your last position?"

Now this is the juicy part, where you start to reveal all the reasons that you are here. The employer is asking you this because they want to know why things didn't work out. Was the other position just not right for you? Did you leave your last job for a similar reason that you might end up leaving this job at this company you are trying to work at? They're going to want to know what happened to get a better insight into what went on. Spare them the dramatic details and keep it professional.

"I left my last position because I felt as though there was no room for advancement. I lacked creative control and I felt that my voice wasn't being heard. I needed a positive change in my life because I want to continue to grow and move forward."

"How did you find out about this current position?"

The reason that employers might want to know this is because it will reveal even more about you. First, they are going to want to know if you know anyone that already works there. This gives them a personal recommendation which can be helpful in understanding who you are. They are also going to want to know if you were actively job-hunting and being proactive about finding a new position, or if this is just something that slipped into your lap. They are also going to be interested in figuring out if any of their marketing tactics to reach out to other potential candidates are working or not.

"I actually found a listing for this job on an online job board. I have been looking and applying to several places and the objectives and job description of this position intrigued me."

"Can you tell me about a time where you went above and beyond and did even more than what you were expected to do?"

This is a hard question because it will put you on the spot. Employers still want to see if you can come up with information like this quickly and without another prompt. Though challenging, you will still want to have a specific example so that they can truly see the nature of your character. You will want to pull preferably from a time period when you were working somewhere else. Don't lie and make yourself sound extra good – they will be able to tell. Be honest and speak from experience because it will be easier to remember this event when it comes time to talk about it then. Describe not just how you were able to go beyond what you were asked to do, but how you also managed to help the business out in some way as well. This would be a good answer, but remember to keep it specific to the scenario and not to base it verbatim of ours:

"There was a time when I used to work at the ice cream store in my hometown. At night, it would be our duty to clean the place up and then clock out. The morning staff would be responsible for setting up for the next day. One night we were rather slow, so I decided to do all of the morning prep. The next day, the workers came in and didn't have to do much at all, making their morning start off easier. On top of that, they were able to open early and let some people in the store who had already been waiting."

"How would your last boss, manager, or supervisor describe you as an employee?"

This is another great question that they will likely ask you in some form or other. They want to know not just what you are like as an employee, but as someone who takes orders from the higher-ups. Were you feared by them? Did they have trouble telling you things? Were they your best friend? This previous relationship with the higher-ups will be important in helping them see what benefits you might bring to the position as an employee.

"I would say that I had a pretty good relationship with my last supervisor. We had open communication and instead of her always telling me what to do, we worked together to delegate tasks that I was better at to me and delegate tasks that she was better at to her, always checking in with each other to make sure both of our needs were being met."

"Can you describe to me a time in the past at a different position in which you were faced with a very challenging scenario, and what you did in the moment to resolve the issue?"

This is a good question where your answer will show that you are recognizing what you might have struggled with in the past, and how you handle pressure when you are faced with an obstacle. Remember to stay honest, and don't feel the need to go into every last agonizing detail about this.

"There was a time when I worked retail at a small gift shop. I noticed that a woman was stuffing some smaller jewelry pieces into her purse. She was standing right by the door, so I feared that she was going to make a run for it. I asked her if she needed any help and showed her some merchandise at the back of the store to buy me time while I talked to the owner. She was about to leave when I asked her if she was going to pay for the items in her purse. After retrieving the items, the owner and I decided to let her go since it was less than $30 worth of merchandise, but we made sure she wasn't allowed back in. I panicked at first and wanted to stop her immediately, but that could have turned into a messy situation, so I tried to remain as calm as possible and work with my supervisor to find the right solution."

"What is something that you saw a different employee do that you wouldn't do yourself? Can you describe a time when a coworker did something they shouldn't do? How did you handle this?"

This question might be phrased in a few different ways, but it's an important one that will give them insight into what you believe a good employee should be like. There are a ton of employees who do the wrong thing, so when you can show that you recognize the difference between right and wrong, it makes you all the more trustworthy. Don't shame anyone, don't use names, and make sure that you aren't being rude. Simply state what they did wrong, why it was wrong, and how you would have corrected the situation. Here is an example:

"There was a time in my last job when my coworker would always leave her leftover tasks for the person that came into the next shift. Even though she worked a slower shift, there would still be leftover tasks that she didn't bother to complete. Initially, I confronted her about it. I made sure all my tasks were done and left a note asking to help out during the slow shifts since ours were busier at night. She ended up ignoring this, so I had a discussion with my boss, and we came up with the perfect task list that fairly delegated the right amount of duties."

"What was the best part about your last position?"

This is a question that will let your interviewer know what you value the most in the workplace. When you can discuss with them the benefits of a position, they will be more likely to see what things you are passionate about.

Be honest with this, but of course keep it professional. You might have enjoyed that you had a few hours a day to sit on your phone after the boss went home, or maybe you liked that you got a free meal every shift. Keep it professional. Say something like this:

"One of the best parts of my last job was the sense of community that was there. Everyone got along and we all managed to work together in a harmonious way, playing off each other's strengths and weaknesses. It was unfortunate when I had to leave, but luckily, I still keep in contact with many of the same people and have no issue including them in my life to this day."

"If you were in a position where you had to fire someone, how would you do it? Have you ever had to let someone go in the past? What is your method for doing so?"

Not every position that you are interviewing for is going to require you to have to fire someone. There might still come a time when you have to be a part of the process of letting someone go. This is a challenging scenario that requires someone empathy, but also strong enough to reveal the truth. Even if you don't think you'd ever be in that position for the job that you are interviewing for, it's still important to have an answer to this question. Start by saying something such as this:

"I never have had to do this in the past, but I would imagine it would be a difficult scenario. If I ever had to, I would start by ensuring that I am in a private room with the person so as not to embarrass them. I would let them know the reason there is an issue in the first place, and then gently reveal to them what is going to happen next. I'd give them the remainder of the day to clear out if they wanted to but give them the freedom to decide when to leave during the day."

"What has been your greatest achievement in life? What about in your career?"

This question is usually asked because they want to know what your biggest accomplishment is. Think about what has been the single most important time in your life or something that you are proud of to share with others. They want to see your passion as you talk and find out how you might have been able to improve your own life.

Make sure that when you share this you give a personal or a career related answer, depending on how they might end up asking.

"My greatest achievement was certainly getting my Master's degree. Before I even applied to graduate school, I was nervous. I thought I wouldn't be able to do well because I had a bad semester as an undergrad. I let this become my source of motivation and graduated at the top of my class! Whenever I doubt myself I don't use my degree as a reminder, but instead, my dedication that was required for all the hours of studying and homework to remind me of all the things that I'm capable of."

Chapter 4: Talking About Your Advantages And Disadvantages

"Tell us about your pros and cons" - this is probably one of the most common questions in the interview. Someone is offered to name three of their weaknesses and three strengths, others are asked to describe the personality traits that hinder or help them in building a career – there are a plenty of options how recruiters formulate this question.

First, let's understand why this issue consistently ranks among the most frequently asked during the interview. What recruiters want to hear from the candidates? Honest confession of laziness and lack of organization or pompous speech of "I have virtually no weaknesses"?

Neither one nor the other. By asking the applicant about his advantages and disadvantages, a specialist of recruitment wants to know how mature is a person sitting in front of him, what is his self-esteem, if he is able to work constructively, including on himself. as it is known, there are no people without flaws: we are all woven of good and bad qualities. Namely in their recognition psychologists tend to see a sign of a stable and mature personality.

However, you do not need to invent anything to show recruiters that you fully meet the job requirements. Lying at the interview will not help you make a career. Be honest, but think over your answer in view of the given recommendations:

Lows in the pros. Psychologists believe that the best practice is response to a question about the shortcomings at the interview indirectly pointing out own advantages. "Friends think I'm meticulous. I really scrupulous, like checking all the details, and it annoys people. But I'm trying to learn to look at things more widely," – this is an excellent response of the applicant applying for the position of design engineer. "I think I am over-talkative, perhaps this is a consequence of my profession" - a good option for a candidate for the position of PR-manager or marketing specialist.

Another option of answer to the question about the shortcomings is to mention the lack of professional knowledge, not directly related to the desired position. Thus, you will demonstrate your recruiters frankness and willingness to develop. For example, if you are applying for a position of news feed reporter, you can safely admit that so far have not mastered the genre of the essay: in this work, you likely will not need this skill in the near future. However, you should still be careful not to harm yourself - think carefully about the answer.

Think about how the qualities which you are going to tell recruiters will create for you a competitive advantage over other candidates. For example, do not point to your leadership skills where they are not needed. "I'm pretty ambitious," - says the candidate for the post of accountant in a company with an established structure and ... left without a job offer. But in the young company, vigorously seizing market, such quality may well come in handy.

How to answer personal questions during the interview?
In preparation for the interview, many job seekers think through in advance the answers to possible questions - about the professional accomplishments, the reasons for leaving previous job, career goals. But personal questions are often taken by surprise. What recruiters want to know, asking, for example, about the reasons for divorce or the presence of chronic diseases in the child? How to respond to such questions, and whether to do it?

In most cases, questions about the private life are not caused by idle curiosity of recruiters; they have very specific goal - a more or less accurate psychological profile of the candidate. Experienced hiring managers know that often information which, at first glance, is not related to the professional qualities of the applicant, says more about him than he was talking about himself. That is why many HRs go for a violation of ethical norms and show interest to the private life of the candidate.

For the successful employment psychologists advise not to neglect the possible answers to personal questions: "What you care about that?" "Why do you want to know?" - such counter-questions to address HR management hardly will benefit your career. Try to find an opportunity to respond, and if the question seems too personal, politely and gently turn the conversation in another direction.

"Do you live with parents or separately?" - it would seem, what does this have to do with future work in the position of sales manager? Meanwhile, detailed response to this question can talk about such personal characteristics of the applicant, as the maturity, independence, responsibility towards the family, as well as on the level of his income. If a candidate talks about high earnings in the previous place of work, but he lives in a studio apartment with his parents or other relatives, recruiter may begin to doubt his sincerity, and hence the level of professionalism.

"Do you have your own apartment or rent it?" – this is another frequent question during the interview. At first glance, what interest business recruiter has to jobseekers property? Most likely, in such way the personnel manager is trying to understand the structure of your costs. It's one thing if the candidate has his own housing, the other - if he is forced to save each month rather big amount to pay the rent of apartment, and the third - if he pays the mortgage. In addition, the answer to this question will help supplement your psychological portrait of valuable information - whether you are willing to bear a serious responsibility to the credit institution.

Many young women have heard on interview questions like, "When you are planning to have a baby?" Of course, this is a very personal question, and often job applicant lost in answering it. After all, it is not always possible to accurately plan the birth of a baby: it is a question not only of the desire but also the state of health.

Desire of recruiter to know about your plans is clear: not all employers are willing to invest in the adaptation of the employee, which soon plans to leave on maternity leave. How to answer this question - directly or evasive, you decide. "In the near future we do not plan to have children" – such a response do not oblige you to anything, and thus dispels some fears of employer.

By law, you cannot be refused to be accepted for a job if you want to become a mother, or are already pregnant. However, it is likely that the true cause of refusal in this case will not be communicated.

"How often your child is sick?" is one more personal question, often asked by women during the interview. At this, for recruiter it does not matter what the temperature accompanies a cold in a baby - he is more concerned about the frequency and duration of your sick lists. It is better to answer frankly, because it is important also for you: the HR manager asks you to prioritize. If the career for you at the moment is no less important than the education of offspring, boldly answer that there is someone to look after baby. "The child is sick as often as other children, but grandmother (nurse, husband, etc...) is ready to stay with him" - this answer is quite satisfactory for the employer.

"What are you fond of?", "Do you have any hobbies?" – asking such questions recruiters are trying to figure out what are your temperament and character, whether you are suitable for the position by personal qualities. If, for example, the candidate claims to PR-manager position in a young and rapidly growing company, but says that he spends weekends in a chair knitting, the manager on staff will have reasonable doubts in his sociability.

"What is the last book you read?" – this is a question for revealing the overall development of the candidate. What he reads - only professional literature or finds the time to reread the classics? Although the objectivity of this method could be argued, it is still applied. There is no need to compose a list of literature, which, as it seems to you, makes you smarter in the eyes of a hiring manager. It is better to call the two books that you really have read recently: one professional and one fiction. Thus, you show that you develop not only as a professional but also as a person.

Personal questions are not uncommon in the interviews, and how you respond to them, to some extent, the decision about accepting you in a new team depends on. Therefore, talking with recruiters, be polite, diplomatic and sincere. If you do not want to respond to some particularly personal question - calmly and kindly tell that you are not ready to discuss it.

Chapter 5: Power Words to Blow Them Out Of The Water

Your goal in an interview is to make an impression and stand out from the crowd. There are some words that you can use to do just that. Barry Drexler, an interview coach, has conducted more than 10,000 interviews, and with his experience in HR, he has come up with 12 of the most powerful words that you should use in the interview process.

Leadership and management

You may not be applying for a position as a manager, but many companies want to know that you have some experience in this area, because you may be called upon to lead a team or give orders in some capacity. Even Burger King has some supervisors. So, if you can say things like "I managed a team of workers or I led a group of colleagues," then you can have a leg up in the process, because you demonstrate that you have skills that can eventually lead to leadership opportunities, even within this company.

Strategy and plan

Employers view candidates who have a strategic plan in mind more favorably. If you have experience with roles or responsibilities that required strategy, it shows that you have a background that is necessary to take on challenges and difficulties that may come your way in your new role. If you have a plan, then you know what to do and what steps you need to take to achieve the goals and complete tasks that are required for the job function. It also shows that you are a visionary who will carry out a plan to completion.

Established

Drexler says this word is powerful, because it shows that you have been able to complete a project and it demonstrates your authorship of a strategy or plan that was carried out. For example, you could say that you established a certain plan for a company. That would carry a lot of weight, because you authored the plan that was completed and accomplished a goal for the company.

Results and achieved

Employers love it when you talk about what you have achieved. This shows that you were able to reach the objectives that you had set. It also shows that you are a committed employee who always follows through on promises, goals, and other objectives that are set. It also gives you a sense of credibility and proves you are trustworthy as a worker. It is powerful for the interviewer to hear about the goals you have achieved.

Influence

Another word that is important is influence. When you show that you have influenced others, then you show yourself to be both a reliable and interesting candidate. You can talk about how you influenced the management to carry out some kind of plan. Instead of saying, "My managers really liked my plan," you could say, "I influenced the management to carry out this action plan, which succeeded in growing the business."

Recommend and suggest

When you use these words, you show that you are willing to contribute to the growth of the organization and want to do your best to promote your own plans and persuade the management to follow your advice and ideas. For example, you could say, "I recommended that my boss do _____, and they listened to my counsel. In the end, the business succeeded in _____."

Collaborate

When you use the word "collaborate", you indicate that you can work well with others. You're not just working for yourself. Instead, you're proving that you can be a member of a team and contribute meaningfully to it. You can talk about how you collaborated with others and how you were a key member of a group. You could say something like, "I collaborated with the marketing team to produce a strategy that worked for the company."

Example

Isaac is in an interview to get the position of data analyst.

Isaac: As you can see on my resume, I collaborated with many members of the data analysis team at my previous job. We were able to accomplish numerous tasks which enabled the company to move forward.

Interviewer: Isaac, would you tell us about a time where you had to lead a team?

Isaac: Yes, in fact, I led a team last year. We analyzed a survey that had been carried out by Coca Cola, and we were able to accomplish a goal. I collaborated with the members of the team. We succeeded in _____. In addition, I recommended to my manager that we do

_____. In the end, my recommendation helped the organization to achieve the aim of _____.

Isaac used several keywords that were powerful and would wield influence over the decision of the HR team. He used to "accomplish", "collaborate", "succeed", "achieve", and "recommend", all of which would be helpful in securing him the position on the team.

Conclusion

It is important that you find ways that you can become more confident during an interview. You can use some power words to get you going. Always remember to be positive and reflect on your past experience, emphasizing what you were able to take from each aspect of your background. Strengthen your case by talking about your accomplishments, how you overcame adversity, and the skills that you can bring to the position. The main thing is matching your skills and experience with the position and proving why you would be the best candidate for the job. You have to find persuasive ways to do that. It all starts with your language and the words you choose to project your image. Remember that you have all the background and skills necessary to do it. All you need to do now is to communicate it and make your case. Then, you can achieve your goal and snag your dream job!

Chapter 6: People Skills Questions

Employers don't just care if you can do the job—lots of people can. What they want to know is if you want to do the job (your motivation) and if you'll fit in with the rest of the people you need to deal with (your people skills) on the job.

For this reason, behavioral interviewing is very common, which means the interviewer will ask lots of nosy questions about your past behavior, believing there's no better way to predict your future actions than by hearing about your previous actions in similar situations. You may also encounter situational interviewing, in which you are asked hypothetical questions so the interviewer can see how you react in imaginary situations, which may or may not take place in this job.

Behavioral interviewing asks lots of questions about your past behavior, because of the belief that past actions are the best predictors of your future actions in similar situations. Situational interviewing poses hypothetical questions like "what if or "let's say" to see how you'd behave in possible situations.

What is your management style? Or: Give me an example of when you had to show good leadership. Or: Describe your leadership style or skills...

What the interviewer is asking/looking for: In most industries, the ability to manage people is considered important to advancement in your career. Because of this, the interviewer wants to know how you lead, plan, organize, and control things—the four main components of management.

Good answer: Think about times when you got things done with the help of other people—if not at work, then in your volunteer, leisure, or school activities. Then think about good bosses and bad bosses you've had and why they were good or bad. Perhaps your bad boss used to give you deadlines and then ask a week before the due date where the project was, or yell at you without explaining what you did wrong, or hog all the credit.

You learned by negative example that a good boss gives credit where it is due, communicates clearly, and is fair. In addition, criticism of your work should be constructive, pointing out what you did wrong and what you need to do to improve without attacking you personally. Your answer should reflect some of these good traits, and be ready to give an example or two from your experience.

Bad answer: Anything that shows you haven't managed people at all or thought about how you deal with them. Or that you display the hallmarks of a bad boss.

How do you motivate people you manage?

What the interviewer is asking/looking for: He or she wants to see you are generous with praise and credit for a job well done, and possess enough insight to know different people are motivated by different things, instead of following a cookie-cutter management approach.

Good answer: Show that you aim to inspire and teach the people you manage and respect their individual differences, instead of being an autocrat who issues orders with no explanation.

Bad answer: An answer that reveals you don't bother much about motivating your underlings—and as far as trying to understand their differences, forget it.

Tell me about your track record for promoting your staff...

I had a team of 12 sales people and 8 of them got promoted in the last two years.

What the interviewer is asking/looking for: The interviewer wants to know you have the "right stuff" in terms of identifying talented workers and helping develop their potential so they can contribute to the best of their ability to your organization.

Good answer: Having staffers who rise in your organization reflects well on you as a manager, so hopefully your success ratio in this area is good and you can give an example or two to prove it.

Bad answer: An answer that shows you never met an underling you liked enough to develop them, which does not reflect well on your skills as a manager.

5 years ago (as an assistant) he really wanted to leave the company but I managed to convince him not to do so – and now he is the operations manager.

What the interviewer is asking/looking for: He or she wants to see that you can spot talent and potential, and point out a flaw that can stand some improvement tactfully, without losing the employee.

Did you watch The Apprentice, the hit TV reality show where job-hunters compete for a top, well-paying spot in Donald Trump's company? Well, lessons from the series are being taught at top business schools nationwide, as MBA students study how the job-seekers learned to think on their feet, take risks, choose their team, and defend their actions. Some major lessons from The Apprentice include:

• Bosses want to hire people who are like others on their current team.

• Pay attention to what the boss says are his or her company values.

• You're always being interviewed.

• You have to fight to get the job.

• Show respect for your peers.

• All companies want team players who pitch in.

Good answer: Give an example that shows how you were able to smooth a diamond in the rough's edges, or clarify how to produce good results in your organization, to enable the employee to reach his or her potential.

Bad answer: An answer that shows you are not skilled at people-problem solving, and don't really know how to salvage a talented employee with a flaw or two.

Describe a time when a personal commitment interfered with a business crisis or last-minute meeting...

I had a last-minute meeting with the CEO and the same afternoon my son had a very important soccer game, so I asked my wife to record it with our camcorder. The next day me and my son watched the entire game at home (eating popcorn, hot-dog, things like that) and it was fun!

What the interviewer is asking/looking for: He or she wants to know if, when the going gets tough, you'll be running off to a personal appointment, or you can be counted on when your employer really needs you.

Good answer: Give an example of how you rescheduled your personal commitment, or arranged to have someone else handle it, to show how loyal you are when your employer is in a crunch.

Bad answer: A remark or nonverbal cue that shows resentment and/or incredulity that your employer may ever expect to come above your personal life in your list of priorities.

How did you get along with your last work team?

I worked well with my team and their different personalities.

What the interviewer is asking/looking for: Trust me, the interviewer does not want to hear the gory details about the ghastly coworkers you are forced to put up with, any more than hearing about your boss, the head ogre.

Good answer: Give an example of how the team pulled together to achieve a goal. Show that you are cooperative and pleasant as well as a good worker.

Bad answer: A litany of how lazy, incompetent, or mean-spirited your team members were, in contrast to you, a saint.

Lace your answers with "we" and "our," not just "I," to signify you are a team player who has the employer's interests at heart, not just your own.

Can you give an example of how you increased sales, saved money, saved time, or improved efficiency at your job?

I handled my workload more efficiently by holding calls and returning them at a certain time of day to give me uninterrupted working time.

What the interviewer is asking/looking for: These are an employer's major goals, so the interviewer wants to know if you've ever brought "added value" by making a meaningful contribution in any of these crucial areas.

Good answer: Tell the interviewer about any time you brought in new business or made a suggestion your employer acted on—a potential client to pitch, an advertising or publicity campaign you dreamed up that increased a client sales and led to more business with your firm, an employee you referred, researching a cheaper way to deliver a product you worked on.

Bad answer: You can't think of any time you demonstrated "added value" to your employer. Isn't it enough you come in 9 to 5 five days a week?

Substance versus style: Most employers want both. They want to know you can do the job well (substance) as well as act appropriately with people you have to deal with (style).

What would you describe as a good work environment?

It is where talent and hard work are recognized and rewarded.

What the interviewer is asking/looking for: He or she wants to feel a work atmosphere you can thrive in mirrors their own, and is eager to avoid a bad fit like a very laid-back person in a pressure-cooker environment, which you will feel impelled to quit at the first opportunity.

Good answer: If you have any idea from your research what the work environment is like at this employer, try to reflect it in your answer. If not, say something like an atmosphere where people are motivated to pull together to produce a quality product or service. Who can argue with you?

Bad answer: An environment that bears no resemblance whatsoever to the employer in question, which means your days there will probably be numbered or you will do your work perpetually disgruntled.

Constructive criticism points out what you did wrong and what you need to do to improve without attacking you personally (for example, by berating you as stupid or incompetent).

How do you handle rejection?

I don't take rejection personally, but as an abstract turn-down of a product or service I am representing.

What the interviewer is asking/looking for: Because rejection is a crucial part of any job in sales, which includes public relations, customer service, and telemarketing, the interviewer wants to make sure you are secure enough to bounce back after being rejected, instead of taking it personally and feeling miserable.

Good answer: Rejection often gives you helpful information about how to convince your next sales prospect or overcome the objection of your current prospect, thus increasing your success ratio.

Bad answer: Any clue that you are insecure and will act devastated, defensive, or nasty after rejection, which will interfere with doing your job well.

How would your coworkers describe you? Or: How would your supervisor describe you?

Enthusiasm, reliability, integrity, and being a team player.

What the interviewer is asking/looking for: This is a cagey way for the interviewer to find out what you're really like at work, in the words of coworkers and bosses.

Good answer: Hopefully they will have recognized some of your greatest strengths. Cite some strengths employers tend to admire.

Bad answer: Blurting out how coworkers and your supervisor see you unfairly, and how they are wrong.

How far do you want to rise (or see yourself rising) in our organization?

As far as my skills and the employer will allow.

What the interviewer is asking/looking for: He or she wants to gauge your level of ambition and future orientation. Giving them a sense of how motivated and goal-directed you are is more important than naming a specific job title.

Good answer: Obviously, your advancement will hinge both on your doing well and your accomplishments being recognized and rewarded by the employer, so try something noncommittal. If your goal is to head the department you would be joining, or become sales manager for a larger territory, say so.

Bad answer: Anything that shows you have given no thought to your future beyond the job you are applying for. On the other hand, saying "I want your job" generally is a bit too bold for most interviewers.

Summary

"People skills" are important, and by now the interviewer has a pretty good sense of how you get along with people, manage people, and cope with people when they're difficult.

You've now described your style with examples of how you've acted in the past, while he or she already knows your substance or qualifications. He or she also has a sense of what you think is a good work environment, if you've ever brought added value by increasing sales or saving money (which is dear to any employer's heart), as well as how far you want to go.

• Be prepared to give examples of how you handled past situations at work.

• Be prepared to describe how you are a team player who gets along with many different types of people.

• Be prepared to give examples of how you increased sales, saved money or time, or increased efficiency at work.

• You may be asked how you would handle hypothetical situations at work.

Chapter 7: Industry Related Questions

Tell me about a time when you went above and beyond expectations for a project or assignment.

Question Type:

Behavioral

Question Analysis:

One of the most common performance ratings for a hardworking and competent employee is "meets expectations" however, there will be opportunities when an employee should think outside of the box and go above and beyond the call of duty. Interviewers want to know that the candidate is willing to embrace these opportunities instead of shying away from them. You should discuss an example of a time when you identified an opportunity to exceed expectations and took advantage of it to bring value to your team or to a customer.

What to Avoid:

You should avoid opportunistic dialogue such as "I always exceed expectations." The interviewer will know this is not a realistic response. You should avoid examples that would be expected of any normal hard-working employee such as "I had a tight deadline coming up, so I worked 50 hours one week instead of my normal 40."

Example Response:

S/T: In my previous position as a web developer, I was assigned to a project to help a new customer integrate a payment processor for their ecommerce platform. As I was reviewing their website code, I noticed some unrelated HTML errors that were hurting their search engine optimization. I estimated that it would take me an extra twelve hours to fix the code, but I had no extra time in my schedule.

A: I explained the situation to my manager and asked for permission to do the work for the customer outside of my current work commitments. She was impressed that I took the initiative to bring additional value to a new customer at the expense of my evenings over the next week. I informed the customer about the errors and explained the SEO value it would bring if I corrected them.

R: Both my manager and our customer were appreciative that I was willing to work the extra hours at no additional charge to correct the issue for them. They ended up choosing our firm for a major project three months later and mentioned their earlier experience working with me as a deciding factor.

Tell me about a time you had to meet a tight deadline. What was the outcome?

Question Type:

Behavioral

Question Analysis:

The interviewer will ask this question to assess how well the candidate works under pressure and to see if they are willing to go the extra mile. You should provide an example of an unexpected situation that involved careful planning and required you to go above and beyond normal expectations.

What to Avoid:

You should avoid providing an example that is associated with a routine task such as "our monthly report was due the next day, but I had not started it yet" because you likely would have known about the deadline in advance, so it can appear as though it is only a tight deadline due to poor planning. Unless there was a significant unforeseen circumstance, you should also avoid discussing an example of a tight deadline which you or your team were not able to meet it.

Example Response:

S: In my previous role as a systems analyst, I lead a project to implement an EDI integration for a client's new procurement software.

T: Two weeks before the project deadline, the client informed us of a significant issue with their legacy software which was having a major impact on their day-to-day business. They asked if we could accelerate our timeline to deliver our project in five days. My manager and I discussed the situation and agreed to let the client know we would do everything we could to meet their new request.

A: I brought our team together to explain the situation and let them know that we would be focusing our time exclusively on this project to try to meet the accelerated deadline. I mapped out all remaining tasks on a whiteboard and we agreed on completion dates for each task over the next five days. I also scheduled daily update meetings to ensure we were staying on track and available to each other when issues came up.

T: We worked 14 hours per day over the next five days but through our collaboration and perseverance we completed the project on time. The client was extremely happy with results of the project and our manager gave each of us three extra vacation days for our hard work.

Tell me about a time you disagreed with your boss. How did you handle it?

Question Type:

Behavioral

Question Analysis:

The interviewer will use this question to assess how well the candidate handles a disagreement with someone in an authoritative position. The response will say a lot about the type of working relationship the candidate might have with a future boss. Your example should show that you have confidence in speaking candidly with your boss while still respecting their point of view and authority. You should try to think of a situation in which you disagreed with a situation but offered an alternative solution.

What to Avoid:

In your example, you should avoid personally criticizing your boss. This can raise a warning flag about your character. You should also avoid examples in which you raised the disagreement with your boss in the presence of other team members. Unless your boss encouraged feedback in a group setting, disagreements with those in authority should be handled in a one-on-one setting.

Example Response:

S: In a prior role as a procurement analyst, I was on a team that worked on procurement process efficiency through the measurement of purchasing history and inventory turnover trends. In an effort to add more reporting functionality to our purchasing history, our boss worked on a project to switch us over to a new software package.

T: Although the reporting functionality had improved, the new software did not integrate directly with our company's ERP system, so we were required to manually upload our purchase history which often took us hours to do.

A: I set up a meeting with my boss to explain my experience and concerns with the software. I first told him that I appreciated his hard work in seeking to find better reporting solutions. I then explained that I felt the benefits of the new software were outweighed by the time it took our team to manually add the purchasing history data which slowed down our analysis. As an alternative solution, I showed him documentation of research I had done on comparable software that could be integrated with our ERP system.

R: My boss was appreciative of me being upfront and honest about the change. He also thanked me for my research on the software solution I came up with and one month later we ended up switching over to it.

What do you like most about working in this industry?

Question Type:

Industry and Company Specific

Question Analysis:

The interviewer will ask this question for a couple reasons. First, a new hire is an investment for the company, so they want to validate the candidate's passion and long-term commitment to the industry. They will also use the question to see how well the response aligns with the duties of the job. When discussing your favorite aspects about the industry, be sure to highlight those that are highly relevant to the position.

What to Avoid:

You should avoid discussing characteristics that do not pertain to the position. For example, if you are interviewing for a marketing position and the job description desires competency in Adobe Photoshop, you would not want to express how much you love working with Affinity Photo (Mac competitor to Photoshop). You should also try not to be too vague in your response. "I love that I get to work with people" does not sound nearly as good as "I enjoy working directly with clients to diagnose their challenges and offer solutions that bring them a better return on investment on their advertising budgets."

Example Response:

The thing I enjoy most about offering software solutions in the sales industry is that no two days are ever the same. I have the opportunity to work with such a wide range of clients who possess diverse challenges and needs for their human resource systems. I take pleasure in fostering client relationships. To me, success looks like a client reaching out for help with confidence that I can solve their problem. Believe it or not, I also really enjoy the travel associated with this industry. I consider it an opportunity to be able to explore new cities while I am traveling to meet with current and prospective clients.

What was the most difficult decision you have made in the past year?

Question Type:

Behavioral

Question Analysis:

Candidates without management experience will often get tripped up over this question because they have not had to make what would traditionally be considered a difficult decision such as cutting a budget or laying off an employee. However, there are plenty of opportunities to discuss difficult decisions outside of management roles. The interviewer is looking for an answer that demonstrates rationale and strong problem-solving skills. You should discuss an example that shows your ability to weigh options and critically think through the situation before coming to the decision. Some examples of tough decisions include: reporting unethical behavior, providing a negative review for a co-worker, choosing a new vendor, and turning down a promotion.

What to Avoid:

You should avoid discussing personal decisions that are not relevant to the position such as "I decided to purchase my first home last year" or "three months ago, I decided it was time to break it off with my fiancé." The interviewer is looking for your decision-making capabilities in a professional setting. Your answer should include the result of your decision, so you should avoid examples where the decision lead to an unfavorable outcome.

Example Response:

S/T: In a previous role selling professional services for IT projects, I was offered a promotion to be our company's Midwest resource services manager. I was honored to be offered the promotion and asked my boss for a few days to consider it. The new position would have increased my responsibilities while offering a raise in pay. At the time, I was in critical stages of a few projects with my clients. I was also making inroads with prospective clients that would soon lead to new business. Before the promotion came up, I had a strong interest in exploring future opportunities within the company's marketing team which would be a change to a new department.

A: I set up a meeting with my boss to discuss my desire to remain in my current position as well as my inclination to find an opportunity in the marketing department for my next career move.

R: At first, he was a little surprised that I decided to turn down the promotion, but he agreed with me that I brought the most value to our clients by remaining in my current position. He thanked me for my honest assessment and connected me with a manager in the marketing department to discuss future opportunities.

What motivates you?

Question Type:

Ambition

Question Analysis:

Candidates often struggle with this question because it is so broad in nature. The interviewer is typically using the question to understand what type of work is encouraging and fulfilling to the candidate. Coming up with an answer does require some personal reflection but ultimately your response should be centered around positive results or characteristics in the professional setting. Ideally, your motivation comes from something that aligns well with the company's culture.

What to Avoid:

Some candidates see this as such a broad question that they answer it with personal examples such as "my husband and kids" or "my lake cottage" but the interviewer is typically looking for motivation from a professional perspective.

Example Response:

I am motivated by a team culture that encourages collaboration and innovation. When team members are encouraged to work together to change things for the better, it brings lasting value to the whole organization. There is nothing I like more than envisioning a better way to do something and seeing it come to life.

What do you like to do outside of work?

Question Type:

Background and Personality

Question Analysis:

This may seem like a "softball" question but the interviewer will be paying close attention to your response to see if you are a good fit for the company's culture. Employers look for candidates who make the most of their free time. Your answer should be focused on activities that benefit your own wellbeing and the wellbeing of others in the community.

What to Avoid:

You should avoid discussing activities that sound unprofessional such as "I enjoy drinking and tailgating every Saturday during football season" or "I play video games each night." You should also be careful not to provide a dry response that makes it sound like you have no hobbies. This can create a negative perception about your personality in the eyes of the interviewer.

Example Response:

I am an avid golfer and fly fisherman. I try to play at least one round of golf each week during the spring and summer and I just got back from a fly fishing trip in Yellowstone National Park. I also enjoy giving back to the local community.

What is your management style?

Question Type:

Background and Personality

Question Analysis:

This question is very common when interviewing for management or supervisor positions but may also come up for any role that requires some level of leadership capability. The interviewer wants to know if your management style would be effective for the position and align well with the company's leadership culture. You should focus your response on your leadership traits that would fit well within the company and bring value to the position.

What to Avoid:

You should avoid using absolute words to describe your management style such as "always," "never," or "must." For example, scheduling regular team meetings to encourage team discussion and collaboration is an excellent tactic but if you say, "whenever an issue arises, I always schedule a group meeting to collaborate until we find an answer," it sounds like you react the same way to every problem. You should discuss your style with an emphasis on being able to adapt to a specific situation or to the unique personality traits of your team members.

Example Response:

I believe that the most effective managers are capable of adapting their style to the unique traits of each team member to empower them to reach their full potential. My typical management style is to lead by example, use clear and concise communication, encourage collaboration, and provide constructive feedback. As I get to know my team members, I will often make adjustments to my style to help bring more value to the team. For example, I typically like to meet with each of my team members once per month to discuss their concerns and offer constructive feedback. Last year, I noticed that one of my new team members was second guessing her work which was causing her to fall behind on a project. I decided to adjust my meeting schedule with her to once per week, so I could offer her more regular feedback. I immediately started to see an increase in her confidence which lead to better efficiency in her work. Eventually, she felt comfortable enough to reduce our meeting schedule to once per month. She mentioned that the weekly feedback I offered was a key element in helping her build up her confidence on our team.

Why should we hire you over the other candidates?

Question Type:

Background and Personality

Question Analysis:

This question is almost identical to question #3 but when some candidates are asked to compare themselves to the other candidates, they feel a sense of pressure to oversell themselves to the point of sounding like a used car salesman. However, it is important to remember that you will typically not earn the job offer on a single "grand slam" response. It is earned over the course of a full interview. The interviewer will use this question to learn more about the candidate's strengths and any type of unique value they would bring to the position. You should focus your answer on your strengths that correspond well with the job requirements and try to discuss at least one unique trait that would be attractive to the company.

What to Avoid:

Even though the question invites you to do so, you should avoid making any assumptions about the other candidates such as "I would work harder than any of the other candidates." Negative statements about candidates you likely do not even know can come off as presumptuous and arrogant. Instead, you can acknowledge that you cannot speak for the other candidates, but you feel confident that you are the right fit for the position.

Example Response:

Well, I cannot speak with regard to the other candidates, but I can tell you why I am an excellent fit for the position. My experience leading the development of over 25 successful web applications has put me in a position to understand what it takes to strategize, plan, and execute any type of coding project. My experience leading teams has taught me strong organizational and motivational skills. Aside from my strong skillset that aligns with the position, I am always looking to bring added value to any process or project through innovation. I am never content with a system or process if there is a more effective or efficient way. I typically drive innovation by collaborating with both internal and external resources and by leveraging new technology.

Tell me about a time you set a challenging goal for yourself. How did you ensure that you achieved it?

Question Type:

Behavioral

Question Analysis:

The interviewer will use this question to get a better sense of the candidate's ambition and initiative. They also want to know the strength of the candidate's planning skills when faced with a difficult challenge. In your response, you should focus the discussion around the planning and analysis that enabled you to take calculated actions to achieve your goal.

What to Avoid:

If you have professional experience on your resume, you should typically avoid discussing personal goals such as "I set a goal to lose 50 pounds" or "my goal was to complete a marathon." Instead try to draw on a goal you achieved that relates to your profession. You should also avoid trivial goals such as "I set a goal to arrive at work by 8:30 AM each day."

Example Response:

S: In my previous role as an IT security analyst, I noted that all managers and directors in my department had the

Certified Information Systems Security Professional (CISSP) certification in their email signature. I spoke with my manager and learned that the company highly encouraged the certification for IT employees who sought promotions and leadership opportunities.

T: I wanted to place myself in a position to be considered for growth opportunities in our department, so I set a personal goal to pass the CISSP exam within three months. The exam is six hours long and covers eight different subjects, so I knew I would need to create and execute a detailed plan to achieve my goal.

A: Before I started studying for the exam, I reviewed the study materials and spoke with co-workers who had passed the exam to determine the expected number of study hours. I looked through my calendar for the next three months to identify study time outside of the working days and on weekends. After determining that I would need roughly 100 hours to study for the exam, I created a robust plan assigning sections of the preparation materials to each study session on my calendar.

R: It was a strenuous three months, but I remained focused on my end goal to ensure I stayed on task with my study plan. I ended up acing the exam and I accepted a promotion within our department later that year.

Chapter 8: Informational Interviews

Informational interviews are a means to gather information about some specific career field or job. You can conduct these interviews and ask the participants questions before choosing your career.

Advantages of Informational Interviews

Informational interviews are very useful because they help to:

- Narrow down your options

- Prepare you for a specific career

- Discover occupations that you didn't know existed or weren't familiar with

- Gain self confidence and experience when interviewing with professionals

- Discover the types of personalities that thrive in particular career fields

- Have realistic expectations related to employment in particular fields

- Obtain an accurate idea of the existing job market

- Expand your connections with professionals in the field of your choice

How to Start

Choose an Occupation

You should select one or more occupations that you wish to investigate. Decide what information you are interested in acquiring about them. Write down all of the questions you want to get answered.

As with other interviews, it is recommended that you read and gather as much information about the company or organization as you can before you go to the interview.

Identify the People to be Interviewed

You can contact anyone for this type of interview. Start with a list of those people you already know such as your fellow students, friends, neighbors, people who worked with you in the past, or your present coworkers and supervisors. You can visit the alumni office or career center of your college and get the names of those who are currently working in the fields you are interested in. You can approach your family members' acquaintances or public speakers for an interview. Organizational directories, professional organizations, and the yellow pages are some other good resources. Besides this, you can also call a company and ask to speak to someone who has a particular job title.

Conduct Research Before the Interview

In order to conduct an effective informational interview, you cannot go in blindly. It is essential to prepare beforehand. You must do research about various things such as the company, its products, and the person you are going to interview. If you know enough about the company, you will be able to ask in-depth questions related to the job and organization. This in turn will give you the confidence to communicate efficiently.

There are a number of benefits to doing research.

- You can ask more relevant and intelligent questions.

- You can respond more thoughtfully if the interviewee asks any questions.

- You will not waste time by asking questions that can be answered easily by doing some research.

Think about what you want to know about a particular occupation and then figure out the people who may be able to provide that type of information. You can ask the organizations for their pamphlets and brochures to get additional information. The college's library can also be useful for this purpose.

Schedule the Interview

You can contact the person you want to interview in several different ways. You may send a letter or an email, make a phone call, or meet the person personally. You can even ask an acquaintance of the interviewee to get you an appointment.

Letter or Email

You can write an introductory email or letter similar to a cover letter that does not include a job pitch. It can be typed or printed neatly. It must include:

- A short introduction about yourself

- Your purpose for writing to the person

- A brief description of your interest or experience in the individual's field, location, or organization

- Why you wish to talk with the person

- Be straightforward and say you are seeking advice and information

- When and how you will be contacting the person again

Proofread and save the copies of all of the correspondence. Make it a point to contact them again as mentioned. You can call the person on phone and get an appointment. Do not wait for the prospective interviewee to call you on his own. If you are unable to contact the person, you can find out the most suitable time from the receptionist and call again.

Phone or in Person

People who participate in informational interviews usually allot around twenty to thirty minutes to talk about their professional expertise. You should be flexible about scheduling the interview because these interviewees have other commitments. In case a particular volunteer interviewee is too busy, ask him when you can call back and discuss setting up an appointment. Different techniques can be used to request an informational interview. Some good approaches are:

"Hello, I am so and so. I am doing career research related to your occupation. I would like to meet with you and talk to you for around thirty minutes to learn more about this particular job."

"Hi, I am so and so. I am studying at ABC college. I found your name in the organization's directory. I am interested in one day working in a career similar to yours. I hope you can help me to learn more about the job and career options. I would be delighted if you could spare twenty to thirty minutes for an informational interview."

If you want to personally ask the person for an appointment but are unable to meet with him, you can use the receptionists and other support staff as a resource to get information. You can ask them your questions because they may know a lot about the company.

They may be able to tell you how the company works and the job requirements and also name the key people. You should explain to them what you are seeking so that if they feel someone else is better suited to answering questions then, they can refer you to that person. Make it clear that you want to get direct information and will be happy to hear any information they have to share.

Most prospective interviewees are willing to spare twenty to thirty minutes to respond to your question. They may be ready to talk on phone or meet you in their workplace. If you are given a choice between the two, choose to have the interview in the workplace. This will enable you to learn more and make a stronger connection with them.

The Phases

Before the Interview

You should call the person the day before the interview to confirm the appointment. If you are not sure where the interviewee's office is located you can ask at this time. Plan to arrive ten minutes before the interview.

Ninety percent of job openings are not advertised. You may learn about job vacancies that are not found in the newspapers or employment offices through such an interview, so prepare yourself so that you make a great impression. Choose clothing that you would wear for a usual job interview.

During the Interview

Take a pen and notebook: Pretend to be a reporter. It is not necessary to write down everything. However, there might be some phone numbers, names, and other information that you will want to remember.

Take a copy of your resume: Find out what qualities and qualifications the employers look for while hiring. If the situation is appropriate, you can ask the interviewee to review your resume.

Introduce yourself: Once you arrive, you will typically be met by a front desk employee who will introduce you to the interviewee. When you meet him, thank him for taking the time to speak with you. Once again make it clear that you want to learn more about the person's particular career field. Adopt an informal style of conversation during the course of the informational interview.

Be courteous and professional: Maintain good posture and eye contact. Make positive remarks and be light hearted but professional.

Show interest and be enthusiastic: Talk in an informal way and show interest. Ask concise and direct questions. You can refer to the list you have prepared to keep track of your questions but do not curb spontaneous discussion.

Share some things about yourself: You may share some facts related to yourself, but remember that your main purpose is to gather information and learn as much as possible about the field in preparation for a future career.

Many times, the informational interviews turn into employment interviews. If this happens, verify that there is a job opening and emphasize your skills and how they are related to the particular job.

Do not ask for a job: You should not ask for any job during an informational interview. Employers agree to such an interview only because they are sure that it will not be used as an opportunity to seek a job.

If, in the course of the interview, you determine that it is a good job for you, wait until the next day to speak to the employer. The next, call the employer, tell him that the interview helped to confirm your interest in that career, and you wish to formally apply for a position.

The interviewee might offer you a job or an internship. There are many instances where employers have offered jobs to the people who have conducted such interviews. If it is a good offer, go ahead and accept it.

If you ask only for information, you will be treated differently than people who are only interested in a job. Approach the employer by seeking job advice rather than an actual job.

Stay on the right track: Do not waste time asking unnecessary questions.

Listen to them: Listening is a very important part of communication. In addition to asking questions, you should listen carefully. Show them that what they are saying is important to you.

Expand your network of contacts: This interview is like an investment. You spend time with the interviewee sharing information about yourself, asking questions, and getting advice. You are investing your time with him in the hope of gaining something. By spending time with you, he is also hoping to gain something. It is a good idea to keep in touch with each other after the interview ends so that you can both continue to benefit from each other.

Even if the interviewee does not offer you a job, he may be able to refer you to other employers.

Ask for referrals: Before leaving, remember to ask the interviewee if he knows other people who might be willing to speak to you. Ask permission to use his name when contacting potential interviewees.

After the Interview

Thank people: Make sure that you send a letter or card within three days to thank the interviewees. This will help to stay in touch with them. Them that talking to them has been very helpful and that you are grateful to them for taking time out of their day to meet with you. To add a personal touch, you can include a quote they said during the interview. You may also want to ask them to send you any information that they think would be helpful for your career. Include your phone number and address at the end.

Record, analyze, and evaluate: After the interview, remember to write down all of the information that you have gathered. This includes the names of potential future interviewees. Store all of the information together for when you need it. It will be useful for you when you conduct more occupational explorations. Employers are generally impressed by activities like that. It can help pave the way to your ideal job.

When you evaluate the interview, you should ask yourself:

- What is it that you have learned from the interview (consider both the negatives and positives)?

- Does this information that I have gathered match with my interests, values, goals, and abilities?

- What is it that I still have to find out?

- What should my action plan be?

Conclusion

Asking questions can help you to learn about unpublished job opportunities. Even if you do not adopt some formal procedure, just chatting with people on the bus or while waiting in line can lead you to unknown job opportunities.

Questions Asked in Informational Interviews

Here is a list of questions that can be asked during informational interviews:

1. How did you become interested in this particular field?

2. What led you to your current job?

3. How do the knowledge and skills you learned in college apply to this job?

4. Describe your typical day in this job.

5. What future trends do you see for this particular career field?

6. What is your most satisfying accomplishment in this job?

7. What do employers look for in candidates who apply for a job in this field?

8. What is it that you like the most or least about this job?

9. What can I do now to prepare myself for a similar job after I graduate?

10. What advice would you like to give to college students who are interested in this career field?

11. What are the things you learned about this work that you did not know when you graduated?

12. What job search techniques would you suggest for those who have recently graduated?

13. What should I look for in a boss when applying for jobs?

14. What is the "typical" path of this career field?

15. How do employers in this field feel about employees who have a liberal arts degree?

16. Does your organization participate in any internship programs? Can you tell me about them?

17. What are training experiences, trade journals, or professional associations that may help new professionals in this career field?

18. Could I use you as a contact when I start looking for a job or an internship?

Chapter 9: The Power of Storytelling

Storytelling is the ability to tell a story in a way that the listener feels they relate and understand. Anyone can tell a story, but it takes a special type of storytelling for the listener to be able to actually feel what is happening. When you are in a job interview, and the interviewer asks you to tell them about a time something happened, they want you to tell them a story about your past. If your story is uninteresting and not personalized, it is not going to be something that stands out to them. However, if you have a story that they can relate to, and they feel connected to, it could possibly be something that they remember you by and it could even be something that lands you the job.

How can you use this strong tool in your interviews? You can use storytelling when you are answering any long question that requires you to give an example of a time you did something in the past. Examples of these questions are:

● Tell me about a time when you faced a challenge at work, and how you got through it.

● Tell me about a time a decision was made at work and you disagreed with it. How did you handle this situation?

● Tell me your greatest professional strengths and how you have used it in your past employment.

● Tell me about a time when you saw a problem at work and explain how you solved it.

● Tell me about a time when you made a mistake at work and how it was resolved.

● Give me an example of a time when you worked on a team and what helped you accomplish.

These are all questions that are commonly asked in interviews that could benefit from being told an answer in a story format. To do this, you will need some skills in storytelling in the context of an interview. We will look into these skills now.

The first thing that you need to do when telling a story related to an interview question is to remember that the interviewer is looking for the answer. The story can help them to relate to you in a personal way and to see how you have had to deal with struggles in the past, but they want to know the answer to the question. For this, you should always start with the answer. Start with one sentence that completely answers the question. As an example, if you are telling them about a time when you faced a challenge at work and how you got through it, begin by saying that you once had all your staff called in sick on the same day, and you solved the problem by creatively moving staff around in the office to make sure that all of the important tasks got done before the ones that could wait. After you insert with a one-sentence solution, then you can start to tell the details. The details are still helpful, but you want to start with the actual answer so that the interviewer hears it right away and that they know you are responding to exactly what they are asking. Answering the question in the first sentence also shows you are confident in your answer and that you knew what to say right away.

After you answer the question, you can start to provide the background information. The interviewer will likely be interested in this information because they want to know exactly how you accomplished solving your problem. They will want to know all of the details so that they can tell what you are capable of. You can provide the context of why the challenge occurred and why you were the one that had to solve it. Any related information will be interesting and helpful to the interviewer who is listening to your story.

After you provide the context, explain why you were the one that had to deal with the challenge. You'll want to explain your role in the process, talk about how you were the one to solve it, and why it was not the responsibility of everyone else. It can also make you seem like someone who sees problems and fixes them. The way that you word this part of the story is important because it will reflect who you are considered by the interviewer. The interviewer will more than likely love to see you as a leader or someone who sees problems and fixes them. They may not, however, love to see you as the person who made a mistake. For this, it is important how you word this part of the story. You want the story to show all of the good attributes that you have. This is another reason why it is helpful to plan the story out in advance. If you go through the story in advance, you can define your role as something that the employer actually wants to see.

After you define your role, you will want to share the results of the story. This is when you tell how the problem worked out. You can tell if your problem solving worked or if you had to figure out something else afterwards. You do want to keep this step in mind when you are choosing your story that you would like to tell. This is because you want the story to have positive results when you tell it to the person who is interviewing you. You do not want them to see you as a person who failed or someone who does not have the results. Stories of failed results are not stories that should be told in interviews unless they're asked for. For this, you also want to keep this part of the storytelling in mind when you are choosing a story because you want your role to be a positive one. You want your role to portray who you can be, and that is the perfect employee for the opening that the employer currently has.

After you finish telling your story, consider taking some time to make sure that the lesson of your story is clear. You do not want to tell the story in an interview that does not have a purpose or point. You do not want to tell the story that has nothing to do with the question asked. If you think your story only slightly relates to the question, or that its relation was not clear, it is your job to make sure that the lesson of the story is shown clearly by the end of your speech. You can't simply state what the lesson is, or you can use an example to show it to your interviewer. You do not want the interviewer to get the wrong impression; you want them to see the side of you that you were trying to portray. After all, you did just tell an entire story to show why you would be a good fit for a job. Do you want the story to be worth it and come across the way you actually intend?

Let's look at an example. Think about a person who has interviewed you and asked you the question, "Tell me about a time you made a mistake at work, and how you recovered from it." To answer this question in a story format, you could write something like:

"One time, I gave the wrong order to a customer, and I had to fix this problem before the reputation of the business was ruined. When I was 16, I worked in a little old grocery store in the middle of my small town. This grocery store was one of the few establishments in a few miles' radius, so it had multiple different functions. One of the things the grocery store had was a deli counter. Behind the deli counter, was a broiler. This meant that people who came into the grocery store wanted to get fresh broiled chicken. My job, as a teenager, was to cook this chicken.

One day, I got a call that a customer wanted one dozen chicken legs. This was our first order of the day, so I knew we had plenty of chicken. The customer would come in two hours later, so I figured I would just cook the chicken in an hour and a half so it would be hot and ready when they arrived to pick it up. However, when I went over to cook the chicken a half hour before the customer was going to arrive, I found out that there were only 11 chicken legs thawed and ready to cook. This was a big problem. I told the customer that I would have 12 chicken legs ready for them, and I could only have 11. To handle this, I put the 11 chicken legs in the broiler along with a few extra pieces of different parts of the chicken. I then went right to the phone.

Once I got to the phone, I called the customer who ordered the 12 chicken legs. I called them to explain the problem and to offer any solutions that may help. I gave the customer three choices. I told them that they could either wait an extra hour for another chicken leg to unthaw, that they could have a discount on their 11 chicken legs, or that they could have some other pieces of meat along with their chicken legs to make up for the missing piece.

I could have just ignored this and given the customer the eleven chicken legs, hoping that they did not notice that one was missing. This would have been bad customer service, and it would have given the grocery store a bad reputation. It would have affected my job, as I'm sure my boss would have heard of it. It would have affected my guilt level as well because I would have felt bad about not giving the customer what they wanted and what they paid for.

It was not easy to call the customer. It was actually difficult. I had to tell them that I messed up and I did not have what they wanted. However, they appreciated my customer service. They appreciated that I called and told them the truth that I had made a mistake and that I wanted to fix it. They chose one of my three options and happily picked up the chicken. They never complained of the situation, so they must not have been too upset.

The moral of the story is I did not carefully check we had enough chicken before telling the customer that I could give it to them. However, I did help solve the problem in the right way. The story shows me that honesty is always the best policy. Even when I make mistakes, I always need to own up to them to fix them. I learned this at the young age of 16, and I have been perfecting my morals and work ever since."

Looking at this example, it started by telling the answer to the question. It then gave the context and some background information, explained the mistake and finished by sharing the results and making the lesson clear.

Telling stories can be a strong tool in interviews, especially when the interviewer is asking to hear one. Make sure that you have your stories ready in advance so that you can tell the ones that portray your best sides when you are actually in the interview. Make sure to follow the five steps when telling the story so that you can tell it in a way that stands out and shows them everything that you want them to see. If you follow these tips and tricks while telling stories in your interviews, your interviewer will see more into your personality through them, and your stories will show what you are truly capable of. This will make your stories a great addition to your interview skills and help you land your dream job.

Now that we have looked into all of the ways that words and verbal communication can help you and your interviews, let's look into how your nonverbal communication can help you as well.

Chapter 10: Emotional Intelligence in your Job Interview.

First of all, you cannot understand the functioning of the whole world, without understanding yourself. Using emotional intelligence is the first step to be able to look critically at the people around us. Social competences, such as empathy, assertiveness, confidence, cooperation, are essential aspects of your personal life. It depends on it whether we will be the soul of the party, liked, and accepted. We will not achieve this only due to high IQ or scientific knowledge.

It is also worth realizing that during the interview, it is our qualities such as the ability to behave appropriately, the ease of establishing interpersonal relationships, understanding the situation, the skill of persuasion makes up the first impression and can determine whether the employer will see us as a future employee.

Communication Skills at Job Interviews

You have come too far to mess things up. You have done a lot of research, spent your time to gather all that you need for the interview, and even groomed yourself for the occasion. It would be a pity to lose it all for mistakes you did on the actual interview. Remember the objective of your interview is to land a job offer. To realize this objective, you will, by all means, have to prove that you are the best there is. If you are waiting to do big things to blow away your hiring managers, it is time to wake up and smell the coffee. It is the little things that matter and that will possibly work for you or against you.

What to do during the interview

Say Hi to the receptionist

It is common courtesy to greet people you meet. You do not have to start up a conversation, as a matter of fact, it is not recommended that you do. If you can, also get his/her name if it is not on a tag somewhere. This is very important since some hiring managers seek to see just how keen you are and aware of your environment or even friendliness by asking you the name of the receptionist or even the guard at the door.

Which might seem harsh but valid. Hiring managers do not want to hire robots or persons who say they are friendly and do not care enough to know the name of the receptionist or even the guard.

Have the right body language

Your body language will communicate just as much as the information you offer to your hiring managers. You do not want to be in a situation that you say you are confident but your body language reeks of lacking in confidence. Try as much as you can to have your body language convey the same message as your words. If you say you are confident, do maintain an upright posture, maintain eye contact and have a convincing tone.

If slouching, fidgeting and looking down are bad habits that you possess, you can get rid of them by practicing in front of a mirror. Pull up a chair and observe your body language.

Also, avoid flattering behaviors like biting your lower lip or winking. You might be unaware that you wink at people or it is just something you picked up over the years, regardless, you might have to actively subdue them.

Have the right tone of voice

Like your body language, your tone will also speak a thousand words. You could repeat that you know how to do your job a thousand times but if you do not sound like you can, your words are worth nothing. Have a tone that will inspire confidence in your hiring manager.

So, how does one sound more confident during a job interview?

Take your time to think over the question, gather your thoughts before you answer. The recommended time to take for this is five seconds. Now it might seem like such a long time and awkwardness might set in but the interviewer sees it as you giving your answer some consideration.

Always have an interested tone though factual and straight forward. You should keep away from rising your pitch towards the end of your statements as this will turn them into questions making you seem uncertain of what you are saying. You should however vary your tone depending on the question and what it relates to. Do not overdo it though.

Do not apologize for being nervous. Doing this will actually put more scrutiny on just how worried you are about your performance.

Use a firm handshake

There are individuals who are sucker for firm handshakes. There are those who can tell who you are from the way you shake their hand. Just ensure you do not hurt your hiring manager while you are at it.

Sit only when you are asked to

When you walk into the room, only take a seat when they ask you to and not before. It is a sign of politeness. It is the same thing as when someone is at your door. They should wait until you invite them in (especially if you are not as close).

Have your loose items on the floor right next to you

You should never place your items on the interviewer desk unless they say that it is okay that you do so. Have all these items placed comfortably on your lap or on a coffee table right in front of you. As for your briefcase, have it right at your feet or on your side.

Have your mobile turned off

You do not want to have disruptions during the interview. Setting your phone to vibrate just won't cut it.

Thank your interviewer

The fact that they choose you out of the hundreds and thousands of applicants is worth saying thank you.

What not to do during an interview

Do not assume the interview is done until you are out of the door

From the moment you walk in the office the interview is on. Everything from your behavior, use of words to attitude is under scrutiny. As such, you should be overly careful of what you say. After all, everything you say and do will be held and used against you. Be at the very top of our game until you walk out that door, or better yet, out of the company building. You never know who you will bump into on your way out so be respectful to everyone.

Do not be too relaxed

Sure, the interview is a platform for you to gauge is you will love the job and you are encouraged to be relaxed. You should however not treat your hiring manager like your long lost friend (even if he/she is). You should be friendly, but remember you are seeking to be impressive. Being too relaxed may have you slipping up and saying the wrong things altogether.

Never badmouth your old job

Maybe your former boss was the devil incarnate and is probably the reason why you left your previous job. But be it as it may, you should not point it out to your hiring manager. As far as your hiring company is concerned, you should get along with everyone you are given to work with no matter how difficult they are. So rather than badmouth your previous boss or company, speak of the achievements you made as a team. Doing this will also keep you from coming across as self-centered.

Do not freak out if you do not know the answer

Some hiring managers are known for putting their interviewees on the spot. And since you never know what kind of hiring manager you will get, you should always be prepared. Never freak out when you are presented with a question that you do not know the answer to. Freaking out will make you lose all sense of rationality making things even worse. So how should you hand yourself in such a situation?

First, and most important, you should calm down. Freaking out will rise your heart beat rate, rise your temperature and cloud your judgments. Be sure to take deep breaths and convince yourself that all is well. After all, it is okay not to know the answer to a question.

Second, even when you do not know the answer to the question provided, never say that you do not know the answer without giving it a try. Also, as you try to give your answer, do not make things up. Hiring managers are not stupid and will be sure to see right through the crap.

You also have the option of asking follow up questions to ensure you understand the question right. Ask for clarification and more details that will help you provide a better answer.

But even after the clarification, if the question still proves difficult to answer, be sure to iterate what you do know rather than what you do not know. Also, you should spell out the steps that you could take to get to the answer of the question presented. This way, even while you may not have the answer at the moment, you assure the hiring managers that you have the ability to get to the answer if afforded more time.

Never lie

You should, by all means, be straight forward with your hiring manager. It is as they say, the truth always has a way of coming out. When lying, you may not be able to hold a sincere flowing conversation with the hiring manager and this might be a major turn off. Truth be told, honesty is the best policy. Even when you land that job position you will have started on the wrong foot and it is only a matter of time before your lies catch up with you.

Chapter 11: Can You Coach Others?

Interview Question

What have you done to help a peer understand skill areas to strengthen? Give an example.

Why do they ask this question?

Bad Answer

An example of a bad answer to this question would be:

I once had a group member in school who struggled to understand the basic accounting concepts in our accounting class. I knew the person was going to take some time to understand the concepts, so I just ended up doing their work for them so that we could finish the project in a timely manner.

Taking over for the group member helped us get a good grade·

Why this is a bad answer:
Even though you show that your group member has room for development, you don't really show the steps you took to develop them. You don't show that you were interested in developing them. For this question, you have to show

willingness to understand another person's weaknesses, and the desire to help them.

Good Answer

An example of a good answer to this question would be:
I once had a classmate in my tax research class ask me how to get better at tax research. I helped them understand what skills and knowledge to strengthen by asking them a series of questions. I asked them if they knew hierarchy of authority in tax research, and I also asked them where they started once they received a research topic. By understanding the person's approach and current knowledge, I was able to develop a plan for them to improve their skills.

Good Answer

An example of a good answer to this question would be:
I once had a group member who had a really bad attitude during a group project, so I took the person aside and spoke to them. I told them that they seemed disinterested in the work, and I asked if there was something bothering them.

It turns out that there was something bothering them. They had just failed a project in another class and that is what was affecting them. The group member apologized to me because they weren't aware that they were coming off as disinterested. In this case I was able to provide the feedback in an appropriate manner without embarrassing or offending my group member.

Why this is a good answer:
This is a good answer because it shows how you provided feedback in a tasteful and appropriate manner. You took the person aside and had a personal conversation. You also were not harsh to the person's face.

Interview Question

Give me an example of feedback received and how you put the information to use.

Why do they ask this question?

Are you able to receive feedback without taking it personally?

Can you take feedback and improve on it, or does it go in one ear and out the other?

Bad Answer

An example of a bad answer to this question would be:

One of my prior bosses told me that I was too ambitious and that I didn't need to work so hard. I hear that a lot actually --- that I work too hard.

Why this is a bad answer:

Don't say this in an interview. This is a very typical answer. Nobody like someone that tries to show off by saying that their biggest weakness is working too hard. Just think of a couple of examples where you've received constructive feedback and use those. Do not say your one weakness is that you work too hard or care too much though.

Good Answer

An example of a good answer to this question would be:
After a project in school that involved public speaking, I received some feedback from the professor that I was monotoned and slumped over. It was hard for me to take the feedback at first, but I knew that improving my public speaking is key to my success in business. I took the professor's advice, and I also started attending toastmasters to improve my public speaking. After taking the feedback and analyzing it, I performed very well on my next public speaking project I had in school.

Why this is a good answer:
This is a good answer because it highlights not only your ability to take feedback but to also improve on that feedback. This candidate not only received the feedback from the professor, but they also improved their performance in the future by taking the professors feedback positively.

Chapter 12: Master Your Phone Interview

Being interviewed over the phone is a unique and challenging experience. In a limited amount of time, you have to be prepared to sell your appropriateness for the opportunity in order to secure a spot in the next round of interviews. In order to succeed, you will need to understand the different types of phone interviews you may encounter, how to respond most appropriately to the questions asked and what to do in order to gain clarity for the next steps in the process.

So, what is a phone interview? Of course, it is an interview that takes place over the phone but there are a few permutations of the phone interview to prepare for. Sometimes, you may not even realize that you are being interviewed.

The role of the person on the phone is often that of recruiter. The first type of phone interview is not really an interview at all: a recruiter contacting you with the intention of setting up an-in person interview. The recruiter would like to confirm your interest in the position and provide you with the details of when your interview will take place and who you will be meeting with. The recruiter has every intention of setting up an interview for you at this point unless you give her a reason to be concerned.

There could be variety of reasons that the phone call is eliciting concern on the recruiter's behalf such as:

- You answered the call in an unprofessional manner and seem confused as to why you are receiving a phone call. You may not be expecting a call and you are treating the recruiter like a telemarketer until you figure out what the call is concerning.

- You seem uninterested in interviewing for the position.

- You are asking several basic questions about the job, demonstrating that you do not remember much of anything about the company or the role.

- You do not sound professional on the phone. Perhaps you are too focused on the salary or the hours for the position or you are being too candid or lax in your language.

- You cannot be heard or understood. You may be in an area with bad cell phone reception or trying to whisper at your current place or employment or your kids are trying to talk over you when you are on the phone.

As a recent college graduate several years ago, I attempted to answer a call in Times Square from a recruiter representing a large media company. Needless to say, one of the busiest places in the world was (and is) one of the loudest as well. After a few responses of "Can you repeat that?" the opportunity was lost. I was told by the recruiter that he would call me back but that never happened.

- You are inflexible in your availability to come in for an interview. The recruiter may have proposed several times for you to attend an in-person interview but none of those times work for you due to your work schedule or other commitments.

While the recruiter may have called you with every intention of setting up an interview, a point or two of concern may have eliminated your chances. You will be told that you will be contacted once the company has made a decision rather than being called in for an interview.

In some cases, the recruiter attempted to reach you but was unsuccessful in doing so or experienced an area of concern that eliminated that possibility. That may include:

- An unprofessional voicemail message. Your first verbal impression might be your voicemail message so make sure that it is professionally appropriate. Provide a message that clearly states your name that you are sorry that you missed the call and that you will return the call as soon as time allows. Avoid any voicemails messages that include extended words of inspiration, attempts at demonstrating your vocal or rap talents or allowing your kids to record a cute message on your behalf.

- A voicemail message that is not in English or you do not state your name. The recruiter has to know that she reached you. Always provide your name in your message and if you expect that many of the callers to your phone are non-English speakers, provide at least a message in your language of preference as well as one in English.

- Your phone is out of order. Whether it is a permanent change in number or you have used up your prepaid minutes, an out of service phone will lead to a missed opportunity. Unless you possess unique skills that are unlikely to be found in other candidates (and even then), a recruiter is not going to chase you down to find you on social media or email.

- Someone answering the phone who does not take a message for you with all of the necessary details.

So, how can you ensure a smooth phone screening and no stumbling blocks to the in-person interview?

- If you do not recognize the phone number, assume that it may be a recruiter. Answer the call with your name and in a professional manner.

- Be prepared to talk when you answer the phone. If you are unprepared to talk, let the phone go to voicemail.

- If you are prepared to talk but you see that your cell phone reception is very weak or your train is about to go underground, let the call go to voicemail.

- If you planned to be able to talk but something came up unexpectedly, take the recruiter's name and number, and ask when you may call back.

- When you are job seeking, you should have a general idea of your schedule of availability so that setting up an in-person interview is not an arduous process.

- It would be difficult to access every application you have made over the last few months in order to be prepared every time the phone rings but it would be helpful to maintain a basic list that you can quickly peruse for information to refresh your memory once you are contacted.

- If you absolutely have to, fake it until you make it. Make it clear that you are interested in the opportunity when speaking on the phone until you have a reason not to be interested. Do your best to show enthusiasm while you are trying to figure things out.

By following the suggestions above, you will be able to avoid the pitfalls of the seemingly "simple" process of setting up the interview when the recruiter calls you.

All conditions being perfect, it is best to answer the call then and there but sometimes it is not the ideal time. It may be difficult to reach the recruiter later but it is better than to pick up the phone in a bad reception zone or a noisy area.

The next style of phone interview is a pre-screening, which involves being asked a handful of questions to determine if you match the basic criteria needed for the role. The recruiter is trying to avoid having to meet in-person with candidates who are clearly not a fit for the job.

One of the challenges of this type of phone interview is that you may or may not be given a warning in advance. Some recruiters may email you to set up a time for a brief phone screening whereas others will just launch into their questions. What this means is that you must always be prepared. These brief few minutes are your opportunity to sell yourself for the role. The recruiter will not give much consideration to whatever was going on at the time of the call that may have been a distraction to you or hurt your chances of putting your best foot forward.

While you cannot anticipate all of the questions that may be asked, the questions do tend to veer to the basics during a phone screen. A recruiter will generally not have an expert knowledge of the position that you are interviewing for. He will be looking for a basic skills match and looking to weed out people with major question marks in their backgrounds.

The key here is that time is limited. The recruiter is trying to determine your basic fit for the role. Similar questions may be asked by the same person during an in person interview, which you can answer with greater depth and detail at that time.

No matter what questions are asked, consider the following:

How can I demonstrate that I am a great fit for this role when I answer this question? An interview isn't about you but an opportunity to show why you are a great fit for the job.

Without having the opportunity to see someone in person, there is a connection that is lost over the phone. Try to project a good level of energy and enthusiasm over the phone. If normally you are subdued and a quiet talker, you may need to push yourself outside of your comfort zone for the phone interview. In order to project your voice and maintain your enthusiasm, you may want to stand up for the phone interview and speak a bit louder than you normally would. Although it might be tempting, avoid pacing around. Your phone might hit certain bad reception areas if you are walking around so avoid having the phone cut in and out.

If you are given the opportunity to prepare for the phone screening, there are several steps that you can take to put your best foot forward:

Research: When you know that you have a phone screening to prepare for, don't be reliant upon remembering what you learned about the company when you submitted your resume. Look up the company website and read current articles about the organization.

Review: Reread the job description for the position (you saved it, right? If not, a Google search might help you to find the old posting), the cover letter that you sent as well as your resume.

Consider: What questions you might be asked about your background and determine how you can explain any bumps in your career journey- such as an inconsistent work history or if you have ever been fired.

If you need to, admit to any mistakes or errors in judgment but focus on what you have learned as well. Try to stay light on the negativity and focus on the positive.

Space: Find a quiet area where you will be taking the call. If you are at home, make sure that your family knows that you have an important call at that time and you will let them know when you are off of the phone.

Do not ask about the salary over the phone. Just like it is not appropriate to ask about the salary during your first in person interview, it is not appropriate to ask here either.

The recruiter might ask what salary you are seeking as a way to weed out candidates over the phone. Provide a wide salary range as opposed to a number. Once you have responded, you can inquire as to what range the company has in mind.

When you are asked if you have any questions, don't focus on the hours of the job or the fringe benefits. Use this as your opportunity to gain clarity on the next steps in the process as well as the recruiter's contact information.

Ask what are the next steps in the process and when you can expect to hear back. This will provide you with a timeline for your follow up strategy. If you are told that you will hear back within two weeks, it would be acceptable for you to contact the recruiter again somewhere in the range of two and a half to three weeks later.

Make sure to get the recruiter's full name and email address. Email the recruiter a thank you note within one day of your phone interview. Avoid a generic note that can be used for anyone at any time. Include a couple of specific details that were discussed and a reference as to your strong qualifications.

"Dear Ms. Thomas,

Thank you for taking the time over the phone to discuss the position of Systems Analyst. I enjoyed learning more about the organization's planned expansion into the South American market. Given my knowledge of the region and relevant experience in the areas of banking and finance, I am excited to learn more. I am looking forward to the next steps in the process.

Regards"

The third, and final, type of phone interview is not a pre-screening but your actual "first interview". The most common reason that the first interview takes place over the phone is for logistical purposes: candidates from outside of the geographic area are being considered for the position and to be respectful of everyone's time, the phone interview is replacing the need to travel to an in-person interview. This style of interview is becoming less commonplace as interviews with remote candidates are more commonly being conducted over Skype or similar web based application.

Being able to participate in a formal interview over the phone does have some advantages for the applicant. As you cannot be seen by the interviewer, you can keep your notes in front of you. This might include a list of the questions that you want to ask, reminders of particular accomplishments that you want to be sure to mention and possibly even your resume.

If there is more than one person on the other end of the line, you have to pay special attention as to when it is your time to talk. The first interviewer may have just finished talking and you are ready to respond but the second interviewer has something to say. When there is more than one interviewer, allow a brief moment before you respond to each question before you respond.

As opposed to a briefer pre-screening interview, you should provide answers that go more in-depth and paint a picture of your strong qualifications for the job.

Chapter 13: Reviewing The Interview

You've articulated your strengths, you've learned to tell your story, and you've practiced to become your very best. Now what?

Even though you've gotten much better at interviewing by learning how to communicate your story, you probably won't deliver a knockout performance in every interview. The truth is that there is always room to get better, and there is one thing in particular you can do to get even better at interviewing. Evaluate how the interview went and think about your perceptions of the organization *before* they give you a job offer.

Why bother thinking about something that just happened?

People have a tendency to believe that any given outcome was inevitable once it has happened, even if they didn't know what the outcome would be before it happened. If you wait until you hear that an organization is not interested in hiring you, you may think that you knew this was going to happen all along. When you think back on the interview after having been turned down, it will inevitably seem like it went poorly. You may blame yourself, the interviewer (perhaps they didn't ask you the right questions), or someone else (perhaps there are many overqualified job seekers in your area, and they're taking all the entry-level jobs that should be given to younger people). Your memories will have faded and you'll think back on only the negative aspects of the interview.

Alternatively, what if you're offered the job? It's tempting to believe that this means that your interviewing skills are absolutely amazing and you couldn't have done any better. You might feel that you don't even need to practice the next time you decide to look for a job. After all, you're a master, and getting future jobs will be as easy as showing up to interview on the scheduled day. (We hope you can read our sarcasm.)

Putting an interview experience out of mind as soon as you walk out the door can also lead you to make the wrong decision about accepting the job. If you're presented with a strong job offer, you may find yourself deciding that you really like the organization. Perhaps the hiring manager said a lot of great things about you when they called with the offer; maybe they talked up all of the benefits you would receive if you worked there. If you have received an offer without already deciding whether the organization is right for you, it will be really difficult to objectively evaluate their offer. That decision is too important to let someone make for you.

And if you're still not convinced that you need to reflect on your job interview, do it for another reason. If nothing else, writing down the questions that you answered well, or the questions that you didn't address particularly well, gives you great content for a thank you letter.

For all of these reasons, it's best to evaluate the interview experience before you learn its outcome. It is very important to *write down* your perceptions so you don't forget them later. With written notes, you'll have an objective impression of how the interview went that you can then use to improve your interview skills in the future as well as to decide whether you want to accept a job offer.

How to Reflect on Your Interview Experience

As soon as you have a moment to yourself after the interview is over, think about your overall impressions.

Then think about the interview in chronological order, stopping at each memorable event (walking into the office, shaking hands, greeting your interviewer, and so forth) and again at each interview question that you can remember. Evaluate each of these in your mind and then compose written notes.

After thinking about the interview by yourself, talk about the experience with several people. Ideally, these should be people who will ask you a lot of questions. Conversation will help you to reflect on things that may have escaped your attention. For instance, a friend might ask if people were smiling in the office. If you talk about this on the same day that you had the interview, you'll be able to remember whether you saw people who seemed to be happy to be at their jobs. If you try to remember this next month when you're evaluating the job offer, your recollection won't be as accurate.

Next, jot down what you learned about the company. What are the expectations that were communicated to you? What did you learn about the company culture? Were they asking questions that focused on specific tasks or skills? If so, these will probably be key to your success on the job.

Finally, think through the highlights, lowlights, and what you plan to do in future interviews. To help you along in this process of evaluating your interview, we've created an Interview Evaluation Guide.

Interview Evaluation Guide

Overview

● **How well prepared did you feel walking into the interview?**

● <u>Which questions surprised you or caught you off guard?</u>

The positives

● Which of your answers best communicated your story? What worked about those answers?

The negatives

● Which of your answers did not communicate your story very well? Why did they fall short? (Perhaps your answer didn't fit with the rest of your story or was confusing. Maybe you just couldn't think of an answer.)

The company

● **Did you get a clear sense of what you would do on a daily basis?**

● Do you know who you would work with? Who would you report to? Who would you interact with on a daily basis? Who would you interact with only occasionally?

● Do you think you could get along reasonably well with the people you met? (Include everyone you interacted with, not just the interviewers.)

● Do you think this position will allow you to use your skills and knowledge and help you meet your career goals?

● Do you know what will be expected of you, how you will be evaluated, and what you will need to do to excel in this position?

● <u>Are you excited about the possibility of working for this organization and with these people?</u>

For the future

● What might you do differently during your next interview?

Disliking an organization

If you don't like to fail, you may find yourself writing something like, "I don't think I liked this organization." That way, you'll be able to soothe your ego if they don't extend you an offer. You'll just say to yourself, *that job would have been awful—I'm glad they didn't bother calling me back!*

It's fine to write down negative opinions if they are in fact true. But try to avoid being pre-emptively negative in order to save your feelings. This is a little like breaking up with someone just so they don't break up with you first. Why not give it a little time? It's okay to like a job or an organization even if you're not exactly the right fit, right now. That doesn't mean you'll never get to work there. In fact, a better position may open up in the future, or your future work experiences may make you a more desirable candidate.

If you evaluate an organization negatively just to feel better about rejection in the future, you'll also be less likely to be happy or satisfied with the job offer when it does come. You'll look back at your written reflections and think, *oh, but I didn't like this organization. Maybe I shouldn't accept the offer*.

If you're always evaluating jobs or organizations negatively and you know that it's not because you're afraid of rejection, you may be applying to the wrong jobs. In this case, it's time to do more research about organizations before you bother applying and going on interviews and to honestly evaluate whether this is indeed the field you want to work in. For instance, if you find yourself frustrated that every banking job in New York City requires ridiculous hours, perhaps you need to consider living in a different area or working for a less prestigious firm where the expectations may be a little lower.

Success is Not Measured in Job Offers

You should always remember that whether or not you get a job offer shouldn't define how well the interview went. You can make a great impression in the mind of an interviewer and still not be the best fit for the job. If you are considering a job offer and reflecting on the interview, keep in mind that the cost of a bad fit is high for both you and your employer. If you don't think you can deliver what the job requires, it may be best for you to pass on the offer. And instead of thinking about whether you aced an interview, instead of letting the outcome dictate how you feel about the process, you can define for yourself whether or not the interview was a success. If you can remember this while you're in the interview itself, it will help you be more objective and less nervous. It will also help you to stay positive throughout the whole job search process.

Chapter 14: Dealing with Realities

A well thought out job search that focuses on the right fit starts with some definitions.

- What industry or industry segments do you want to work in?
- Do you want to work in an established company or one new to the industry?
- Where would you most like to work or where else would you be willing to accept a relevant job geographically?
- Given your present circumstances, how much of a risk-taker are you?

Clearly, your perception of yourself, and how you are convinced that others see you, helps you rebrand yourself. Positive results that are relevant to the needs of your target company, and presented credibly, are what will get you in the door and give you the opportunity to excel. But to get there, you have to deal with realities: besides company financial status, try to measure the quality and staying power of the management.

You should understand the status of products and services, morale factors affecting productivity or turnover, and the gaps and pains the company needs to resolve to improve its competitiveness and profitability. The level of your success depends heavily on how well your experience and results can help close the gaps and manage the pain.

Before you get too far into your decision making, make sure to check your priorities and share your thoughts with the people who most matter in your life.

Where do you start?

Unless you're single and responsible only for yourself, your first reality check is your family. If you're married, start obviously with your spouse. Hopefully, there are no surprises. If you've been out of work, your spouse is well aware that you need to produce income and also well aware of what kind of situation can restore your confidence, make you happiest and probably most successful.

If an important new job requires a move, then what? One of your many considerations may be spouse employment.

Do you go alone for a while until you're sure things will work the way you envisioned while your spouse continues to work and maybe starts his/her own job search? What about children? Do you have kids in school? If they're very young, they're probably also very malleable. They can move and make new friends in days and this can turn out to be wonderful adventure for them. If they're older, not so easy. It depends on what grades they're in school, what outside activities and, maybe more than anything else, what close friendships they may have to leave behind.

The importance of family support

Your family is your main source of support. If you really like the new opportunity, you may need to sell a lot to get them onboard. Selling in this case is to illustrate benefits to them, dealing first with emotions like fear, anger and insecurity, especially over losing friends and facing the changes inherent in a strange new place. While they may resist and experience some temporary setback, you need to first overcome the emotions and then convince them that this new situation is good for them. Not an easy task. But an extension of your role as a salesman.

If you force them to go literally kicking and screaming, or with arms folded across their chests, and given to spurts of anger or crying jags, can you possibly focus enough on your new job to make positive impressions? Maybe you can clear your head and focus during the day, but what about coming home? How much resistance can you put up with and for how long?

Add to that the possibility of leaving behind, or taking with you, elderly or sick parents and the various complications you can imagine.

None of this is meant to scare you or turn you off to what you think could be a great opportunity. It is meant to condition you to the realities, including all of the circumstances you need to be aware of in this life-changing decision.

You want a job with growth potential, where you can excel and maximize your income. Getting to that point is not as simple as finding an ad and acing an interview. It is hard work. Maybe even tedious work. And it takes thoughtful, disciplined research. You never want to make a decision, particularly if it involves a move that can blow up in your face because of factors you didn't know, and, therefore, didn't anticipate. What do you do then? Go back into a job search and possibly move again after your family has gotten settled?

Even if you are fortunate enough to find an opportunity that does not require a move, is it possibly a temporary relief from a problem that could wind up being worse sometime down the line. Make sure to uncover both the good and the bad of the company and its management. Whatever you decide, keeping up the confidence, respect, security and support of your family is fundamental to your success.

Never give up on research

If you can read between the lines and understand where I am going with this, your smartest approach is to invest as much time and effort as possible into meaningful research. And, if you can, find ways for your family to help you. You may be surprised by ideas they come up with and people they may know who can be valuable sources of information. You want to do this right.

Find that situation that lets you excel, where your family, each member, sees something positive. For your spouse, maybe a better job as well, or a better house, better neighborhood, better activities or social circles. For the kids, maybe better schools or camps or colleges than you couldn't have afforded before, along with greater, affordable social opportunities. Maybe a car. You get the picture.

If they are all happy, it is much easier for you to approach that new job with a vigor and excitement that wins you recognition. And it is much easier to come home at night to smiling faces eager to tell you about their new experiences.

My appreciation, and love, of research was instilled in me early in my career by some of the toughest critics I could possibly imagine. They shaped my thinking in ways that have served me well throughout my career. I am grateful to them for whatever successes I have had. And, in retrospect, I've thought many times how glad I am that I was receptive and eager to learn from them. I hope in this book, and particularly in this chapter, that I can pass on some of their wisdom.

As a young journalism student, I had the good fortune of learning from seasoned, street smart newspaper editors who were not impressed by academic writings, but insisted on "clear, correct and concise" articles on any subject. Those words became a mantra. They insisted on the use of correct words, corroboration of facts and background for stories along with absolute adherence to deadlines. I think back sometimes to what I thought were excellent pieces of copy that wound up being slashed and marked up beyond belief. And sometimes even ridiculed.

I once used the word "penultimate" in writing about a tennis player advancing to the semi-finals of a tournament. The loud "you got to be kidding me" response from my instructor obviously has stuck with me as a reminder to express, not impress, with my writing.

An editing assignment a little later on in which a New York Times writer referred to a car "careering" over a curb and into a wall served as another long-time lesson. I confidently changed the word to "careening."

The instructor, who, at night was the editor of The New York Times foreign desk, called me out in class and asked me what "careening" meant and I confidently answered him (to sway to the side). Then he asked me what "careering" meant and I made an attempt to answer, defending my change and learning a lesson in research when the editor asked me publicly if I had bothered to look up the word or had just chosen to assume I knew more than the writer.

I had mistakenly changed the writer's meaning and imagery. Careering, I learned, meant plunging straight ahead, not swaying to the side. My argument that the word "careering" didn't fit the "clear" part of the mantra fell flat and I learned quickly to make frequent use of both a dictionary and a thesaurus.

A few years later, Journalism degree in my pocket and a graduate of a Defense Department training program, I was an intelligence analyst at the National Security Agency, where research is a challenging and demanding full time business. I collected and analyzed data on a variety of targets, then had to learn to write reports using only precise adjectives and strictly supportable facts. Adjectives like "long" or "short," "big" or "small" or colors like "red" or "blue" or "green" can be interpreted in so many different ways by different people as to be generally meaningless and unsupportable.

The rule of thumb was that each fact had to be proven with input from five different sources and, where possible, was appended with statistical research and photographs. The work was painstaking and exacting, but the sensation of having reports accepted for distribution was exhilarating. With all the bad raps NSA has taken in the past few years, I learned to respect the dedicated professionalism that went into intelligence products. I am still influenced by what I learned there many years ago.

You'll probably never have to write with only absolutely precise adjectives and prove everything you say from five sources, but you will need to learn the discipline of looking at facts through clear eyes, without prejudgment. That will help you analyze and assess industries, companies and people who may influence the rest of your life.

Getting into your "best" company

So, you've identified the industries, the companies and the people you want to pursue. Now what? You want to capitalize on all of the effort you've put into finding industries where you would have the most comfort and expertise and then companies within those industries where the past results of your skills and experience could be most valuable.

Using any sources, including the internet, see if you can find speeches or articles by key executives to get insights into what is going on right now or in the immediate future. With luck, you might find something from an executive in your area of specialization that could be extremely useful in both gaining entry to the company and in interviews.

Don't hesitate to write to someone whose article or speech has impressed you. Look also at press releases to get a better sense of how the company wants to be perceived by its various publics, especially shareholders and customers.

Sift through your notes and drop companies that give you concern. Consider what you're doing as a step towards a long-term relationship. Are you willing to commit long hours, enthusiasm and passion to this organization which may, in fact, consume most of your daily thoughts, not to mention time? Maybe even more than your home life. Are the potential rewards worth the potential risk? As much as possible, make up your mind objectively, with research as your basis.

Don't be talked into a job where there are serious questions. That said, no company, and no job, is perfect. There will always be some level of anxiety. Go back to the earlier thoughts about knowing yourself and make a reasoned decision based on the best intelligence you have been able to muster. Imperfections in a company may be opportunities for you depending on your experience and ability to fix them.

By now, you should have a short list. Maybe even a single company. But, remember, there are no sure things. Hedge a bit. Have alternatives. A Plan "B". Maybe more.

In preparation for your approach to a company, find out what you can about the executives, particularly those who conceivably could influence your future. How old are they? How long have they been with the company? How successful have they been here and in previous organizations? Did they by chance go to the same school or schools that you did? What outside organizations are they involved with?

Most importantly, is there anything in their backgrounds that ties to you? Or to someone you know well? That also could aid your entry into the company. Your very valuable business librarian should be able to steer you to biographical references, by name or by company.

If you can find, or get introduced to, current or former employees of your target companies, ask about these executives. What do these people know or hear about them? Do they have a reputation for fairness and a history of supporting and developing subordinates? Ask their impressions of the company and, while you're at it, check out Glassdoor and similar websites that can provide insights into the company. If you don't know people personally, one of the best ways to find them is through LinkedIn.

Keep moving forward

As in intelligence work, you'll rarely find everything you would like to know. But the more you do find that objectively satisfies your interest, the more your enthusiasm should be piqued. And, presumably, you can find valuable information that can get you in the door and be knowledgeably impressive in interviews. The quality and usefulness of your research should allow you to separate yourself from your competition and give you an opening to prove your worth.

You are now ready to move into the next phase of your strategy: Getting in the door. You might get lucky through your research and establish contact with a key executive, in person, at a business meeting or by phone or letter, or through networking. If you got that person's attention, most likely he/she would contact HR and have them interview you. That's a plus because it moves you to a short list (maybe the top) and requires that the HR people report the results of the meeting to the key executive.

Remember, the comment earlier about being the CEO of You? Well, now you're in charge. Excel in the interview and your chances of landing the job have just soared.

The most likely scenario is that you will need to network into a position which, because of an implied endorsement, may be more powerful than the direct contact. It involves an extra step or two but helps you build relationships for now and the future.

Especially after you have the advantage of learning how to effectively use principles and strategies of networking.

Conclusion

In summary, a job interview is one of the most important meetings in the working life of a person. Interviews serve as a good chance for the employer to assess a prospective new team member, while the candidate assesses their potential bosses. Interview preparation offers candidates the necessary tactics on how to conduct themselves to increase their chances of having a successful interview. Conversely, lack of preparation leads to nervousness and mistakes during the interview process.

As a basic guideline, this book equips a job candidate, whether starting up or experienced candidates, with necessary techniques to ace their next interview process. It offers a step-by-step guide on things one needs to know and do before an interview, things to do during the interview, and things one needs to know and do after the interview. It portrays the significance of reading prior to an interview since it shows candidates how to market themselves to the prospective employers and to be able to assess if the job offer is suitable for them in the process. It also offers insight into the things that should be avoided during an interview. If this guideline is followed, a candidate is assured of ultimate success in their next interview.

INTERVIEW PREPARATION

How to Improve your Job Interview skills and Be Yourself. Stop Worrying and Be More Positive with Amazing Interview Answers

Jim Hunting

Introduction

Interviewers are not superhumans that can do all things. They may seem to wield more power than you because they can decide if you are hired or not, but at the end of the day, they are still human just like you. They are not infallible and make mistakes. You shouldn't put them on a pedestal and think that they are better than you. They are similar to you in many ways. They are susceptible to the same psychological and cognitive biases that you are. In that way, they can catch on to things that are seemingly minute, but reveal something important inside of the interviewee.

There are things that you can do to make yourself a more likable person who is going to be perceived as outgoing, friendly, and an overall pleasant person to be around. In the game of the interview process, this manipulation tool can help you land a job. Let's look at all the ways that you can work with the interviewer's psychology to get the job of your dreams.

1. Schedule your interview for late morning on Tuesday

Likely, this is a time when the interviewer has gone past the craze of Monday that can be stressful and time-consuming. Once Tuesday rolls around, things are much calmer and more relaxed. If you can arrange for the interview to be late morning on a Tuesday, things should be pretty smooth. Still, you must work around the interviewer's schedule to make sure you have a good time, but when you can arrange the interview around your own, then you can choose a time that you think will work to your advantage; this is at the time when the interviewer is at their best, because that will score you more points, and you will likely have a better outcome.

2. Don't interview on the same day as the strongest candidates

Research has shown that the interviewers base their scores on the other interviewees who have been there on the same day. If you have a series of stronger candidates before your interview, then you will likely be scored down and not get the job. However, if you are after a series of weaker candidates, then likely your score will go up. You may not know who is interviewing and when, but if you have any knowledge beforehand of the people interviewing, then you should choose to come in on a day that has less qualified applicants than you, because you can score more points and have a better result, which could put you in the running for the second or third round of interviews that may come after.

3. Choose what you wear very carefully

Research has shown that orange is the absolute worst color you could possibly wear to an interview, so you should definitely avoid wearing that color. A CareerBuilder survey revealed that many applicants preferred wearing blue, because it indicates that you are a team player and can work well with others. Whereas black suggests that you have leadership potential. Gray suggests that you are logical and analytical. White indicates that you are organized. Brown means you are dependable. Red shows that you can exercise power in your job.

4. Work your hand motions as they will reveal a lot about your character

You should hold your palm outward to show a sign of sincerity, because that will demonstrate that you are a man or woman of integrity and can share well. You can also hold your hand to make the shape of a church steeple, which indicates that you are confident. Conversely, you should not hold your palm downward, because it can indicate a sign of dominance. Don't hide your hands, because it may seem like you're trying to hide something. Also, if you tap your fingers, you are displaying a sign of impatience, and if you fold your arms, you may be indicating disappointment. If you do these actions, then you can start focusing on projecting the most positive image possible.

5. Find something that you have in common with the interviewer

Often, the similarity attraction hypothesis comes into play when you can find something that you have in common with the interviewer. Maybe you're wearing a similar style as the interviewer; you can emphasize that. Or, if your interviewer mentions something about a recent basketball game and you can chime in about it, then you can continue the conversation. You can also bring it back to the interviewer's interests as you go about the process. That can resonate well with a person, because it can seem a little bit like emotional flattery, and you can help the interviewer feel like you appreciate them and could work well with them.

6. Body language mirroring

One way to flatter your interviewer is to do exactly what they are doing during the interview. If they are sitting back in their chair, then you should do the same, or if they are sitting up straight and leaning forward toward you, do as they do. It can help show that you can conform to their pattern of behavior and that you can adapt to different environments.

7. Give compliments to the company without self-promotion

Another thing you should be careful about is offering compliments to your interviewer or the organization. You don't want to sound like you're flattering in order to help your personal profile. That could backfire easily and make it more likely for you to not get the job. Be wary about how you give compliments to the organization that you're looking into working for.

8. Be excited about it

It has been shown that the more enthusiastic and excited you are about the role and the interview, the higher the chances you will get asked back to another interview or even get the position. There are many applicants who are looking to get the job, but you should try to find ways that you can project your excitement and energy, because that can definitely work in your favor. When you show that you are highly engaged in the interview, you demonstrate an interest in the company, which could help you in the whole process.

Examples

Qualities to describe Nick: Intelligent, warm, friendly, talented, and hardworking, but slightly overly confident.

Qualities that describe Frank: Overly confident, hardworking, intelligent, warm, and friendly.

The two candidates are very similar in the adjectives that are used for them, but one is clearly better than the other due to the order of the adjectives that are ascribed to them. It makes a difference in the interview process, because we always seek out the positive first in a candidate and can easily sidestep the potential drawbacks within a person.

13. Emphasize your efforts over your success

One thing that you can do in the interview is to emphasize your hard work and dedication over the success that you have experienced. Instead of saying, "I am successful," you can say, "I struggled during this time with XYZ, but I was able to accomplish XYZ after a lot of hard work and effort." When you do so, you demonstrate kindness, amicability, relatability, and humility, all of which are positive attributes of a potential colleague. Such attributes will help the interviewer to sift through the various candidates and find a humble but likable character who could be a good fit for their organization.

14. Prepare to ad-lib and go off script

One thing that many interviewers expect is for their interviewees to have a pre-programmed script in their minds, which will lead the interview in a certain direction, ultimately to land the person the job. However, this is not always the way it needs to be. There should be a certain amount of natural spontaneity in the conversation that makes it less canned and predictable. Instead, you should say things like, "Let me tell you what's not on my resume..." When you can bring new information that is not evident on the resume, then you can demonstrate what knowledge and expertise you bring to the table. You can do so by wowing your interviewer with the variety of information that you can present to them without being so predictable that they know every word that you are about to say; that is just not very interesting.

15. Ask the interviewer why they invited you to the interview

Another key tip for the process is preparing to ask the interviewer why they brought you in. It shows initiative and humility, but you automatically draw attention to why the interviewers want to talk to you about a potential position with them. This can play to your strength, because then the interviewer will see you in a positive light.

To conclude, show what you can do to prepare for an interview and what you can do to prepare psychologically, as well as to think about the way an interviewer will perceive you when you arrive at the interview. Furthermore, you should play up your strengths so that you will be viewed in a favorable way. That will help you greatly in the application process and make you a candidate who stands out.

Chapter1: Job Hunting

Job search is the most difficult game there is. There are many reasons why this is so. Here are a few of them:

- It is a game that requires us to play in a certain way.

- Most jobseekers know that they are supposed to sell, or promote themselves, but they hate the idea of selling. How can anyone perform well at a task they despise?

- All job seekers are selling, whether they want to or not, but virtually everyone of them has adopted the worst possible sales style, as I will soon illustrate.

- Jobseekers are required to sell the most complex, hardest-to-sell product in the world— themselves. This is difficult because most people are uncomfortable promoting themselves.

- Successful job search requires us to understand the value we represent, and then confidently express this value. But it is hard to be objective about ourselves. Most jobseekers struggle to understand what their strengths are for many weeks.

- Jobseekers are required to sell this incredibly complex product under the most pressure-packed circumstance: the job interview. This isn't a seven-game series where you can lose three games and still advance. If you lose in the first round, bye-bye. You may have been a close second, but there is no medal for second place.

- The job interview is a complex sale and few people—even salespeople—understand this approach. Most jobseekers have never received an hour of training in the art of complex sales. Worse yet, there are few resources that do a good job covering this subject.

- Finally, the game requires you to be upbeat and confident, even though you may have just received the leveling, painful blow of job loss.

Is there any wonder why most un-coached jobseekers, when they are handed the ball, take off in the wrong direction? Sending an untrained person to an interview is like taking someone who has never driven a car and giving them the keys, pointing out the location of the brakes, accelerator and steering wheel, and setting them free on the German autobahn for their maiden voyage. Godspeed!

GOOD NEWS FOR THOSE WHO HATE SELLING

The complex sales approach that you will learn from this book has the following great advantage: It does not feel like selling to either you, or to the hiring authority. This is by design, because people love buying, but don't like being sold.

I remember taking a potential customer, and her team, to dinner, escorting them through a plant tour the next day, followed by our "sales presentation." We presented problems we had uncovered and their potential solutions. We spoke about their goals and how our product might lead to their achievement.

Lunch and a short walk to a waiting limo ended our time together. Before the buying authority entered the limo that was headed to O'Hare airport, she turned to me and said words I've never forgotten, "I've been with you for two days, and you've yet to try and sell me anything."

I smiled and said, "It's all my fault. Have a nice flight back home." But while I said that I thought, "I've been selling you from the moment you arrived." It did not feel that way, but she was sold. She did buy our system.

If you master this system you won't feel like you have been selling anyone, and that is just one of the many reasons why the system works. Remember, Jack was and is an engineer. Engineers tend not to like selling or have a strong urge to pursue a career in sales. Yet Jack adopted my approach and, as we will find out later, is still using some of its techniques to be successful in his new job.

MASTERING THE GAME

I hate golf and I can't understand why people take golfing vacations. I went to St. Andrews' University for my junior year abroad. It's the birthplace of golf. Golfers who learn of this always ask me, "Did you play on the Old Course?" Their eyes sparkle with delight, but their glimmer dies quickly when I answer, "Nope. Never even made it to the driving range or the putting green. But I did drink my fair share of pints at the Niblick." The Niblick is a pub that is very close to the Old Course.

What stands behind my aversion? I stink at golf. I don't like it and it doesn't like me. That is one of the reasons why people hate interviewing: They stink at it, and know this deep inside, even if they cannot consciously admit it to themselves.

If you seriously apply yourself to master the lessons in this book, then you will master the game of job search, and this can make interviewing enjoyable. I know this firsthand. I got to the point where I enjoyed interviewing. But I wanted to see if this was true for Jack, after two grueling days of eighteen interviews. His experience would be something of an acid test. So, I asked him if he enjoyed the experience and he replied:

As far as the interviewing experience, surprisingly I did have a positive experience. I felt very prepared and felt confident that I could convey my experience and skills sets in a very effective manner (clear, concise and with stories).

Note how he continues to emphasize stylistic points like clarity, eliminating wordiness, and using stories. He learned valuable lessons about how to communicate effectively, and his continual repetition of these insights indicated he was not going to forget them.

Jack's experience reveals a key to job search success. We need to make the interviewing process enjoyable by mastering it, and by getting rid of our conventional, simple sales pitch.

THE SIMPLE SALE

Here is the crowning irony of job search: Those jobseekers who hate the idea of selling are unwittingly adopting the worst possible sales style. They typically use a simple sales approach that I will briefly describe so that it can be avoided at all costs.

In the simple sale there is typically one decision maker, because the price tag for the simple-sale's item, or service, is low. When the price is low, the risks of making a bad-buying decision are also low. If the decision maker purchases something that doesn't work out, his attitude is, "No big deal." He learns from his inexpensive mistake and moves on. For this reason there is no need to waste the time of multiple decision makers, or put a complex decision-making process in place. There is no committee making a buying decision in simple sales.

The simple sales approach looks like this:

Salesperson: Hi, I'm Bill. I represent Acme, Inc., the ballpoint pen suppliers for most of the school systems in the state. The reason why we're twice as large as our next largest competitor is because of the quality of the product and the low cost. Most of my customers are placing their annual stocking orders right now, have you placed yours?

Buyer: Nope.

Salesperson: So how many pens do you need to fill your stocking order? [Followed by...] That order would cost _____. If you place your order now you can get free shipping and it will arrive by next week. Deal?

Buyer: Maybe. I'll think about it.

Salesperson: That's fine. But if you think about it, you've got a hundred more important things to think about. How about we take this item off your to-do list and get you set up for the school year with the best quality pens at a discounted price?

Buyer: You're probably right. Use this P.O. number.

I rattle off a few of the most impressive facts and then I close, close, close. Ask for the order! If an objection arises, I answer it and then close, close, close. However, in the complex sales process I never asked for the order. Not once, much less three times.

Now let's apply this simple sales approach to the job interview to see what it looks like.

THE SIMPLE JOB INTERVIEW

The simple sales style can work during an interview, but only for a simple job opportunity. These are the low-skilled, low-paying jobs where one person meets the candidate and often makes the hiring decision on the spot. The downside of making a bad decision is low so no hiring committee is ever formed.

Take, for example, a dishwashing job. The interview might go like this:

Kitchen Manager: You here for the dishwashing job?

Interviewee: Yep.

Kitchen Manager: We pay the minimum wage and the hours are Tuesday through Saturday night, from five in the evening to one in the morning.

Interviewee: Cool. I work hard and show up on time. Do I start tonight?

Offer a few reasons why you should be hired and ask for the job. This is a very direct and rational approach, and for the simple job opportunity this makes sense. The hiring authority is exposed to little risk if he makes a bad decision. If things don't pan out, then another warm body can quickly be found. Emotion will only enter the equation when the stakes are higher, the compensation and responsibilities are greater, and it becomes a higher-risk, higher-reward decision. Then the process becomes more complex. Several people interview multiple candidates, and the "sale" is no longer simple.

JOBSEEKERS SELLING POORLY

They interview as if driven by this philosophy: *Whoever presents the most reasons, and the best reasons, will win the interviewing contest*.

Whether they've thought about it or not, they act like the hiring decision is a rational one. After all, how could something so important to their life and career be irrational? "Doesn't the hiring authority want to hire the best?" their thought process goes. "And don't I need to show them I am the best by piling up the evidence that this is so?"

If the interviewer was a computer that could hear every reason why we are the best candidate, immediately calculate its worth, and simultaneously compare these weighted reasons to those of the other four candidates, then they would choose us if our qualifications outweighed our competition's. But the hiring authority is human—most of the time—and he can't keep up with weighing the information, organizing it, remembering it, etc., before more arrives.

Now multiply the impact of this data-dumping style times five (you and your four competitors). By the end of the fifth interview, the hiring authority's ears are bleeding and his head is about to explode. He forgets what has been said and who said it. The continuous stream of facts and data creates a data fog, and all of the candidates disappear in it. The exhausted interviewer struggles to associate resumes with the people he met mere hours ago.

THE CAUSES OF THE HIRING-DECISION-EFFECT

This rational, simple-sales approach doesn't work, because the complex hiring decision is caused by emotions, not reasons. If we are to cause a hiring decision, then we need to employ these emotional causes.

Let's compare the hiring of dishwashers to the hiring of professionals. With dishwashers there was a low risk-reward element in the decision. But when it comes to hiring professionals, a higher risk-reward relationship is in play.

If, for example, I hire a disruptive person for my marketing team, someone who destroys my team's chemistry and is disrespectful to authority figures, then I have not only made my life miserable, but I've hurt the productivity of the team, my company and my standing within it. I will now appear to be a poor judge of character and an ineffective team builder. Conversely, when I hire someone who exceeds all expectations, it makes my life easier as a manager, and it reflects well on me.

The risk and reward of hiring professionals introduces emotion into the decision-making process. I fear making a mistake. I don't hire someone who I cannot trust, or who makes me feel uncomfortable. I hire people I like and who I want to be around.

PERCEPTION AND EMOTION
One of the reasons why emotions cause hiring decisions is because they shape perception. Favorable emotions can create a filter that keeps the hiring authority from seeing our weaknesses, while negative feelings can keep them from seeing our strengths. For example, when our interviewing style gets an interviewer to like us, this

influences their perception in ways that favor us, because "perception is affected not only by what people *expect* to see; it is also colored by what they *want* to see."

The hiring authority looks for reasons to hire the candidate they like the most. They begin to see "what they *want* to see." When candidates are liked, then everything they say or do is colored in a positive way. There is a psychological reason why love is blind: We see what we want to see.

Let's return to the woman who said I had yet to sell her anything. She did not realize that the reason why we took her and her team up to the top of the Hancock Building for drinks, then out to a nice dinner, was to generate positive feelings toward us. Then, when we made our presentation, we did not present facts and data, but solutions to problems that caused painful feelings. In short, I was using emotions to cause the buying-decision-effect.

Once we understand the importance of emotion we will take a less rational approach to our quest for employment. We will stop focusing on the limited rational mind, and will make our appeal to another mental system that is more emotional. The way it impacts decision-making, communication, and perception will change our job-search course.

Chapter 2: Securing an Interview

Proper planning and perseverance will be the key to securing a quality number of interviews. It is vitally important to maintain a positive attitude throughout the process of securing interviews. There will undoubtedly be times during this phase of your job search that you will become very frustrated and want to quit. However, giving up at this point in the process will get you nowhere except back to where you started.

It's a common practice for many companies including search firms not to respond to your letters, resumes and phone calls during this part of your job search. Unless they have an interest in your background, they are simply inundated with resumes and lack the resources to respond to every applicant. Learn to expect rejection at this point of your search and try not to take it too personally. Continue on with your search and do not give up just because several people have not responded or simply indicated that there is no interest in your background.

Rejection: Simply Just a Way of Saying No, For Now
Rejection is simply a "No" answer, for now. By properly following up on a rejection letter, you may find that the company does have a need for your skills and invite you

in for an interview. Should you receive a rejection letter pertaining to a position for which you have applied, you should immediately write a letter back to the employer addressing it to the hiring authority. Indicate in your letter that you understand and respect their decision, however you feel confident that you may be an asset to their company. Be specific and explain how your experience and background can benefit their company. Indicate that you have done a great deal of research and have respect for their company's products or services as well as their corporate goals. Follow-up your letter with a telephone call to the hiring authority. It is very important that your letter and phone call be sent to a key decision-maker for the position you seek.

Speculation and the Law of Averages

Your ability to find and secure the job of your choice is a speculative process. You can increase your chances of a successful search by adopting and working with a principle called "The Law of Averages." A career search method that utilizes the "Law of Averages" is what I have termed "The Bullet Approach." This approach is based upon a systematic method of sending resumes to key decision makers using your target list of fifteen to twenty companies. By using this approach, you dramatically increase your chances of securing interviews with companies specific to your interest and skill match. If your particular skills and experience match those of a company you have targeted, the opportunity for a successful match increases significantly.

Another career search method that is often used but provides poor results is called "The Shotgun Approach." This approach also uses "The Law of Averages," but does not use the law properly to achieve a statistical advantage. "The Shotgun Approach" works on a principle similar to that of a real shotgun where a large number of pellets are propelled out of the gun in somewhat of a uniform pattern hoping to hit part of the target. Applied as a job search method, you literally present as many resumes as possible to companies hoping for a response. It is nearly impossible to effectively follow-up with such a large number of companies versus the fifteen to twenty I have advocated with "The Bullet Approach."

When you apply "The Bullet Approach" to your job search, you are not limited to the initial fifteen to twenty companies you have selected. It is wise however to try and limit the number you target at any one time. If you target too many companies you may not be able to properly research and follow-up with each company. As you begin to follow-up with companies on your initial target list, continue the process of researching other potential companies of interest. Begin to add other companies to your target list in the same proportion of those you eliminate.

If you target a company where your experience and skills do not match a particular job profile, your chances of securing the position is limited. A job match is similar to an organ transplant, where there must be a near perfect tissue and blood type match. If there is no match, the body will reject the organ. For example, if you are a computer sales representative selling computer hard drives, the probability of securing a position with another computer company selling hardware is significantly enhanced. This opposed to trying to obtain a position outside your known field of selling chemicals to the food industry.

However, if you want to change careers, you will need to present and sell your talents and skills in a different manner. Suppose you have made the decision to seek a sales position with a company whose products are unfamiliar to you. Emphasize your sales skills, including your ability to build a business. Emphasize your sales achievements and all other related sales skills including your exceptional negotiating and closing abilities.

You have taken an important step in your job search by identifying and researching companies that meet your career requirements. The next step in your job search will be to secure an interview with the proper hiring authority at each of your target companies. Making contact with a hiring authority is an important key to the success of your search. View this essential step of the process as if you were a private investigator trying to locate a missing person. Who are you trying to locate? What is that person's name, title and function within their business?

If you are a sales representative seeking a sales position you should make contact with the Vice President or Director of Sales. If however these are positions you seek, direct your contact to an Executive Vice President or President of the company. The most effective method for making contact with company managers is to start high on the company's organizational chart, i.e., President, Vice President, Director, etc. It is always beneficial to be able to indicate to a Director or Regional Manager that the Vice President or President of their company has asked you to make contact with them.

This type of referral represents a higher level of authority and gives you instant credibility with mid level management. This important telephone call enables you to establish a one on one conversation with the proper hiring authority. The more personal contact you have with the hiring authority either by telephone, mail, email, personal meetings, etc., is key to securing the position you desire.

Develop a system to follow-up on each telephone call to a potential employer or contact. It may be beneficial to create a spreadsheet on your computer using a program such as Microsoft's Excel. Create your own form indicating headings such as: Date, Contact, Title, Company, Address, Email, Web, Telephone and Fax numbers including a Purpose/Results section. In addition to developing a spreadsheet to track your contacts, there are a number of very sophisticated contact databases such as ACT, which are excellent tools for tracking your contacts and any action taken with them.

Because you have targeted fifteen to twenty companies you should make at least fifteen to twenty follow-up telephone calls after sending your resume. How well you handle each follow-up phone call to a proposed hiring authority may determine whether or not you will secure an interview.

Human Resources, Proceed with Extreme Caution!

You may want to make contact with the personnel office specifically with the Vice President, Director or Manager of Human Resources within the company you are interested. Proceed with extreme caution when making contact with a company's personnel department! A friend of mine commented during his job search that he often felt the personnel department was like a giant black hole, where everything was sucked in and nothing came out. Without entirely degrading personnel, as they do have a function, it is my view that you should initially avoid the personnel area. Your first contact should be the hiring authority and if they are interested in your background, personnel will be copied on your background and will become involved. It is my experience that individuals involved in the personnel department tend not to fully understand the intricacy of hiring, as this is only a small percentage of their total duties.

I have only had the pleasure of working with a few true professional personnel individuals who understand the complexity of hiring people. The problem is that most personnel managers do not view people as individuals, but rather as a stereotyped group of people called applicants or candidates. If you decide to send your resume to a company's personnel department, it is important to address your letter to a specific individual ideally a senior manager within the department rather than simply "Personnel."

As previously indicated, it is important to develop a system of follow-up with your company contacts. I often hear about job seekers sending out cover letters and resumes but never personally following up with a telephone call to their contact. Your follow-up telephone call is one of the most important aspects of the job search. It enables you to establish a one on one conversation with the proposed hiring authority. Without direct personal contact with the hiring authority you will not be able to secure a position.

Before you make your initial follow-up call, I have found it very helpful to write out your proposed conversation. Your notes will act as a script that will assist you to stay focused on the purpose of your conversation. A key factor for any follow-up telephone call is to determine the purpose for your call. Realize that you are selling yourself, your skills and knowledge to the prospective employer. Ask yourself the question, what is my purpose for calling this person, and what do I hope to accomplish. Try to anticipate any questions the employer may ask you and what your response will be. If you have ever played chess, checkers or any other game requiring strategy, you understand that the ability to anticipate a challenger's move is an extremely important aspect of winning the game.

An example of an initial follow-up call after you have sent a cover letter and a resume to the hiring authority known as Mr. Robert Morris, Vice President of JEM Computer, Inc. may be as follows:

"Hello, Mr. Morris, my name is John Powell. I recently wrote to you regarding my background in the area of computer hardware sales, specifically in the area of high-resolution computer screens." (Your specific product or service experience stated should be of interest to Mr. Morris and his company.) "The purpose of my call is to introduce myself as a potential candidate for a sales position within your company. I recently sent you my resume. Do you have a moment where I might discuss with you how I can be an asset to your company?" Stop! Let Mr. Morris respond to your initial statements. A myriad of responses from Mr. Morris may follow your introductory statements. He may simply say, "Yes, I am in receipt of your resume, and although you have an excellent background, we do not have a position available at this time commensurate with your experience."

Don't give up at this point in your discussion. Ask Mr. Morris if he foresees, in the near future, a position where your background in the area of high-resolution computer screens may become available. Consider the fact that it is possible that the position you seek with JEM Computer, Inc. may open up in the near future. If Mr. Morris says, "Yes, in fact a position may be available in about a month, however this particular job is within another division." Ask him what the specific duties of that position are. Who does the position report to? Can you speak directly with that person? Is it okay to indicate that Mr. Morris referred you to that individual?

In addition, ask Mr. Morris if he is aware of another company that may be expanding or have specific personnel needs where your background would be a potential fit. If Mr. Morris recommends a company to you, ask him if he has any contacts within the company. If he refers you to a particular contact, ask him if it is okay to indicate that he was the source of the referral. This approach will give you instant credibility with the referred company and may be the key to securing a new position.

Finally, it is always wise to send a thank you note to Mr. Morris expressing your appreciation for the time he spent with you regarding his company and your potential role within his company. You should also express your continued interest in his company and a desire to speak with him further should a position become available. If Mr. Morris was able to refer you to another company, thank him for his referral as well.

Depending upon the level of rapport you have developed with Mr. Morris during your conversation, you may also want to ask him if he has some time to meet with you. You should indicate to him that you have done some research on his company and that it is a firm you are very interested in working for. Even though there isn't an open position at the present time, you would like to learn more about his company should a position become available in the near future. If you are able to arrange a meeting with Mr. Morris, treat it as any other interview you have secured. You may be surprised by the results. Mr. Morris may like you, and he might create a position for you within his company. If he does not have a position commensurate with your background at this time, you may want to ask him if it would be okay for you to speak with his Director of Computer Sales, Sales Manager, or both individuals. They may be able to direct you to other contacts within the industry that may lead you to other job search leads.

The larger and more enhanced your network becomes, the probability of securing a position with a company or organization that you desire becomes greater. It is important to remember that locating and securing a job is a calculated numbers game where the law of averages is always a factor for success. If you make contact with the proper hiring authorities within a select number of targeted companies, your chances of landing a position is high. Put into practice the motto of my Executive Search firm of "Quality versus Quantity," and you will succeed in your job search.

Chapter 3: Researching the Organization

Before your interview, find out as much as you can about the company. It will help you answer their questions better and think of good questions for the interviewer at the end. There's a wealth of information available online that you can use. Follow our top tips to gather information.

● *Visit the company website.* The company's website is the first place to look when doing your research. Most companies have an "About Us" page where you can read their mission statement, history and what they say about their company culture.

● *Use LinkedIn.* LinkedIn company profiles can give you plenty of information. You'll be able to see if you have any connections there who may be able to help you. You can also see new hires, promotions, company statistics and other jobs they have posted. Find your interviewer's profile to gain insight into their job and background.

● *Google the company.* Do a Google search for the company, focusing on the web and news results. Have they recently achieved something noteworthy?

What are the latest company developments? Avoid any bad press, or anything which gives a negative impression of the company.

● *Speak to your connections.* Do you know anyone who works there? Ask if they can help. Find out what they may know about the company that isn't in the news or available online. This will give you advantage over other candidates who don't have your connections.

● *Read the small print.* When you are on the company's website, use the sitemap to find pages that may not be easy to find. You'll be surprised how much information could be hidden away!

● *Speak to your recruitment agency.* If you secured this interview through an agency, speak to your consultant about the company. They will know a lot about them, as they would have worked and looked for candidates for them before.

1   Make a list. Think of things you may want to find out before you start. Here are a few examples:

2   How old is the company

3   How many people work for them?

4   How many countries do they operate in?

5   What are their main products and services?

6   Who are their customers?

7   Who are their competitors?

8   Where is their head office based?

9   What training programs do they offer?

10   What does their Annual Report or accounts say about the business?

● *Make some calls.* Call the company's human resources department and ask about the company. They may be willing to share some information with you.

● *Use social network sites.* See if they have a Twitter account or Facebook page. By liking them on Facebook or following them on Twitter, you will receive all of their updates and posts. See if they have a blog and read some of their posts.

What Are They Looking For?

There are three main things the interviewer wants to know, and your answers to these will depend on how you respond to other questions and how you act and react during the interview.

19. *Can you do the job?*

20. This relates to your skills, knowledge and experience, and when you have done similar roles before.

21. *How will you do it?*

22. This relates to your personal qualities, for example, whether you are good at speaking to customers, your networking abilities, if you keep calm under pressure, or what type of a manager you are.

23. *Will you make the tea?*

24. What we mean by this is "How will you fit in with the company culture and the rest of the team?" You will spend more time at work than you do with your family during the day, so a prospective line manager will be asking themselves, "Will this person get along with the team and me?" You and your colleagues don't have to be best friends but you do need to get on.

So how do you find out what exactly the company is looking for in an employee? The job description should give you an idea. You can use this to structure your answers to show your interviewer that you are the right person for the role.

Let's say the job description is for an admin assistant who will work as part of a large team in the complaints department.

You can use your previous admin work experience to answer the first question. How you deal with customers, e.g., staying calm even when confronted am angry client, will answer the second question. Your ability to work with your teammates will answer the third question.

Technical Interview

If you're going for a role that requires a high level of technical knowledge, you might find yourself having to undergo a technical interview. It may also be in the form of a written test or presentation.

In each case, preparation is the key. You are unlikely to get the job if you cannot demonstrate your technical knowledge to the required level, under pressure.

Do not panic. Approach each problem logically. If you require further clarification, do not hesitate to ask, as this type of test may include impossible or "**trick**" questions. These are designed to assess your problem-solving skills and logical thought processes, as well as your technical knowledge.

Assessment Centre

This type of interview normally takes place over one or more days in a specially selected location. As a candidate, you could be subjected to different types of interviews.

You are also likely to take part in several group or individual activities. These can include mini-assault courses or group tasks, such as constructing items from provided materials within in a certain time frame. These activities will be used to assess your problem-solving skills, ability to perform under pressure and your communication, negotiation and teamwork skills.

You may be asked to give presentations to the group or to the panel of interviewers. You may also have to undergo written tests designed to assess your literacy, numeracy and technical knowledge. The company may also use psychometric testing to evaluate your personality.

This type of interview is extremely tough and is normally reserved for graduate and higher level positions. Rehearse for all types of interviews, do some IQ and psychometric tests, and brush up on your literacy, numeracy and problem-solving skills. Tests and resources are readily available on the internet.

Keep in mind throughout the process that your performance is constantly being evaluated. Many companies will put on a lunch or dinner for candidates and interviewers in order to assess their social skills. If you are a smoker, do try and limit the number of breaks that you have and ensure you freshen up after having one.

Second interview

If you do well enough to go through the first interview, you might then be asked to return for a second one. By now the company will have a shortlist of potential candidates and may need to whittle this down to make an offer to one candidate. The second interview could take the form of any of the interview types already discussed, so be ready for anything.

If you have faced assessment centers or panel interviews in the first round, the second interview will more likely be to see how you will integrate into the team. You may even have the opportunity to visit the place where you will be working or to meet some of your potential team members.

Treat each succeeding interview with as much attention as the first. Do not assume that the next interviewer knows what you told the first one. Be prepared to repeat yourself, if necessary. Do not get complacent and think that as this is your second or third interview, you are a definite shoo-in for the job. Yes, you are one step closer, but you still need to give it 100%.

Chapter 4: Interview Skills That Will Get You Hired_

In competing with so many applicants for any given job and throughout the hiring process, what does a hiring manager look for which will differentiate you from other job candidates?

1. Knowledge of the Company

In the same way a hiring manager is interviewing you and investing in getting to know you, and whether or not you're a good fit for their company, a hiring manager is also looking to see if you've also done your homework. Take the time to research the companies you are applying to work for, including their strengths and weaknesses; and demonstrate this by asking intelligent questions about the company.

3. Great Attitude

Most people do not like to work with or hire a grouch. Put on a smile, develop an authentic "can do" attitude, and let this shine through when you interact with hiring managers. Remember, if the hiring manager doesn't enjoy being around you and your attitude, they can be fairly sure your would-be co-workers also wouldn't enjoy you, and you probably won't make the cut.

4. Team Player

Employers are interested in hiring those who work well with others and who recognize that greatness is never achieved in a silo. Demonstrating that you are a team player to a prospective employer is powerful. As you share your past work experiences, demonstrate your ability to work in a team by highlighting the strengths of the teams you've worked on in the past and praise others for their contributions in addition to mentioning your own.

5. Flexibility

Employers want to hire professionals who can flex. A person who is stuck in their ways and doesn't demonstrate adaptability tends to be harder to work with. This is especially important in today's corporate climate where job scopes change and evolve day by day to meet a company's needs. Employers know they can get more mileage out of a professional who can adapt to a variety of job requirements and company needs.

6. Growth Mindset

This is perhaps the most misunderstood and yet the most important skill that will affect the impression you leave with a hiring manager. A growth mindset is not meant to indicate you are a professional intent on growth within an organization, upward mobility, and a desire to advance in your position. Rather, a growth mindset means you look at your job, your company and your work responsibilities with the eye of someone intent on personal growth and development. You are a professional who will continue learning, perfecting your skills and learning new ones, and someone who is agile and capable of growth and change. You may have held the same position for ten years, but every single year you enhance your ability to do your job better, more efficiently, and to a higher degree of professionalism. A growth mindset is less about career advancement and more about demonstrating that you are a flexible, adaptable, forward thinking professional.

7. Self-Starter (Highly Motivated)

Self-motivation may be one of a hiring manager's most sought after attributes in a candidate because it directly correlates to how a hiring manager will need to invest their own time and effort in managing an employee. Employees who are motivated on their own and don't require constant supervision and prompting from their manager are more likely to be low-maintenance and highly productive additions to a team.

8. Excellent Soft Skills

Beyond how your background, education, experience, and industry knowledge qualifies you for a position, hiring managers want to know if you have the right soft skills to be a good fit for their team. These are the skills that most degrees and years in an industry won't teach you, but they are what can make or break your ability to convince a hiring manager you are a worthwhile addition. Respectful, hardworking, dependable, positive, organized, confident, works well under pressure, effective communicator, and a problem solver are a few examples of highly desirable soft skills.

9. Ability to add Value to the Organization

Think about a time you've purchased a vehicle. Beyond the year, make and model, you are interested in the additional assets a car possesses which will add value to your purchase – a sunroof, a backup camera, remote keyless entry, for example. Presenting yourself to a hiring manager is like showing yourself off as a car to a potential buyer. If you can demonstrate value in yourself as a candidate, including attributes like superior knowledge, skills or job-related abilities, you have a better chance of showing a hiring manager that you can add value to a company. What is the skill or attribute you have that will make you invaluable to a hiring manager?

Find that answer and then sell that in your interview and on your resume as a way of differentiating yourself from the pack of other candidates.

Chapter 5: The Secret of Interview Etiquette

Principles of Interview Etiquette

I cannot think of a situation more difficult than walking into an interview room with a stranger who has the upper hand and who questions everything you say or do. It is easy to lose your composure and confidence, which then makes everything else go haywire. As you prepare to attend the next interview, remember to equip yourself with business etiquette as it is a core pillar to successful interviews.

Your etiquette determines whether or not you get to the next level of the recruitment process. Most job candidates spend much of their time and energy thinking about their skills and qualifications to present to the interviewer and forget about personal conduct. Good manners determine the success of a business relationship since they determine how you establish rapport with other people. Your manner of behavior toward others is equally important as your résumé and any kind of experience. It is no surprise, therefore, that recruiters are interested in individuals who will fit within their business family.

The following guidelines reflect the principles of interview etiquette that show you how to avoid some mistakes job hunters have made and which derail them from reaching their goal.

How to greet your interviewers

Interviewers are most often referred to by their first name. Chances of offending someone by referring to them by their first name are minimal since it is the universal standard of meeting someone for the first time. However, calling someone by their last name shows a sense of respect and it directly tells them that you consider them important. Remember that the employer is looking for suggestions that you will be easy to work with, fully understanding the organizational management structure and respecting it.

Table talk

After greeting, the interviewer should remain standing until or unless you are asked to sit. Once you are offered a seat, refrain from feeling comfortable to the point of placing your belongings, such as a handbag, on the table. Be humble enough to place them under your chair or beside your legs. Only a professional binder should be placed on the table near you. Remember to turn down the offer of a drink politely if one is offered. Finally, sit up properly without moving your feet around.

Ensure your cell phone is completely off

An interview is definitely one of the most crucial gatherings in your life and a phone distraction is not worth ruining such a meeting. Interviewers are keen to notice a phone's vibration; thus, it should be totally off. If possible, do not enter the interview room with your phone. At this moment there is nothing more important than your conversation with your potential employer. They will want to know if you can serve their clients without being distracted by your own personal gadget. Therefore, make sure to avoid the distraction at all costs.

Let the company take the lead during the conversation

Sometimes your interviewer may be laid back or soft-spoken, which may tempt you to get things going. You may start assuming the lead position and you eventually become inconsequential. Refrain from giving in to the temptation and let the interviewer take the lead regardless of their style. Go silent and do not look bored whenever they go silent. After all, you have nothing to worry about if you are well prepared. So just relax. Talking too much is a common mistake that interviewees make. It is easy to begin explaining things that are uncalled for when your employer is a person of few words.

Do not talk over the speaker

The most disturbing aspect in an interview is stepping into the interviewer's last two to three words of a statement and talking over without even extending the courtesy to letting them finish their statement. In this chapter, it comes off as a principle of etiquette. Show that you would respect the management and that you have good listening skills, which are so valuable in today's business world.

Take notes during the interview

One of the items that you should bring with you into an interview room is a professional-looking binder. Remember to make it useful during the conversation. Taking notes indicates that you are candidly interested in the job and the company, and it also helps you to pose a query when you are given a chance. Talking of an official folder, invest in one that looks first class. Do not use an electronic gadget such as a tablet to take notes in the interview. Such gadgets can only be used if you are interviewing for an Information Technology position or something similar. Also, remember that providing your professional references and résumé copies is a positive note.

Chase the position tirelessly even if you feel like the interview has already gone wrong

It is not unusual for someone to be having a rough time during an interview and to even create conclusions about the company, which may impact their ability to deliver the best version of themselves. The best thing you can do during such a time is to maintain professionalism and finish the interview without showing any signs of backing down. Remember you are not being forced to take this job, after all. You are still in the driver's seat in the end since you can always turn down an offer or respectfully withdraw from the process. Job candidates can be fond of prejudice toward the interviewers and they end up regretting it later. Ensure that you have collected all possible facts before making an ultimate judgment about the organization. Leave the interviewers with a good impression of you as it could pay back later in unimaginable ways. Imagine having poorly interviewed with this employer's biggest client who is now your boss.

Remember that your interview is not over until you walk out of the gate

From the moment you walk through the gate, how you talk to the receptionist or any other person, including the premises' cleaners, matters a lot in your hiring process. Some employers have taken time to ask parties such as the receptionist how you greeted them on your way in.

Hiring managers could watch a candidate as they exit the interview premises. Conversely, some interviewees have some outrageous behavior such as starting to make calls or lighting up cigarettes right outside the premises. Remember to maintain official conduct until you are far from the premises.

Arrive about fifteen minutes early but do not show up at the interview door more than five minutes early

It goes without saying; you never want to be late for an interview. It is one of the biggest deal breakers if you cannot keep time on the first day. If you are not five minutes early, then you are late. It is recommended that you arrive early and get accustomed to the organization's ambiance. If you are uncontrollably running late, make sure to call and inform them of your delay. Always have the contact information of the person organizing your visit for such a reason, but make sure to overcome all obstacles to arrive at the scheduled time. It shows that you are punctual and you can be trusted with routines or to hit deadlines, or even to save time for the company. Conversely, arriving too early gives employers the first reason to start judging you from a negative light.

Close the interview the right way

Express your gratitude toward the interviewer for the interview as it comes to an end and restate your interest in the role. Feel free to make an inquiry on how long it would take before they could reach out. Finally, greet everyone in the room by the hand if possible and also use their name as this shows your attention to details and courtesy. Greeting other people in the outer office shows good manners as well, although it may not be a strategy per se. Remember to keep smiling until you leave the premises.

Send a thank you note after the interview

Thanking the hiring manager for the interview counts as an important part of your etiquette principles. It reminds the interviewers about you and shows them how courteous you are. Also, take this chance to clarify anything you feel you need to reiterate. Refer to anything that the interviewer said during the interview that intrigued you. Reiterate why you think you are fit for the position.

Chapter 6: Inside the Mind of an Interviewer

We'll let you in on a little secret. Interviewers don't want to have to interview. They'd rather you were already hired. Of course, especially in growing organizations, they'll have to interview people frequently, but in their ideal situation, these future interviews would always be for new openings. What interviewers really don't want is to have to interview candidates for the position that's currently open. Ever again.

It's not that they hate interviewing, although it's certainly not everyone's favorite task. And it's not simply that interviewing regularly for the same position can be a drain on an organization's resources. Interviewers also don't want to be proven wrong. They don't want to be the person who recommended hiring someone whose performance turns out to be lackluster. They don't want to be the person who recommended hiring someone who later needs to be fired. They don't even want to be the person who recommended someone who quits after ten months.

Succeeding in job interviews involves understanding both sides of the conversation, your own and that of the people who want to fill the open position. If you can manage to think like your interviewers, you will be able to speak directly to their concerns and put yourself that much closer to landing a great job.

In order to understand what's going on in the minds of hiring managers and your potential bosses, it can be helpful to think about how the process often goes wrong. Here are a few profiles of people we've worked with over the years. To be clear, none of these profiles represents a single real person, but they're characteristic of many coworkers whom we've known. Each also indicates an interview process that could and should have gone differently.

The square peg. The square peg might have been great in the interview setting, but he can't actually do the job. To the interviewer, his previous experience seemed highly relevant, but it turned out to be insufficient for the present job. His coworkers might appreciate his water cooler banter, but his bosses must double-check or reassign most of his work. What's worse, the extra coaching and training that they provide don't seem to help. In worst-case scenarios, his employers have to fire him in order to protect their workflow, and this brings down office morale. Suddenly, people who didn't work closely with this misaligned employee are thinking, *Why* *are people being fired randomly? Is my job at risk? Maybe I should start looking for a more secure position myself.*

The slacker. Unlike the square peg, the slacker may be perfectly capable, but she doesn't seem to do much of anything. She can't be bothered to learn the details of a project before an important meeting with a client. She sometimes closes the door to her office and chats with her mother all day. (Office doors don't block out noise *that* well.) When she's in a meeting, she "secretly" plays games on her iPhone. (It is wholly obvious when you're checking your work email and when you're on Facebook.) To make matters worse, the slacker's inaction upsets her coworkers, whose jobs are now harder than they were before she was hired. They're silently aware that the slacker is being paid a salary to do nothing at all.

The troublemaker. The troublemaker is often capable, and he usually does the work that is asked of him. But he does something else that is certainly not asked of him. He creates unnecessary tension in the workplace. This may be done in the form of subtle (sometimes less-than-subtle) gossip: "Do you think Mark is gunning for a promotion? I heard he had coffee with the VP of finance yesterday." Or "I'm pretty sure this new so-called security protocol is actually a system to keep track of how much time we spend at our desks." This person complains about his coworkers, office policies, and employee pay, but always to other employees and never to someone who actually has the authority to answer his questions or remedy the problem. This person is rarely fired for failing to complete his work, but he's also less likely to be given a second chance if he makes a mistake. For most employers this is an even bigger disaster than it seems. The toxic culture created by this person makes his coworkers dissatisfied; indeed, sometimes these employees leave, giving the troublemaker a chance to begin again with new hires.

The achiever. The achiever is more than capable, highly engaged, even respectful of her bosses and coworkers. She's a dream employee except for one major issue: she wants more recognition, a better title, and better pay and she wants these things faster than the organization can accommodate. The achiever may do wonderful things and do them quickly, but she jumps ship and signs with a competitor as soon as she has new accomplishments to display. Suddenly, the organization's top competitor has a great employee, while they themselves are back to hiring.

The prima donna. Watch out. The prima donna may be a good, even a talented, employee but his performance is out of line with his self-perception. Like the achiever, he wants a raise and a promotion, but unlike the achiever, he has an unrealistic sense of the demand for his skills. He may not want to leave his job (indeed, he may be unable to do so), but he demands as much as he can while he waits for something better. A prima donna doesn't necessarily produce further rounds of hiring, but if your interviewer is an experienced hiring manager, they will do their best to avoid hiring this character. A prima donna creates tension. His manager is always saying no or bending over backwards to give him what he wants, like the best office or best projects. And if he gets what he wants and is paid more than his equally effective peers, his coworkers may become aware of that inequality and feel less satisfied with their own situations. He's also often the first person out the door when the economy goes sour, because cutting his salary from payroll is the best bang for the buck.

The job hopper. The job hopper also shares an important trait with the achiever. She's a competent worker, but she's not fully committed. She questions, *Am I meant to check tax returns or should I be in a forest in Canada, studying the migratory patterns of rare birds?* Or perhaps her boyfriend has a job offer across the country, and she wants to follow. The job hopper leaves as soon as it's convenient for her, regardless of how her schedule fits with her employer's needs.

These are caricatures, of course. Good interviewers don't try to force people into boxes. And there can be good reasons to act in each of these ways. Some are truly great reasons, like trying to achieve your real earning potential or supporting a loved one as they take up a new career. The important thing to keep in mind is that interviewers don't want to have to hire more often than needed for the same position. It's their task to determine not simply whether you have the right experience, an excellent degree, or a winning personality; they need to know that you'll serve the organization's larger interests.

What Type of Employee Are You?

To determine what kind of employee you are, a good interviewer will try to glean several pieces of information. Some of these pieces of information are really important. We call these *major considerations*. Nearly all interviewers think about all of the major considerations, and they think about them for nearly all job candidates. The other pieces of information that an interviewer wants to learn are *minor considerations*. Only certain interviewers care about the minor things, they may care about them only for certain jobs, and they may not think about them for all candidates.

All of these considerations are reliant on one thing: that you come across as being accurate during the interview. Interviewers need assurance that you are self-aware and that you are accurately describing your experience. If they think you're talented at saying what you think they want to hear, or that your self-perception is wildly different from the way others perceive you, they won't believe anything you have to say. Show yourself to be a reliable source of information by sharing examples that back up your claims.

Major Considerations

From the standpoint of any organization, having to fire and then hire again is much worse than having to hire again because someone quit. Firing employees is unpleasant and costly, and it lowers morale. For this reason, the major considerations are competency, fit, and interest. If new employees don't meet the basic requirements for these considerations, they put their organizations at risk.

Competency

Basic competency is often the first quality that an interviewer tries to evaluate. It's good to remember that the evaluation of your competency begins before any representative of the organization shakes your hand or calls you on the phone. Before any interview, someone in the organization (usually multiple people) reviews your cover letter and resume. During this initial review, they ask themselves, "Can this applicant do the job?" And in order to answer this question, they'll look for relevant experience, knowledge, and the presence of particular skills.

If you're like many people (remember the obviously-strong-candidate approach?), you may be thinking that you spent hours and hours on your resume and it already explains your skills and abilities perfectly well, thank you very much. Why would an interviewer ask you about the same facts that you carefully listed for them already?

In a perfect universe, landing a job would be a simple matter of sending a resume. Alas, this is not the case. Resumes have a few key faults. What's more, the language of resumes is highly, if sometimes intentionally, ambiguous: the same description of last summer's internship often masks wildly different levels of experience or proficiency. And finally—and it's unlikely that this refers to you—small numbers of people out and out lie on their resumes.

Interviewers are aware of these faults. And for this reason, they will usually ask questions about how long, how often, and at what level you have actually performed the tasks and duties that you described on your resume. How long did it take you to become a spreadsheet expert? Was that successful branding campaign on social media entirely your effort or did you make important contributions as part of a team? You don't need to have learned everything already, but you do need to be able to speak clearly and effectively about what you know and how you hope to develop in the future.

The final thing to keep in mind about the ambiguity of your resume is that interviewers often test areas that seem like potential weaknesses. For instance, if the job posting mentions that effective employees will need to use Excel macros and you don't include anything about macros in your cover letter or resume, you will need to be prepared to answer a question about your ability or experience in this area. You needn't be an expert in macros, of course, to convey your general competence or your willingness to learn, but good preparation will lead you to expect this very question.

<u>Fit</u>

We've been throwing around the term "fit," but what does it actually mean? Fit is a catchall word to describe the fact that organizations want employees who can adapt easily to their roles, be successful, and contribute to the overall office culture. Fit is an elastic term. It means different things in different contexts.

Fit is sometimes a matter of the job in question. If a company is hiring a customer service representative, they may search for someone who is warm, supportive, and patient. These same qualities might ill serve someone who is a federal prosecutor. (No offense to federal prosecutors!) What's more, if an organization publicly espouses certain values, like its low environmental impact, a warm person who volunteers for local river clean-up days might be an even better fit.

Asking Questions

A survey by CareerBuilder in 2012 found that 32% of hiring managers reported that not asking good questions is one of the most detrimental mistakes job applicants make during an interview. Generally speaking, employers feel that if you don't have some prepared questions that are relevant to the job or company, then you might not really be interested in the job.

In my own experience in interviewing people for jobs, I would have to agree with the above survey. Time and time again I experienced people who did really well in the interview, but when it came time for them to ask questions, they either had no questions to ask, or the questions they asked were poor choices.

You might be thinking then, "What are the best questions I could ask at the end of an interview?" Similarly, "Which questions should I avoid?" In this chapter I will outline some possible responses to each of these questions.

Asking the right questions can help show the interviewer that you have prepared for the interview and that you are serious about this job. Employers respect people who want to know more about the job or the company. It should also be noted that asking questions provides another opportunity to sell you. In considering which questions you might ask, it is important for them to be positive, rather than asking a question that might be viewed in a negative manner by the employer. For example, it would make more sense to ask about the company's mission statement then it would to ask why their profits were down (if in fact you knew this kind of information).

The following provide some examples of questions that would be appropriate to ask in most job interviews:

What do you see as some changes that will be occurring in your organization over the next five years?

How would you describe the leadership style in your company?

What are the major skills and personal traits you are looking for in this job?

What are some immediate challenges you see as being addressed by the person fulfilling this job?

Why do you like working here?

Are there any aspects of this job that we haven't discussed here today that you think I should know about?

What sort of person is most successful in your company?

Does this company offer or support continued education or training?

What is the next step in the interviewing process? It would also be appropriate to ask for the timelines in this process if they are not given to you.

At some point, would it be possible to receive a tour of the company?

What is the most important thing you are looking for in hiring new employees?

The above questions provide examples of some questions you might ask at the end of an interview. I would suggest that you add any other questions that are important to you to this list. After you do this, select 5 - 6 questions that are most important to you. Remember, this is also an opportunity for you to be assessing whether you really want to work for this company.

After you ask each question, don't hesitate to summarize what is said to you, or even ask further questions related to what you have been told. This demonstrates good listening skills which is an important aspect of success in almost any job. If there is strong conversation following any question, it might be advisable to cross a few questions off your list. Two or three questions with some follow-up discussion are better than a barrage of final questions with little or no discussion.

In considering the questions you might ask at the end of an interview, there are some that you should avoid. The following provides some sample questions that you should avoid during an interview (unless the answer is critical to you accepting the job, and even then you have to ask yourself whether it would be better to first be offered the job before asking the question).

Don't ask about salary, benefits, time off, etc. (these can all be discussed further once you have actually been offered the job.

Don't ask what the company does (this is information that you should have researched before the interview).

Similar to this, don't ask any questions that you could have simply Googled before the interview to find the answer.

Don't ask how quickly you can be promoted.

Don't ask whether the company does background checks.

Don't ask questions that relate to your personal needs as opposed to the needs of the company (for example, don't ask if you can have every Saturday off because you play golf).

Don't ask if the company monitors employees' emails.

Don't ask about any rumors or "dirt" you might have heard about the company.

Don't ask if you can do this job from home (unless of course, you expected that this was a part of the job description)?

Don't ask how many warnings does a person receive before getting fired?

As the interview ends, thank the interviewer (once again referring to him or her by name). This is another opportunity for a firm handshake and a smile. If you had some interaction with a receptionist or secretary before the interview, it would be appropriate to say something along the lines of "It was a pleasure meeting you." to this person before you leave the building if it is convenient.

Chapter 7: LinkedIn

LinkedIn can be used as a job search tool, where you can apply for positions or contact potential employers directly, but LinkedIn is so much more than this and can be set up so that people contact you directly about opportunities; this is where the power really is.

Setting up LinkedIn correctly will give you much more online exposure, making you more visible to recruiters and potential employers.

LinkedIn Privacy and Settings

It's important you set up LinkedIn privacy and settings correctly. Follow these steps for maximum online exposure.

At the top right-hand side of your LinkedIn home page, hover over your profile picture icon and click 'Manage' next to 'Privacy & Settings'.

Privacy

After you click on 'Manage'. Click on 'Privacy' near the top of the screen.

Profile Privacy

- Click 'Edit your public profile' (The public profile options page will appear)
- Click 'Create your custom URL' and enter your name or as close to it as possible to create your unique URL.
- Click the button next to 'Make my public profile visible to everyone'
- Ensure all the boxes are ticked then click 'save' and back on your browser.

New or Existing Profile

If you are setting up your profile for the first time you'll see editable sections where you can add the relevant information to your profile. However if you are editing your profile you can do this directly from your existing profile page.

Important Note_

LinkedIn is a business-networking tool and therefore you need to make sure your profile is visible to everyone. Sometime individuals will not upload a profile picture, or hide certain parts of their profile. This is a mistake if you are looking for work.

It is recommended that you switch on all visibility settings and ensure you complete every section when setting up your profile.

The following should be completed.

Personal information

- Insert your name in CAPITAL LETTERS
- Add a photo
- Add your job title followed by your company slogan or personal specialism such as "Professional Writer"
- Add your location
- Add your email address
- Add your phone number
- Add your location
- If you have a Twitter account, add it here
- Add your company website and LinkedIn profile URL

Additional Info

- Add Interests, be sure to add at least five.
- Add Personal Details.
- Add Advice for people to contact you.

Top tip: Ensure your interests are personal rather than work focused. People are also interested to know what you do outside of work.

Skills and Endorsements

Top tip: As well as adding professional skills ensure you include personal ones. People want to get to know you out of the working environment, so add skills that help to build greater rapport.

Courses

Top tip: In addition to courses, you can also add any training and coaching you have received. As before ensure these are both professional and personally focused.

Volunteer

Top tip: Add charitable organization that you are involved with

Languages, Publications & Projects

Ensure these 3 sections are completed as much as possible.

Groups

Top tip: Join groups you are interested in and groups you think your target audience is interested in. Many of your future connections will come from the groups you are a member of.

Influencers

Top tip: Follow influencers, news articles and companies that you are interested in and those you think your target audience will be interested in. Many of your future connections will come from people who follow the same influencers/topics as you.

Chapter 8: The Ten Most Important Interview Questions And How To Answer Them

1) Tell me something about yourself.

What the interviewer actually means is: *"What do you have to offer me?"*

Most interviewees believe that this is one of the most challenging questions an interviewer could ask. It is actually a great open-ended opportunity to share your best features. That said, resist the urge to praise yourself to the heavens. Keep it short and limit your answer to the features that you think will be most beneficial to the employer's business. For instance, you may have both technical computer skills and salesmanship skills. But if you're applying for a position which will require you to deal mostly with the technical aspect of computers, then stick to selling your computer skills.

Fight the inclination to present your whole autobiography. Instead, keep your answer short by providing a brief background and highlighting some of your most notable accomplishments. Connect your educational background with the current position that you're holding. Make sure you cover your educational and career background and your most recent job experience. It is important that you express how your career has taken a logical advancement.

"I grew up in Connecticut and moved to New York where I studied Fine Arts and Art History at NYU. Straight out of college, I got a job at as an art curator at ____. Working in this job allowed me to learn a great deal about my chosen field and to cultivate my skills and knowledge as well as my stamina, my social skills, and my salesmanship skills. From there, I was able to obtain a senior position at ____. That's where I was truly able to develop my managerial skills as well as my ability to handle high-profile projects and manage budgets up to $1 million. Right now, I believe that all the skills and experiences that I've gathered throughout the years make me a suitable candidate for a position in your company. I intend to prove that today. Do tell me, what are the qualities you are seeking in an ideal applicant for this job position?"

With this answer, you were able to answer the interviewer's actual question: "What do you have to offer me?"

The things you are able to offer him are:

● your excellent stamina
● your social skills

- your salesmanship skills

- your managerial skills

- and your ability to manage million-dollar projects and budgets

2) Why do you want to work in this company?

Why indeed? While your true answer may be because you need something from the company (a salary, stability), make it seem as though it's the company that needs something from you.

For this question, mention the features of the company that appeal to you the most. Discuss how the company is the perfect place for you. In other words, show the interviewer why you will fit right in. Proceed to talk about the skills that you possess, which will enable you to benefit from the company while at the same time allowing the company to benefit from you. Demonstrate that you are eager for an opportunity to contribute.

"I'll go ahead and say right out that I'm thrilled with the idea of working in this company. I am seeking an opportunity where my skills will be put to good use and I think that this is the perfect place for me to apply and demonstrate my expertise. For instance, I am very interested in being a part of your company's current project: _____. I am positive that with my experience in cutting costs and maximizing revenues, I can contribute a great deal to this project's success."

3) What makes you certain that you're qualified for this position?

When answering questions like this, you need only to remember that your contribution to a company is often only measured through two things:

- Money
- Time

Therefore, show your interviewer how you can help your employer increase the value of either or both. Thinking of yourself as a product, this is the time where you answer the interviewer with your *benefits* as opposed to your *features*.

"I believe that, considering my experience and skills in my previous job as a _____, I can aid you in saving time by ensuring that the workplace functions smoothly and productively. Coupled with my diligence and skills in negotiation, I also believe that I can lower *our* department's costs while increasing the revenues. By implementing _____, I was able to increase the revenue of (name of previous company you've worked for) by up to 25% in just 4 months' time. I see no reason why I shouldn't be able to do a similar thing for this company, *should I be provided with the opportunity* to work here."

4) Why did you leave your last job?

This can be translated to: If you were doing so well there, why did your employers allow you to leave? Is there anything about you that we should be wary of?

When answering questions similar to this, make it a point to present the facts as briefly as possible and to concentrate on the future. Don't dwell too long on the subject as this may cause your interviewer to grow suspicious. Emphasize that your departure from your previous company/employer was on good terms.

If the hiring manager was impressed with your CV and you were able to leave a great first impression, he'll be secretly hoping that you were not the problem. However, he'll want to have an idea as to how you conducted yourself during the departure. This means you'll have to provide some indication that you handled your departure professionally. How do you do this? By offering references.

Never say anything negative about your former company/employer/colleagues. Don't mention the involvement of other people in your departure. Moreover, refrain from giving more than one reason for leaving your previous job.

Take a look at this example:

"Actually, I've been seeking an opportunity to demonstrate and develop my skills. I'm not certain I would've been able to do this at my previous position. I left on good terms but right now, I'm here because I am certain that I possess the necessary skills to further my career at your institution."

This is a great answer and no one would even suspect that the speaker left a previous employer on bad terms. It's not as though he/she has told a blatant lie. The speaker merely chose to provide an ambiguous, yet smart, response which focuses on the future.

5) What was the most difficult situation that you've encountered and how did you handle it?

Read between the lines. What the interviewer actually wants to know is this: "If you were already working for me, will you crack under pressure and take the whole team down with you?"

Understand that your interviewer is trying to determine your critical thinking and problem-solving skills.

This is the kind of question which calls for one of your on-the-job "war stories." Although you may have encountered and sailed through a bunch of challenging situations, pick the one that is most closely related to the job position that you're applying for. Ask yourself: *What are the problems that I am most likely to encounter in this line of work?* Then determine how you can tie that up with your past experience.

In answering this type of question, concentrate on highlighting your transferrable skills rather than your technical skills. The best skills you can emphasize are your creativity, resourcefulness, and perseverance.

6)   What are your greatest strengths?/What are your greatest weaknesses?

When answering questions about your strengths, the trick is to fit them with the requirements of the position and the unspoken needs of your employer. Ask yourself: *Which of my traits will make my potential employer look good? Which of my skills will make his job easier for him?*

As for weaknesses, don't go so far as denying that you have any. Instead, mention your strengths first and mention lots of them. After that, state only one weakness. Choose the weakness which has the *least* to do with your target job position. For instance, you can admit that you're not very good with numbers if the job you're applying for doesn't really require you to deal with numbers on a regular basis. Don't elaborate on your weakness. Keep it brief and straight to the point. Never mention how this will potentially affect your work performance.

Another trick is to mention a weakness that is actually a "strength in disguise".

Example:

"Perhaps my greatest weakness is that I would sometimes grow impatient with coworkers concerning delays in their part of the task. It's just that missing deadlines bother me a lot."

After this, say no more as though indicating that you're prepared to move on to the next question.

7)   What is your most notable accomplishment?

Whatever accomplishment that you choose to mention should be in line with the target position that you're applying for. You may have a long list of accomplishment and some of them may seem smaller than others. That said, don't measure your accomplishments according to *your* standards. Instead, measure them according to the company's needs.

Even so, if the greatest concern of the company you're applying for is how to gain public exposure, then mentioning the first accomplishment would benefit you more than mentioning the second one.

While talking about your accomplishment, convey genuine passion and pride through your voice and body language.

8)   What are your future goals?

The reason why interviewers ask this question is because they want to know if you intend to stick around or if you're just trying the position on for size until something better comes along. A high employee turnover rate is costly for a company. This increases expenses associated with hiring and training. Regardless of the truth, your answer should focus on the target job position and the company's wellbeing.

Example:

"I intend to grow with a well-established company. I believe that a company like this will provide me with an opportunity for continuous career growth and will enable me to assume more responsibilities in the future as I continue to contribute to the organization's success."

9)   How do you handle competition?

What your interviewer actually wants to know is that you have a positive attitude when it comes to competition. Employers are looking for employees who are up to besting the business competition. Thus, your answer should reveal that you embrace competition not only because you like winning but also because you recognize its positive effects on the business/organization.

Example:

"I would describe myself as a competitive worker. I believe that some competition can be healthy in the workplace as it brings out the best in everyone. Ultimately, competition can benefit the organization as a whole."

10)   How much should we pay you?

This question is like the blade of a guillotine hanging over your head all throughout the interview. It's a question you're afraid to ask but would really, really want to know the answer to. It's a question that your interviewer will inevitably bring up although deep down, you wish he wouldn't. That's because both the interviewer and the applicant are aware that whoever brings up the figure first places himself at a vulnerable position for negotiating. Nevertheless, your interviewer might try to sneak the question in through an inquiry similar to this: *"How much are you making in your current job?"*

What do you tell him then?

Ask yourself these two questions:

- How much are you worth?
- What is your practical range?

Prior to showing up at the interview, make it a point to research your *market value*. That is, the going rate for a professional with your experience and skills. You can search for the figures online or look it up in professional journals related to your field.

The *practical range* refers to the minimum amount that you need to support your lifestyle.

To arrive at a range that you won't be sorry for, bracket the income range so that it slightly goes above the upper range of your market value. It must also be higher than your practical range.

Example:

If, according to your research, your market value is $76,000 - $83,000, and based on your calculations, your practical range is about $77,000, then tell the interviewer that your salary range is: $79,000 – $86,000.

Important: In general, you must avoid the topic of salary until you have been completely informed about the scope of the job and until the interviewer has gained a complete understanding of your qualifications. Delay salary talk until you reach the final interview and until you're certain that you've convinced the employer that his company needs you.

The Post-Interview Phase
So the interview is over. What should I do next?
Don't spend the post-interview phase waiting for the phone to ring. Instead, use it for drafting a professional thank you letter to your would-be employer. Apart from being a traditional act of courtesy, a thank you letter will ensure that your application becomes more prominent in

your employer's mind. If you were unable to close the sale with your closing statement during the interview, this is the opportunity to do it.

A thank you letter is a business letter and not a note or a postcard. It should be printed or emailed. It should contain about four paragraphs.

Start off by thanking the interviewer and stating how pleased you were to meet him. Next, express your excitement over the possibility of working in his company. Include a summary of the highlights of the interview. Remind the interviewer of your selling points. Finally, in the closing statement, restate your understanding of when you expect to obtain a response from the employer.

If you were interviewed by more than one interviewer, make sure that each of them receives a different version of the letter.

View a sample of an effective thank you letter on the next page.

Laura Green

12345 Lakewood Ave.

Chicago, Illinois 60640

Telephone: 000-000-0000

Fax: 000-000-0000

Email: lauragreen@gmail.com

Mr. Paul Smith

Chief Nurse

Mercy Hospital and Medical Center

2525 S Michigan Avenue

Chicago, Illinois, 60616

Dear Mr. Smith,

Thank you for the opportunity to interview for the position of staff nurse. The vitality and intelligence of everyone I spoke with at your offices left a strong impression on me. I am extremely grateful for the warmth and sincerity by which my application was received. I am also thankful for the interest shown in me.

I am thrilled at the prospect of working at Mercy Hospital and Medical Center. You have established a solid team, which I would like so much to be a part of.

I was very pleased with our conversation and especially excited about the idea of the _____ project, which I believe will positively transform patient care. I learned a great deal from that experience and I wish to apply all that I've learned at Mercy Hospital and Medical Center.

Thank you very much again for the stimulating and productive interview. I look forward to hearing from you, as agreed upon, within the next two months.

Sincerely,

Laura green

Chapter 9: Predicting the Questions

The worst part of any job search is the unknown involved with the process overall from top to bottom. Not knowing if you will be called at all, not knowing if you will get a job interview after the call, not knowing how the interview went or if you will get an offer after the job interview. Part of the unknown of the interview itself is what you will be asked and this unknown can be quite scary. However, much of this can be predicted with some digging on your own.

The digging that you must do is to get to know the job itself and get to know what would be the potential questions you might be asked. It would stand to reason that a janitorial job interview may have different questions than that of a cashier, right? Different strengths are necessary and different job pitfalls should be made clear, meaning different questions would be asked.

In order for you to know what might be asked you could start by asking yourself what may be necessary for someone to be able to complete this job successfully? To answer these question let's pretend you are applying for the role of a customer service agent at a large cable company. You could immediately say that the first necessary skill would be the ability to provide quality service, preferably over the phone.

This would be where you start to connect the past experiences and situations you have been in with the potential questions that may be asked. In addition to providing service over the phone another potential question could be about your experience in working in a production environment. This is to say an environment that moves at a quick pace and one that insists on you working fast with a purpose.

More questions could potentially be asked along these lines but this gives you a good start on seeing where these questions could go. Once you have decided on a few different avenues those questions could take you can move on to the next potential question. This set of questions has to do with your perception of what a successful candidate for the position would look like?

In this scenario you should try to picture what a good candidate would look like by picturing what a successful employee would look like. Do you think it would take patience to be able to deal with all of the customer demands levied on the customer service department at a cable company? Wouldn't a successful candidate need to be able to communicate clearly on a personal and professional level with customers?

If these are the qualities that would stand out for a successful candidate then you need to find examples from your past that show your ability to do these things. While you are on this step it is also a good idea to consider what the unsuccessful habits or qualities of a candidate would be. What would be something that would doom someone to fail at this job?

Take a personal story on this from my past as a corporate trainer at a major corporation starting the first day of a new class of new employees. We were going around the room introducing ourselves and telling the group what our ideal job would be. This one particular new employee stated his name and then said that his degree was in a laboratory science and that his dream job was to work in a lab all by himself.

There was no problem in particular with this dream as it was a good explanation from someone who had a dream to pursue. The issue was that the job was one where the individual would be working all day on the phone taking calls from angry customers in relation to insurance claims. Immediately I knew that this fit was not going to work and the individual quit within weeks of working claims. He was a very bright and engaging young man, but the job was a terrible fit for what he wanted to do.

This bleeds over into the next potential question you should ask yourself, why would people leave this position? In the instance my previous job mentioned above it would be a variation of what happened with that individual. People came to our company who had degrees but did not have any profession in mind, many weren't happy on the phones all day and they left.

What will happen during the hiring and training process is that you will be repeatedly sold on the amazing nature of the company and how it can help you. People will tell you how incredible the company treats people and much of it may be true, but the fact of the matter is really quite simple. Aside from a company that is growing too fast, you are being hired because someone else didn't work out or didn't want the job anymore.

In the case of the customer service department at the cable company you may be facing many of the same pitfalls as the company I previously worked for. Lack of patience, lack of communication skills and an environment that was too fast paced were all complaints that were regularly fielded. Consider these and be sure to emphasize how you would or could overcome these potential problems.

This then transitions nicely into the final question you should ask yourself about the job, which is what is the most difficult part of the job? Would it be answering the phones all day or dealing with angry customers one after the other? There could be any number of potential trouble spots and you need to try to dig in on what the hardest could be.

The beauty of this for today's day in age is that you have access to the internet and can do a simple search for the company and people who have left. The complaints aren't always 100% accurate, but if you keep seeing the same complaints over and over it is probably a difficulty that should be considered. Being prepared to explain how you could overcome this could put you over the top of all of the applicants.

Remember that you have the control over your answers and can phrase them in such a way to show your ability to do the job. Predicting the questions can give you a jumping off point to consider what might be asked so that you can consider what situations you should be prepared to explain from your past. With interviews preparation can put you over the top when you do it smartly and correctly.

12 Most Common Job Interview Questions and How Best to Answer Them

No two job interviews are the same. But job interviews generally follow a similar pattern with similar questions. So, you need to arm yourself with the kind of questions you should expect and the best response for each question. Recruiters are also aware of the fact that there are many blogs out there with the title 'How to Answer

Job Interview Questions' and they can tell when you are merely reciting what you have memorized from another source. In other words, this is a guide on how to answer the questions and not exactly how you should answer the questions. I am giving you a pattern and some strategies; for you to tailor these down to fit your own personal experiences.

Here are some of the most common job interview questions and how to answer them:

Tell us about Yourself:

This is usually the first question and asked by practically all job interviewers. You should expect it and prepare for it beforehand. It is however, not an invitation for you to summarize your resume; they have seen your resume already and still want to know more about you. You should talk about your background; and by background, I do not mean your family background and personal life history. Don't mention your marital status or any other personal matters, including religious and political views. No matter how beautiful your family story may be, do not share it because that is not what they are wanting to hear. Summarize your educational history in not more than three sentences, talk about your professional experience if you have any. This is the time to clarify the gaps on your resume if you have any. Talk about your skills as they relate to the position and say a thing or two about your personality. All these should be in line with the role you are being interviewed for. And you should stop talking if you are cut short while you are still answering it.

What Do You Consider to Be Your Biggest Professional Achievement?

This question can be a tough one especially if you just graduated from college and haven't had any professional experience. Preparing for this question will go a long way to affect how you will respond to it. This is an opportunity for you to talk about your internship experience if you have any and what you consider to be your biggest achievement in the process. Do not just give a vague mention of the achievement, give a vivid description of what you actually did and how it helped the company or team you worked with. Talk about results; that's what the recruiter wants to hear.

What are your Biggest Weaknesses?

For every question you will answer, remember that you should provide answers in line with what you are interviewing for. If you are asked what your biggest weaknesses are, make sure that whatever you state your professional weaknesses, not your general weaknesses as a person. Another thing to note is that at each stage of the interview, you are marketing yourself and you shouldn't say anything that will vilify you. You should not tell lies. However, if your biggest professional weaknesses are not something you wish to disclose, you should consider saying something else whether it is the biggest of your weaknesses or not. Pick a weakness of yours and embellish it in such a way that it will eventually turn out interesting. Consider this example from www.inc.com :

Interviewer: What are your biggest weaknesses? Interviewee: My biggest weakness is getting so absorbed in my work that I lose track of time. Every day I look up and realize everyone has gone home! I know I should be more aware of the clock, but when I love what I am doing, I just can't think of anything else.

In other words, your biggest weakness is that you will put in more hours at work and that will be considered as strength for the company.

You can also talk about a weakness you are currently working on and give brief details about the steps you have taken to improve in that area. That way, the interviewer will consider you as someone who goes out of their way to look for solutions to problems.

What are your Biggest Strengths?

This is practically the opposite of 'What are your biggest weaknesses' and you have to be careful with answers as well. You should state what your biggest strengths are but do it in such a way that you will not present yourself as a superhuman. Simply say what your actual professional strengths are and demonstrate with a short description how that strength has helped solve a work-related problem in the past. For instance, if your biggest strength is effective communication, give an instance of when you used that skill to get something done or get other people to do things. And remember to give a sincere answer.

What Motivates you?

There is no right or wrong answer to this question. But then this is a job interview and you need to impress your interviewer. So, like every other question you will answer on this interview, tailor your answer to the role you are interviewing for. You should mention positive things like having to meet deadlines, being a part of a team, being a leader, discovering and learning new things etc.

Where Do You See Yourself in the Next Five Years?

This question can be somehow challenging, especially if you do not have long term career plans. But always remember that you are answering in relation to the position you are interviewing for and avoid mentioning anything outside this. This is not the time to talk about the vacation you have been imagining or how much money you expect to have in your bank account by that time. Talk about how you intend to grow from the experience you will receive from the role and some value you expect to be adding to the company. Give realistic goals and how the position will enhance your chances of reaching them.

What do you know About this Company?

This is a straight forward question, which means that it is expected that you must have done your homework about the company. Describe what you have found out about the company in relation to their competitors and the industry at large. But do not mention if their competitors are doing better than them. Highlight how the company is doing, especially in the area of the position you are interviewing for and how you think it is the best place for you to pursue a career.

How Did You Find Out About this Opening?

This kind of question is another opportunity for you to show that you are interested in the company and not just interested in getting a job. Your response should be specifically about how you found out about the opening. Even if you learned about it through a random job search, try to tell them what caught your attention about this particular opening and how excited you were when received got an invitation for the interview.

What Type of Work Environment do you Prefer?

This shouldn't be a difficult one if you have done your homework about the company. Simply bring in the work culture of the company and how it connects to the position you are interviewing for. It shouldn't be about you alone but about how the kind of work environment you prefer will help you be more successful in your role and add value to the company.

Why do you Want this Job?

Well, why do you want the job? A very simple question, but the way you respond will go a long way to determine the outcome of your interview. Just like every other question you will answer, this should be about the role as well and your overall career growth and development. You should never say that you want the job because you are broke and need the salary. Whether this is the true situation or not, please never say it. Explain how the role and how it is represented in the company fits into your personal career plans. Explain how you think that the company has the kind of environment that will enhance growth and push you forward in your career.

What is your Salary Expectation?

This question can make you very uncomfortable and you may find yourself in between trying not to oversell yourself and also trying not to undersell yourself. If you mention a large salary, you could come across to the interviewer as arrogant. If you ask for a small salary instead, you could come across as undervalued and the quality of what you have to offer will be in doubt.

The best way to go about this is to know beforehand the average salary requirement of the position you are interviewing for. Do your research and find out what the position is worth. Then go ahead and give a salary range. Do not mention a specific amount; that would be too direct. Also let your interviewer know that you are flexible on the salary expectation and it is left for you to accept or reject what they will offer you. Another way to answer the salary expectation question is to tell the interviewer that you will be okay with the company's budget for the position. But if you say this, also make sure that you are willing to accept what they have to offer.

Why Should We Hire you?

This question sums up everything about the interview. "Now that you have told us all these, what other reason do you think that, out of all the candidates being interviewed for this position, we should hire you?" This is an opportunity for you to sell yourself. Emphasize not only how you can do the job, but how you can do it better than any other candidate. Talk about your most important skills and how you can produce results within the company culture.

Chapter 10: Make Your Stories Come to Life

I love doing improv with job seekers. It is so much fun, and although we aren't intending to be funny, we always end up laughing–at ourselves, at what was just said, at the situation. It is certainly a stretching experience to do improv. In the context of a coaching session, it feels very safe. It is just the two of us. If, at the end of this book, you want to venture out a little more, I recommend that you join an improv class to experience it in a group setting. Not all improv makes sense for the job search process. I've culled the list of games to ones that are very relevant to our world–increasing charisma by playing big, being intentional with your eye contact, and staying connected through mime. Jump on a video call with your coach. Or ask a friend to play some of these improv games with you. Through this process we learn a little more about ourselves as it forces to be right here, right now, present. Let's play!

Improve Games That Help with Body Control
Game: Play Big and Play Small
Imagine there are two chairs up on stage. You are sitting in one of the chairs and an improv partner is sitting next

to you. The two of you are facing an audience. The lights are glaring in your eyes and you can see shadows of people sitting in the audience watching the two of you. Your job is to play big without saying a word or making a sound. Sitting on the chair with the use of communicating big with your body, you are to claim that space. Your improv partner next to you is playing small. Using his body, without saying a word, he is playing small. The goal is for you to play big and slowly transform to small over a period of 30 seconds. The teacher in the audience will tell you when it is 15 seconds and when it is time at 30 seconds. Your improv partner's goal is to do exactly the opposite. He is to play small and transform to big over 30 seconds.

Terri and I use video meetings for this game. She starts with being big and I start with being small. In 30 seconds, we switch back and forth from being big to being small.

You can do this at home. Place a chair in front of a mirror and play big. Put on a timer that signals at 30 seconds. And over that period, without saying a word, transform to play small. Pay attention to how you feel when you are playing big and when you are playing small. Try it!

When I asked Terri to explain what she did when she played big, this is what she said:

- I am sitting up

- My shoulders are back

- My legs are spread and out in front of me

- My arms are draped over the arms of my improv partner's chair

- I am looking directly ahead

  - I am looking around directly into my partner's eyes

When I asked Terri to explain how she felt when she was playing big, this is what she said:

- Confident

- Big

- Aggressive

- In control

- In charge

- The boss

I asked Terri, what did you feel when you were playing small?

- Timid

- Scared

- Submissive

- Anxious
- Cautious

Give it a try. For an entire week, play big. And take note at how you feel.

Game: Control Your Eye Contact

Because we do not go through life looking in a mirror, we often aren't aware of how we communicate with our eyes. We may not know that our eyes might be moving constantly or that we might come across as staring. This improv game is one that helps us become aware of our eyes and gain control over what we want to communicate with them.

Imagine you are in a room with your hypothetical improv team. Half of the team, Team A, has a goal to give what they would consider to be intense or too-long eye contact. The other half, Team B, has a goal to avoid eye contact or give too-short eye contact. When the game starts, everyone is to walk around the room acting out their goal. You'll hear nervous laughter and all-out bursts of laughter as two Team A members have a staring contest. Then about 2 minutes into the game, the instructor tells everyone to switch. Team A's job is to avoid all eye contact and Team B's goal is to give intense eye contact. At around two minutes more, the teacher calls time.

In a coaching session, the coach's goal is to give intense eye contact and the client's goal is to give not enough, or fleeting eye contact. Then we switch after 30 seconds.

At home, you could ask a friend to play the role of the coach. Sitting across a table, designate someone to give intense and the other fleeting eye contact. Use a timer and switch after 30 seconds.

Then we debrief and ask to share what happened and what made them laugh, how they felt, which was the most comfortable for them. Typically, the answers are something like the below:

- If I am avoiding eye contact, it is uncomfortable when someone gives me intense eye contact. It feels like an invasion of my space. It feels too intense.

- But when I am the one giving intense eye contact, it is frustrating when someone is avoiding my eye contact.

- It is a bit more comfortable if I meet with someone who is also giving intense eye contact, but if it goes too long, it feels uncomfortable.

- When I am avoiding eye contact and come across someone who is also avoiding, it feels good not to be stared at; however, I do not even see who that person was.

In a coaching session, I will share if I feel that the individual gives a comfortable amount of eye contact. It is a challenge over video conference, and the fact that we aren't looking in a camera at eye level and instead at the person on the screen. However, it is excellent practice since many job interviews are conducted over video conference.

This game helps people understand how it feels when appropriate intensity of eye contact is given. It gives people the opportunity to play around with too much and too little to have greater control over when it is just enough.

Game: Staying Connected Through Mime

A mime is an actor who is generally in black and white clothing, with white clown paint on their face. They act out different things without using their voice. Imagine you are standing in a large circle with other people and you are all mimes. One person starts by holding an imaginary object and doing something obvious with the object. It could be bouncing a basketball or kicking a soccer ball. He then passes or hands the object to his neighbor who then continues doing what his neighbor did with the object. Then he changes it up. Perhaps the basketball shrinks and become a tennis ball. That person then passes or hands the object to the next person. And it goes down the line.

As you can image, sometimes you have no idea what your partner just did. The actions aren't always obvious and you need to make sense of the action. And you'll also realize that it is fruitless to think of something to do ahead of time because you won't know what the object is until it is handed to you.

This game forces us to use our bodies in intentional ways to describe the object and do something with it. It also helps you learn how to not anticipate what you will do with the object because you have no idea in what form the object will come to you. Learning not to anticipate and just be in the moment is one of the most useful things improv can help with in the job search process. It drives out the habit of spinning in your own head. You must just be in the moment.

In a coaching session, I start with an object, do something obvious, and then hand it to the job seeker. She takes it, continues with what I was doing and then does something different and hands it back to me.

At home, you can ask a friend to do the same where you start with an object, do something obvious, and then hand it to your friend. She takes it, continues with what you were doing and then does something different and hands it back to you.

Here are a few ideas of things that you could do with your improv group, whether in a large group or in a pair:

- Eat a lollipop
- Eat a popsicle
- Eat an ice cream cone
- Throw a volleyball
- Throw a baseball
- Use a home phone
- Use a mobile phone

Improv Games That Help with Voice Control

Now that you have learned improv games that help you have greater awareness and control of your body, let's focus on your voice. When you combine body and voice control, you are on your way to making a very powerful in-person impression. Voice control is critical to get invited to a face-to-face interview. Many companies will first want to speak with you over the telephone before they make the investment in coordinating an in-person interview. And I've found that many job seekers aren't sure how they come across over the telephone. They think they are showing up in one way, but my impression of them is slightly, or sometimes very, different.

Many of my clients are across the nation so it is impractical to meet them in person. The first time I see them is always a wonderful surprise, as I'm seeing someone that I've grown to love over a period. It is always a wonderful surprise to finally see someone's animated face and not just an image, like a photo from their LinkedIn profile. And I am always surprised that the person is nothing like I had expected. Which goes to show that when we only speak with a recruiter, they also form an impression of what you look like that is often very different from what you actually look like. The idea is to control that impression as much as you can. Below are a few improv games you can play to gain greater voice control.

Because improv feeds off at least one other person, most improv games are best done within a pair or a group. Improv is an interactive sport. Here are a few improv games that you can play solo if you have a device that can record what you are saying (e.g., smartphone).

Game: Talking Fast and Slow

In high school, I was running for a state position for a national business organization. While I was practicing my speech, my dad kept saying, "Slow down!" It was a struggle to really slow it down. I thought it was so people could follow along with what I was saying; however, what I discovered is that we make assumptions about someone's competence by the speed of their speech. Research says that people who speak slowly appear to be more competent and intelligent.

Use your mobile device or another recording device for this game. Grab some nearby text and record yourself reading it. At first, read it fast, much faster than your normal speech rate, and record yourself. Then read the same page again at a rate slower than your normal speech rate. Play back both recordings and see the difference in how you come across speaking quickly and slowly.

In improv, comedians use voice control to support a certain character they are playing. They will speed up when it serves them. In the same way, you want to be mindful of the rate of your speech so that you support how you wish to come across. For the most part, you will be speaking slowly and clearly to support the fact that you are competent and in control.

Related to speed is the power of the pause. Pauses can be used wisely to make a point. Consider this sentence and placement of the pause: "That project was the turning point for our division. [pause] We saw revenues climb at a steady pace from that point. And I cannot emphasize how vital our cohesion was to our success. Without it [pause] we would have failed."

Try it on for size. For an entire day, be very deliberate in speaking slower than your normal rate and see how it feels. And throw in a few pauses [pause] to make a point.

Game: High and Low

Besides the speed of your speaking, the pitch is also important. Individuals who have a high vocal pitch are seen in a different way than individuals with a lower pitch. People who speak at a higher pitch come across as less confident. Conversely, people with a lower pitch come across as more confident, dominant.

Let's play another improv game with your recording device. Read another page from a book in a pitch that is slightly higher than your normal pitch and record yourself. Do the same and read with a slightly lower pitch than normal. Listen to both recordings and take note of how you come across.

Give it a go. Spend an entire day speaking in a lower pitch than your normal. How did that feel?

Another thing to think about is if you end your sentences on an up note–when your voice goes higher as if you are asking a question. I find that often people aren't aware when they tend to end their sentences on an up note. As with the speed and the pitch, the tendency may leave an impression that you don't want. Research shows that individuals who end their sentences on an up note come across as less confident and more subservient, always seeking approval. Of course, this is not necessarily the case if this is your tendency. Many of my clients who have this tendency are strong, assertive, and confident. They just aren't aware how they come across.

Controlling your voice in and of itself is helpful in the job search process as many of the screening interviews are done over the telephone–no visual used. Combined with body control, you now offer a very powerful package. Let us now mix it in with the stories that were created in the previously and put it all together.

Integrate Body and Voice Control with Your Character: You

During Steve Martin's Masterclass, he encourages comedians to leverage what makes us unique, saying, "There is room for you." In his world, to use our uniqueness contributes to being hilarious. And that holds true for our work as well. To use our uniqueness to be amazing.

Sitting in a room with Jenny, an impressive Communications Specialist, I was heartbroken, as it was obvious to her (and everyone else) that the Vice-President was about to push her out. To me, she was amazing. And it was clear that this organization was not a great fit for her–her unique and creative, out-of-the-box ideas landed too often on glazed faces. Jenny soon left the company and took a job in a firm with the perfect culture for her. She is now the Director of Communications for a global financial services firm reporting to the CEO and creating the most innovative stuff in the field of corporate communications.

There is room for you. Let us mix in You by using improv. First by putting on the skin of someone who is completely out of character for you.

Game: Get Into Character

Let's have some fun and pull these things together with a few improv games. Let us try on a few skins of other people that may be very different from us. Take one of the characters below and imagine yourself putting on their skin. Say the below paragraph in that character using body and voice control to become the character. Try not to break and burst out in laughter. Stay in character. Practice what we've learned in body and voice control to become the person.

Say this paragraph in character. Watch YouTube clips of others in this persona to practice a few times and try it.

It is a beautiful day. The sun is shining and the birds are singing. I'm excited to be alive!

● 16-year-old Valley Girl from California–It's like so beautiful. Like totally kicking. Like the sun is amaaaazing. I'm so, like, you know, OMG, alive.

● Gun slinging, swaggering cowboy in the wild, wild west– (burst through the saloon doors, take a swig from your cigarette and flick it to the floor) Well, if it ain't a pretty day. Sun was shining in my eyes as I shot a bird singing. A good day to be alive.

● A cranky, crusty, pessimistic old man–Pffft. Don't give me all this crap about it being a beautiful day. Stupid sun shining in my eyes. Damned birds singing. Shut up. Not a good day to be alive.

● A 30-foot giant–Fi fi fo fum. It's a beauuutiful day for some delicious bird. Cook it in the sun. Feed my big hungry belly to say alive.

● Martin Luther King, Jr.–I have a dream. One day, one beautiful day. The sun will shine and the birds will sing. We. Will. All. Be. Alive.

● A pirate–Avast you scurvy scum. Shiver me timbers, the sun's out. It's a blimey sunny day. Me burd danced the hampen jig. Son of a biscuit eater.

What Is Your Character? Create an Archetype

Now that we are donning the skins of other characters, let us talk about our own archetype for the interview: You. What is the skin that we will put on as we enter the interview space? The skin of You?

A few years back, I attended a coach training class. On the second day we did a remarkable thing. Carey Baker, instructor extraordinaire, pulled me on stage and asked everyone to throw out a few words or phrases of things people wanted to see more of from me. What was remarkable was that up until this point, we haven't spent a tremendous amount of time together. How could they possibly know me that well? Yet my fellow classmates were throwing out words and phrases at such a fast speed that someone had to write them down for me. This is the list:

- Adventure
- Break the rules
- Be brave
- Step out
- Say F*** YOU

Then Carey asked the group to think of a personality or an archetype that they would like to see me put on. Many archetypes were thrown out, but the one that really stuck

413

with them (I had no say in the selection, by the way) was Motorcycle Mama.

Yes! That is perfect! Motorcycle Mama. We want more of Motorcycle Mama from you, Cara. Kick some ass. Jump on your hog and screech out of here, leaving a trail of dust in our faces.

I've since renamed this archetype to be Badass Motorcycle Mama, and over the years have put on this skin when I've needed to be big and a bit of a badass. And over time, this persona has become more a part of me. So, what is your archetype?

Here are a few archetypes of some of my clients.

- Oprah Winfrey
- Adonis the god of war
- Purring sexy black panther
- Pele, the fire goddess of the Hawaiian Islands
- James Bond
- Dr. Love

If you need help finding your archetype, send me a note, and let's get on the phone. I love helping people find their archetype, and you'll be amazed at how you can do this after a very short conversation.

It's Show Time – Let's Put It All Together

Put on your skin of You, your archetype. Answer the question, "Tell me about yourself." Use your body control and your voice control. Get into the character, stand in front of a mirror, and now rehearse. How is it different in character? Bigger? Bolder? Many job seekers say that they are much more aware of how they come across. And even more important, they can control how they come across. Their stories are more vivid with pauses for effect. Using silence. To make a point.

Ask your coach or a friend to conduct a mock interview. Record the session. Go back and view it. Refine your pitch, your skit, your stories. Ensure that you are coming across as you intend. Powerfully you. You have the tools to show up in a very powerful way. A way that is authentic and true to you. Showing them that you are secure in who you are, what you stand for, and what you can accomplish for them. And with a new awareness of You, your archetype, the skin of which you don as you prepare for and enter conversations with a recruiter. What we've talked about up until this point is how you show up. But as we know, it takes two to tango. There is someone else in the conversation: the recruiter, or the hiring manager, or other members of the team that you will interact with along the way.

Chapter 11: Common Pitfalls

Failure stories. The interviewer will almost certainly ask you to describe a time when you failed in your career or life. Many people make the mistake of trying to spin the example as something that turned out very positive in the end. This is likely because it can hurt to talk about our failures and we want to make a good impression. However, interviewers actually *want* to hear your failure stories. They are expecting something substantial and impactful that. It should be something that was etched in your memory and *hurt.*

For example, when asked about your failure story, a poor story would be "the time you didn't efficiently use the marketing budget and wasted money." This would **not** be a good example because the marketing budget is already set. This failure did not cause much damage.

A better story would be the time you hired someone and realized they were a terrible fit for your culture, and subsequently fired them after five months. In the process, you wasted thousands of dollars, sucked time from managers, and hurt company morale. That is a painful and tangible example. You can, of course, still talk about what you learned from the experience, interviewers want to see that you learned through the failure.

A good, juicy failure story needs to have a real negative impact on others. If you did something wrong in your previous position but faced no consequences, then it is probably not sufficient. When you lose a client and your team suffers — that is bad. When you fail to meet a deadline and a project is canceled, that reflects poorly on you *and* the company.

In the end, this ties back to the leadership principle of taking *ownership.* Make sure to prepare two examples of failures and do not be afraid to speak transparently about your mistakes.

Dive Deep. The reason interviewers dig so deep into the details of your past is to make sure that you actually did what you said you did. The logic is that the best way to discover your true role and responsibility in a job is to grill you on the details. If you said that you were a "sales leader," they want to know the story of how you closed the biggest sales deal. Was your boss in the meeting with you? Did someone else do the contract negotiation? Or were you involved in every step of the negotiation on your own? The depth and scope of your responsibility will come to light through this storytelling.

People who prepare the least for interviews tend to break down when "dive deep" is tested. They get flustered because they are asked to justify their thinking and decision-making process. Frequently, interviewers will ask you, "Why did you decide to take that action? How did you analyze your options? Why did you not push back to your supervisor to try a different option?" You need to be able to explain the logic behind all of your examples.

Diving deep can also be required in the form of *tangible outcomes.* When you describe the size of your marketing budget, they want a number. When you talk about the ROI they also want to know that number. You can talk about your great sales achievement and share a number, but how does that compare to others in the company? How does your sales number compare to the target this year and also last year? Providing context and specific details to describe the impact you made is key.

When you prepare 30 different examples from your previous work, it is unlikely that you are going to remember all of the details and reasons for your decision making. Thus the best way to prepare is to limit the number of examples you prepare to five or six key stories in your career. This way, you will be able to dive deep every time.

Not Answering a Question. One of the biggest mistakes I see people make is when they cop out of answering questions. When you say "I don't know" or "next question please," then you will likely be disqualified immediately. I realize this sounds unfair at first and you might be thinking, *"How am I expected to know all of the answers?"*

This does not mean you have to have a perfect answer to every question. That is an impossible expectation, and interviewers realize everyone might answer differently. Rather, they are more interested in your thinking *process.* They want to know how you break down a problem and how you go about solving it, even if the answer is incorrect. Furthermore, interviewers expects interviewees to think on their feet.

If you need time to think about an answer, then you can simply ask the interviewer to give you one minute to think about it. There is nothing wrong with some silence as you contemplate. Also, you can always request to come back to the question later. Write it down so you do not forget. Whatever you do, the point is to make sure that you always provide some sort of answer!

Long Winded Answers. You will always have more to say than you actually need to. Let that one sink in for a second.

It's important that your answers are never more than a couple of minutes long. If they are, you will be seen as verbose, and it will be marked heavily against you. The challenge is that the interviewer is not going to give you any indication if they want you to stop talking. They will patiently sit there and listen to you while you dig your own grave.

This may sound a little bit harsh, but it's one of the most common traps. People tend to get nervous and ramble, which happens to all of us. To stop yourself from doing this, always use the STAR approach. Second, use a mental timer to keep your answer short and concise. If the interviewer wants more details, they will ask for more. Rather than assume what the interviewer wants to hear, give the concise version of what you're trying to say, and let them probe deeper if they are interested.

Conclusion

Thanks for getting this book. It's my firm belief that it will provide you with all the answers to your questions. Starting a new job can be exciting and nerve wracking. Meeting new people, going to new places, and starting out with a blank slate, are all things which can make you feel insecure and uncertain. Remember that the choice to begin a new position is a choice which was made to help you take steps forward in your career. The fact that you have gained a new position over hundreds of other applicants is a testament not only to your interview skills but you as a person. You were the best fit for the position!

Take time out to enjoy the transition phase of starting a new job or career. Pat yourself on the back and be grateful at the opportunity before you. There are many people who wanted the job you have and were not offered a position. Now is the time to focus on showing your company they made the right choice in choosing you as their star candidate.

Do not be surprised if the position you take shifts and changes over time. It can very well be that as the company gets to know your skills better, they may shift your duties slightly to give you the best chance at success. Be sure to communicate openly with your supervisors, while you continue your work efforts, to be certain you are remaining on the same thought path for your career and involvement in the company.

If you find yourself becoming interested in other aspects of the company do not be afraid to vocalize this fact. The more in tune you are with your goals and desires, and the more you communicate with your superiors, the easier it will be to transition into other positions if the opportunity arises. There is nothing wrong with realizing you desire a completely different career path down the line than what you have accepted. It is best to try and remain in a position, unless given a promotion or are moved by the company itself, for at least three years.

The reason for this is because every company likes to see longevity and commitment to the positions you have already taken. People who move from one position to another quickly are also more likely to jump ship. You do not want your new employer to lose faith in your loyalty and excitement for the position you have taken.

Continue to practice your interview skills even if you are happy within your current position. Take time to practice with friends, even acting as the interviewer, and keep your resume up to date. When you have been in a position for a while it can become way to easy to become complacent and lose touch with what an interview is like. Should you desire to apply for a position higher up within the company you may attempt to rely solely on your work merits. Doing this may keep you from being the shining star you were when you gained the position which started you in the company to begin with. Even though you have started the position of your dreams it is always helpful to remain on your game.

Even if you are happy to remain in your position for the rest of your life be sure to take time for yourself and stay excited about your job and the company. Take your vacation time when you can and allow yourself rest and relaxation. Working too much is an easy trap to fall into as people with flourishing careers often feel they are unable to take time off as they are too pivotal to the company function.

If you are constantly working and never taking time for your private life you will easily burn out and begin to hate the job you originally loved. Keeping the passion alive may require effort but it will not require as much effort as trying to rekindle the relationship you once had should it start to fizzle. Set clear boundaries with your work place when you take your position so you are clear about the expectations of the hours you are required to work. If possible, take time to reaffirm these boundaries if they are being crossed over time because it will be a necessary practice to keep your heart in your work.

Remind yourself over time what aspects of your job you love. Keep positive affirmations at the ready to continue providing a positive attitude for yourself. There will be bad days at your job as every job has difficulties. No place of employment is perfect but you can be extremely happy if you have taken the time to apply for positions which truly fit who you are.

Your job does not define who you are but it is a big aspect of the building blocks that make you. Being in a position which you find fulfilling and rewarding will help you in your career path forward and keep you in a positive and happy mindset in the workplace. That positivity will then transfer over to your colleagues and will create an all-around better atmosphere.

Be grateful for the new opportunity and rejoice in the fact that you have taken another step closer to your achieved dreams and goals. Your hard work has finally paid off and will continue to do so as you keep bringing all of the wonderful talents you pose to the table. Congratulations on your new position and look forward to the future you will manifest for yourself.

Remember, you should play up your strengths so that you will be viewed in a favorable way. That will help you greatly in the application process and make you a candidate who stands out.

All the best!!

Job Interview Questions and Answers

Guide to a Winning Interview with Amazing Interview Answers. Everything You Should Know to Be More Confident and Get the Job You Want.

Jim Hunting

Introduction

Interview questions are designed to help the hiring manager understand you better as a person as well as whether you are qualified and can be successful in the role. Specifically, responses to questions are evaluated across many of the following categories (note that not all of these will apply to all roles):

- Do you have the education/training that is relevant to what this role requires? If not, can you demonstrate you can learn quickly and be effective? (What examples are provided to illustrate this?)

- Are you a team player, or more interested in personal credit and recognition? Will you work well with others? Do you help others even if "not part of your job description"?

- Are you mature? Do you get emotional or have unprofessional reactions to tough situations?

- Do you learn from past mistakes? I've never hired someone who couldn't provide a past mistake and what they learned from it.

- Will you fit in with the team? Will people respect you?

- Do you have critical thinking skills? Can you recognize what is important and not important in a given situation and not get bogged down in details?

- Do you communicate well both verbally and non-verbally? Are you concise, respectful, and able to provide the relevant information in any given situation?

- Can you manage conflict – whether with co-workers, managers, or subordinates?

- Do you put the interests of the company first?

- Are you a "go getter", or will you be a wallflower? I seldom am interested in hiring wallflowers.

Some other key items include never "bad mouthing" your previous boss, company, or co-workers. Always position conflict or reasons for leaving a company in a positive, educational light that made you a stronger person or reflected a change in career path.

One warning sign to watch out for: if a hiring manager asks you the same question, slightly rephrased, twice, then this is a sign you aren't providing the information needed from the question asked. Treat this as a WARNING. It means you need to stop and think a little more about the question and consider why the question is being asked relative to the categories outlined above, and then tailor your response to this.

To be honest, if I have to ask more than 3 or 4 questions over again because of poor responses, this is usually enough for me to terminate the interview, as my decision has already been made not to hire.

Conversely, if more than 2 or 3 responses are too lengthy, ramble and meander all over the place, I'm usually done with that candidate as well.

Remember – concise, relevant answers that don't have any personal, judgmental, or negative connotations in them.

Here are some great general questions to pick from to ask during the interview – *always* augment these with specific questions based on your research of the company and its products/services:

- What are the key challenges you see for this position?
- What are the priorities for the next 3 months for this role? What will success look like at that time?

- Is this a new role in the organization? If so, can you tell me more about the growth that resulted in the need for the role?

- What are the 3 top attributes or skills you think are needed to be successful in this role?

- What brought you to this company – e.g. what excites you about the company and the direction it is headed?

- How would you describe the culture of the company/group/etc.?

- What is your management style?

Chapter 1: Interview Selection Process

By the time you get to the interview, you are competing with people who are similarly qualified, perhaps in different ways. All the time I hear the complaint, "I can't believe they hired so and so when I'm so much more qualified!" Here's a reality check if you have ever felt that way. Technically speaking, you were *both* equally qualified to receive an interview. Your experience level may be different from his, even more than his, but his personality may make him the better match for the position.

When you're selected for an interview, you're in a group of several people a hiring manager decided could do the job. One person's experience or education level might be higher than another's. But after the paperwork was reviewed, the hiring manager determined you were all similarly qualified to be successful. Even if it looks as if someone received an interview because of his social networks, a hiring manager decided he could do the job.

There is a difference between meeting minimum qualifications and being similarly qualified. If you don't meet the minimum education or work qualifications listed on the job posting, your application generally won't even get a review. Similarly, qualified means that all applicants met the minimum qualifications. Thus, all are now eligible for further steps in the process. Now the selection process is about finding the one person who has the perfect mix of skills, personality and potential for success. You want to show the hiring manager that you are that one perfect match.

Beating the Competition

How does a hiring manager determine if someone has the perfect mix of skills to do a great job? Sometimes we get referrals. Sometimes we do a more thorough review of each resume or job application. Sometimes we conduct screening interviews with larger groups of applicants. But it all ends up at the same place: a final interview to see who gets the job. And at that point, how you present yourself is going to determine whether or not you get the job. Not your resume. Not your experience. Not your education. Not who referred you. At that point, it's all about the interview.

Once you're selected for that final interview, it becomes more about your interview performance than your minimum qualifications. You must prepare for that performance. It's partly about the chemistry between you and the interview team. It's also about how you represent the quality of your experience. At the interview, it's rarely about the actual years of experience.

You want *your* work history, whatever it is, to be judged the most applicable to the job. You want *your* answers to be the clearest. You want *your* personality to be likable without being obnoxious. Should you be yourself? Of course! Just be the most articulate, organized, and prepared version of yourself. That way, your experience, qualifications, and personality will shine through and wow the interview panel.

Chapter 2: What's the Best Way to Rehearse?

Most people will have access to, or can get access to, a video camera or a computer with built-in camera and microphone.

Rehearsing on your own is easily done, therefore, if you wish to do this before "showing off" with someone else.

If you decide to have some rehearsals on your own, be sure to act out as realistically as possible the interview situation.

Imagine that you are talking with an interviewer.

Most importantly, speak out - just thinking about it is better than doing no rehearsing, but speaking out your answers and questions is best.

Your mental rehearsals / visualization of your interview success is best done on your way into sleep when you are relaxed.

You should visualize your outstanding performance during the interview, if you wish, but, more importantly, visualize your celebrations after the interview process when you have received the job offer.

The purpose of rehearsal is to reduce your anxieties and fears and raise your performance standards.

Therefore, rehearse as many times as you feel you need and rehearse whatever you feel you need to (e.g. meeting the interviewer, interviews, leaving the interviewer).

Stay relaxed about your rehearsals though, don't get too intense about them.

In fact, have a bit of fun and laugh at your biggest mistakes.

In Summary:

* the best way to rehearse is to do a mock interview with a friend or 'mentor'

* mental rehearsal is also very helpful especially if you visualize success and celebration of it on your way into sleep when relaxed

* you can also rehearse on your own with a computer or video camera, but be sure to speak out.

Exercises to Do:

* test out the quality of your preparation by sharing it (or at least, the key points you have learned from it) with some trusted others, ask for some feedback, learn, do more preparation if necessary etc.

* in particular, prepare your lists of:

- questions you may be asked (arising from your C.V. / resume, and other questions, as illustrated above)

- difficult or awkward questions that you may encounter (from the examples above or from "gaps" in your C.V. / resume)

- questions you plan to ask if you get the opportunity

* practice your responses to the interview questions you have listed and record your efforts on your computer's audio / video system, or with a tape recorder / video camera etc.

* view the replays of your efforts (alone or with a 'mentor') and Analyze your performance both in terms of answers and in terms of your manner, presence, clarity, confidence and communications.

Capture in your learning log key opportunities to improve.

Repeat this exercise……..

* enlist the help of a trusted friend to act as your interviewer and carry out a mock interview using the lists of questions you have prepared. Video tape this.

Seek positive feedback from your 'mentor' / video replay about the strengths and weaknesses of your performance.

Capture in your learning log what you should start doing, stop doing and do differently to improve your performance to "world champion level".

Repeat this exercise........

* on your way into sleep, visualize yourself in the interview situation performing as a true champion.

In particular, visualize the outcome of your interviews when you receive the job offer.

Imagine your family and friends and colleagues congratulating you and everyone, especially you, smiling and laughing and celebrating your great success.

Make this as vivid and real as you can in your mind.

Imagine the colours and sounds. Feel the positive happy emotions that you would feel.

Chapter 3: Background and Personality Questions

What are some characteristics of a successful team?

Question Type:

Background and Personality

Question Analysis:

The interviewer will typically associate the team characteristics in in your response with your own personal working habits and gauge whether you are a good fit within their team. Your answer should focus on characteristics that align well with the company's values and are part of successful team dynamics. Some common characteristics of successful teams to consider are: effective communication, strong collaboration, diverse backgrounds and skillsets, goal driven, strong leadership, supportive, and ability to execute.

What to Avoid:

Even though it is common for teams to joke around and partake in social activities, your answer should avoid unprofessional characteristics such as "knows how to relax and have fun" or "likes to joke around."

Example Response:

Successful teams are made up of people who know how to work together to achieve a common goal. They are centered around strong leadership, effective communication and collaboration, and diverse backgrounds and skillsets. They are also goal driven and know how to complete a task.

Are you willing to work overtime or on weekends if necessary?

Question Type:

Background and Personality

Question Analysis:

Even if there will be very little need to work overtime or on weekends, the interviewer will often use this question to determine the candidate's willingness to be flexible to meet the company's needs. If the company only asks an employee to work odd hours once a year for a one-off project, they want to know that the employee prioritizes their job and has a "whatever it takes" attitude to get it done. Your answer should show your willingness to work when needed but also be honest if you have limitations on your flexibility.

What to Avoid:

You should avoid going into too many unnecessary details about your personal life or commitments. You should also not commit to something if it is not feasible. Be sure to show your willingness to go above and beyond when necessary but also be open about limitations.

Example Response:

I have two young children who are involved in sports and after school activities. For a couple of their teams, I help out as an assistant coach. With that said, I am willing and able to work outside of normal hours when needed. I can be most flexible when I am notified in advance so I am able to arrange my schedule.

Tell me about a time you went out of your way to strengthen a client, customer, or team member relationship.

Question Type:

Behavioral

Question Analysis:

Cultivating strong working relationships requires much more than a technical skillset. The interviewer will get a good sense of the candidate's interpersonal communication skills throughout the interview process, but they will use this question to find out if the candidate only focuses on their own work and objectives or if they are willing to take the time and energy to invest in internal and external working relationships. You should discuss an example that demonstrates strong soft skills and shows your willingness to go above and beyond for a co-worker or client.

What to Avoid:

You should avoid examples that would be expected under normal circumstances such as "When any of our clients send me an email, I always make sure to respond within 24 hours." You should also stay clear of examples that are not professional. "I take a new co-worker out for lunch at least once a month" is okay but it is best to avoid, "I take my team to the bar when we beat our sales numbers."

Example Response:

S: In my previous role as a digital advertising sales representative, I led a team working on a new client project to produce twenty-five digital ads for a social media campaign. We kept our client contact updated on our work at each project milestone. As we approached the wrap up stages of the project, she surprised all of us by changing her mind and asking us to adjust the background colors and design of each ad.

T: Our team was frustrated because we had received positive affirmation on the ads until the very end of the project. We estimated that the edits would take an additional ten hours of work and initially considered asking the client for further payment on top of the initial project fee.

A: Before expressing our frustration and asking for further payment, I set up a meeting with our contact to better understand the situation. Instead of leading the conversation with our frustration, I asked about the changes and found out that it was actually her boss who changed his mind about the ads. She apologized and sympathized with the difficult situation it put us in. I told her I understood that these things happen and agreed to make the edits at no additional charge. We put in the extra work to deliver the project on time and I brought in bagels and coffee for the client and her team at the closing meeting.

R: Our contact was very appreciative of our hard work and willingness to go above and beyond to meet their needs. They had excellent results from the advertisements and ended up hiring us for three additional projects over the next year.

Tell me about a time you did not meet a goal. What did you learn?

Question Type:

Behavioral

Question Analysis:

Like the "describe a failure" question #19, you should not feel uncomfortable discussing a time you did not achieve a goal. As long as you continue to set challenging goals, you will come up short from time to time and the interviewer knows this. The key is to be able to explain to the interviewer why you did not meet the goal and show them that you learned from it.

What to Avoid:

You should avoid placing blame on a co-worker or outside circumstances. The interviewer is looking for an example in which you take responsibility for coming up short. With that said, you should be careful not to provide an example where you failed as a result of negligence or a poor work ethic.

Example Response:

S/T: In my prior role as a business analyst, my manager asked me to create a step-by-step visual tutorial on how to run ten different financial reports in our ERP system. She mentioned that the tutorials were urgently needed for a department project and asked me to estimate how long it would take to have it completed.

A: After reviewing the first couple reports I mentioned to her that I could finish all of the tutorials within two days. Shortly after, I realized I had not reviewed my calendar before making the commitment and I had four important meetings over the next two days which could not be rescheduled. To make matters worse, it quickly became evident that my estimate of time needed to complete the project was too optimistic.

R: I worked thirteen-hour days to try to meet the goal, but it ended up taking me four days to complete the tutorials instead of two. I took full responsibility for the delay when explaining to my manager that I had failed to consider my other obligations and did a poor job of estimating the number of hours the project would require. When setting deadlines for my work, I have learned to take the time to create a comprehensive plan that incorporates all factors and obligations. I have also learned that it is great to set challenging goals, but they should always be realistic and attainable.

How long would you plan to stay with the company?

Question Type:

Ambition

Question Analysis:

Employees are not as loyal to their employers as in the past. Hiring can be a risky investment if a candidate is likely to bounce around to other companies whenever new opportunities arise. The interviewer is looking for the candidate to convince them that they are committed to the position. Your answer should focus on your enthusiasm for the opportunities within the company and position and your desire to remain with the company as long as you are continuing to grow and have a positive impact.

If you do have plans to leave town within a couple of years due to a certain circumstance (such as having a spouse in the military), be honest and upfront about it with the interviewer but if there are opportunities to work remotely, leave the door open to continue with the company.

What to Avoid:

Your answer should avoid contingencies based on promotions or pay increases such as "I'll continue to work here as long as I am paid fairly." You have not established credibility with the employer so an answer like this answer can be off-putting to the interviewer.

Example Response:

I am excited about this position but even more so about the career opportunities working for XYZ Company. The rotational program in the marketing department enables new employees to obtain experience working in many diverse roles over their first three years with the company. I think this program would enhance my skillset and position me for future leadership roles. As long as I continue to bring value and make positive contributions, I would plan on remaining with the company.

If an urgent work situation came up over the weekend, how would you react?

Question Type:

Background and Personality

Question Analysis:

This can be a tricky question for some candidates because they interpret it as the interviewer asking if they will always be "on call." However, this is usually not the objective of the question. Instead, the interviewer wants to know that if a rare and urgent situation arose outside of normal work hours, the candidate would be willing to do whatever they could to help remediate it. You should demonstrate your willingness to help out if an urgent situation came up outside of normal work hours.

What to Avoid:

There is nothing wrong with emphasizing your belief in a work-life balance, but you should never say anything to indicate that you completely ignore work outside of the office such as "I turn my work phone off when I leave the office" or "I ignore all work communication on the weekends." On the other end of the spectrum, your answer should also not be "I make myself available at all times." The interviewer knows this is not possible.

Example Response:

I strongly believe in the benefits of finding a good work-life balance. However, the timing of urgent issues can be unpredictable. If something came up outside of work hours that required immediate attention, I would do whatever I could to help fix the problem.

What are some ways you deal with an upset customer or client?

Question Type:

Background and Personality

Question Analysis:

Individual interactions with vendors, clients, and customers can be reflective of the whole company. The interviewer wants to know that the candidate will be a good representative of the company, especially under pressure and difficult situations. Your answer should show that you know how to remain calm, respectful, and avoid being combative when dealing with an upset customer.

What to Avoid:

You should avoid only discussing how you **talk** to upset customers. Usually, the most important thing to do in this situation is to show the customer you are willing to **listen** to their frustration and sympathize with them. You should also avoid generic canned responses such as "my philosophy is that the customer is always right."

Example Response:

Before I try to offer any type of response or resolution, I first like to show the customer that I am willing to listen to their issue. Typically, the most effective way to calm the situation is to simply take the time to hear the customer and show sympathy for their frustration. When speaking with the customer, I am always mindful of my tone and body language to ensure I do not come across as combative. I try to come to a fair resolution and help the customer in any way I can within the company's policies. If I am not able to come to a resolution or need to look further into the problem, I take down their contact information and follow back up with them as soon as possible.

How do you ensure quality in your work?

Question Type:

Background and Personality

Question Analysis:

The interviewer will use this question to determine how important quality is to the candidate. They are looking for the candidate to discuss procedures they implement to ensure that their work is rooted in quality. You should emphasize your desire for quality work and discuss a process you use to ensure mistakes are limited.

What to Avoid:

The interviewer knows everyone makes mistakes, so you should avoid answers such as "I make almost no mistakes in my work." You also want to stay away from placing the burden on others with a response such as "I usually ask someone else to review my work." The interviewer is looking for you to discuss your own process to mitigate mistakes before it gets reviewed or submitted.

Example Response:

I consider myself to be an efficient worker, but I also take the time to pay close attention to detail in my work. Before I start any task, I step back to ensure I understand the full scope of the work and consider all factors. If there are questions around the deliverables, I make sure to find the answer or reach out to someone who can clarify for me. I would rather get it right the first time than have to go back and redo work. After completing my work, I always go back through it and do a detailed self-review to ensure accuracy and quality. Although I still make the occasional mistake, my process has worked well in maintaining high quality and limiting mistakes before my work gets submitted to someone else.

Are you willing to travel for this job?

Question Type:

Background and Personality

Question Analysis:

The interviewer will typically ask this question only when the job does require some level of travel. They are looking to confirm that the candidate has read the job description (which should indicate the amount of travel) and is agreeable with the travel requirements. Your answer should affirm that you are comfortable with the travel requirements in the job description. If the job description did not mention travel, then you should be upfront and honest about your ability to travel. Be sure to state any travel limitations during the week (such as only able to travel Mon-Fri). If you would like to learn more specifics about the travel requirements, you can find out more with a follow up question at the end of your response.

What to Avoid:

You should never tell the interviewer you are not willing to travel any less than what is stated in the job description. For example, if the description says out-of-town travel is required up to 50% of the time, you should not have applied to the job if you are only willing to travel occasionally. If you are flexible and willing to travel whenever needed, you can let the interviewer know. You should avoid discussing ulterior motives for traveling such as "I never miss a chance to get out of town for a free hotel room and free food" or "I have over 100,000 Marriott points, I would love to get more."

Example Response:

I worked as an account executive in the past and was on the road about 40% of the time. The travel did not bother me at all. When I reviewed the description for this position, it had indicated that travel would be required up to 20% of the time. However, I am flexible to travel beyond that if needed. Would the travel be during certain times of the year or more sporadic?

Tell me about a time you dealt with conflicting priorities. How did you determine the top priority?

Question Type:

Behavioral

Question Analysis:

The interviewer will ask this question to assess the candidate's organizational and decision-making skills. Situations will often come up requiring you to organize your time to manage multiple tasks and effectively prioritize them. Your answer should demonstrate your ability to choose the top priority while not neglecting your responsibilities for the secondary priorities.

What to Avoid:

Prioritizing multiple tasks is much different than "multitasking" which infers that you work on multiple tasks at the same time. You should avoid stating that you like to multitask. Most studies show that multitasking hurts focus, sacrifices quality, and leads to less efficiency.

Example Response:

S: In my previous position selling CRM software, my manager had signed our team up for an out-of-town two-day training event. Three hours before my flight was to depart, the contact at my largest account in the area called me frantically explaining that their software had crashed.

T: My manager was already on a prior flight, so I was unable to get ahold of her at the time. After considering the circumstances, I decided that the best course of action was to drive directly to the client's office to help them resolve the urgent problem.

A: I spent the next four hours working with the client and our IT department until the issue was resolved. I then called my manager and explained why I missed my flight and let her know that the client was very appreciative that I had made myself available right away.

R: My manager told me I made the right decision and said it could have been disastrous if our client had to wait longer to get the assistance they needed. I booked a later flight that evening and made it to the training on time.

Chapter 4: Questions to Understand Your Personality

The employer knows who you are as a person, but they will want to really understand what it's like to spend time with you. How will you fit in with the rest of the team? What will it be like when you have to make a decision? Can you actually lead or are you just saying that?

These are more complex questions to dig deeper into your personality. Anyone can come up with the perfect response to the previous questions we discussed, but these are prompts that force you to be honest about who you are. There is no faking when it comes to crafting these responses!

"Tell me about a time you had to apologize to a friend or family member, and how you were able to rectify the situation."

This can be a pretty tricky one to answer, but there are times that it has been asked in an interview. The point is not to shame you or call you out. What they are looking for is your ability to take accountability. Can you admit when you are wrong? Can you acknowledge other people? Do you understand the various perspectives around a situation? Of course, don't share the most dramatic fight you've ever had, but don't be afraid to be honest! Let them really know what happened and show that you can take responsibility for things. Here's what you might say:

"There was one time when I was on a trip with my Mom and sister. My Mom believed that we should go south to get to a restaurant, and I thought we had to go north. She insisted she checked, but I believed that I was right based on what I remembered from before. Turns out, she was right. I apologized and learned that I should always double check before I assume that I'm certain. Not only did I make myself look silly, but I invalidated my mother's intelligence."

"What would your ultimate dream job be?"

Your dream job might be to lay on the beach and have people pay you to do nothing all day but eat delicious snacks. You can say this if you want, but they will really be wanting to know what type of personality you have. Be truthful and apply it to the job while also refrain from obviously schmoozing them. You might say something like this:

"My dream position would be one where I can have creative freedom while also having a team around me that can help support me with my accountability deadlines, or someone that offers creative perspectives when I'm stuck. I would want a changing environment where I could grow, but one that is also reliable that I know I will have around because job security is important to me."

"How do you motivate yourself when you feel like you don't want to do anything?"

Motivation is a key factor in many positions. The person conducting the interview will simply want to know how you are able to motivate yourself even when you feel like you want to do nothing at all. This is a potential answer that you could share if asked:

"Motivation is best when it comes from within myself. I'll usually try to reward myself. Maybe if I get a project done early then I'll go out for lunch rather than eating what I already packed. If I can't find that motivation within myself, then I like talking to friends and family who encourage me to keep going, or I might listen to some of my favorite songs or read cheesy quotes that help to inspire me!"

"What app on your phone do you use most at the moment?"

This is to get a sense of the type of person that you are. Is it a phone game that you spend most of your time on? Are you someone who is always reading the news? This is just a fun question that will help you to showcase a little bit more about your personality. Be honest! Don't make something up just to sound smarter, because it could be the same app the person conducting the interview uses, and they might want to start a conversation about it that you won't be able to honestly participate in. You might consider saying something like this:

"The app that I probably use the most would be a split between Photos and Instagram. I love taking photographs, editing them, and having memories stored in my phone of my closest loved ones. I also love looking at pictures, keeping up with the news, and chatting with online friends, which I can do through Instagram."

"If you could change one thing about your appearance, what would it be? If you could change something about your personality, what would it be?"

This is a tricky question that might throw you off, but it's also a fun one that gives the person conducting the interview an idea of how you think. What is it that you think is the most important thing to change about your physical appearance? What about your personality? It's going to be important that you are self-aware and understanding of what issues you might need to improve on. You also don't want to be too harsh on yourself. Here is a good answer that you might want to include:

"If I could change one thing about my appearance, I would probably want to whiten my teeth! I think a bright smile is important for spreading positivity and showing that I'm friendly. For my personality, I would also want to be less critical and nicer to myself so that I have more confidence."

"Can you describe a time when you really "learned your lesson," or had an enlightening moment that you still frequently apply to your current life?"

The person conducting the interview is not going to expect that you are perfect. What they will be the most concerned about is that even if you do have a flaw, you know exactly what you need to do to fix it. They want to know that whatever issues you might have, you have the ability to recognize what needs to be learned from the situation and that you had learned the lesson. Life is not about regretting your mistakes, it's about learning from them. Here's what you might say:

"There was one time when I found myself very stressed out from work on Friday to the point that I couldn't enjoy my weekend because I had so much to do on Monday. I had a fun trip planned that was completely ruined by my anxiety over work on Monday. I learned that it was most important for me to get my work done on time so that I could enjoy my time off work more."

"How do you normally interact with coworkers?"

Some environments will be completely isolated, and you won't have to talk to a soul. Others will require complete collaboration. This is a good question to help the person asking to know whether or not you will be able to work well with the rest of the team. Be honest, if you have friends from previous positions, that's great! If you struggled to mingle, share why.

"I can be shy at first, sometimes afraid to let others get to know me, but once I've found my footing and become comfortable, it's easy for me to open up and make friends. Getting along with others is important to me so that I can enjoy my work that much more, and it makes the job a lot more fun as well."

"What is a superficial fear, something not related to being alone or failing?"

This question is one that will be specifically targeted at figuring out what your fears on a deeper level might be. are you afraid of spiders? Clowns? The dark? All of these are perfectly fine! They just want to get to know your personality and want you to avoid the common answer - that you are afraid of failing, because this is what most will answer with. Here is an example of what you might actually want to say:

"I'm pretty afraid of the dark! I don't like when it's pitch black, so I usually keep a night light around. Other than that, I don't have big fears that keep me from working! I actually enjoy situations that might be a little more thrilling, like scary movies or roller coasters."

"Can you describe yourself in three words or less?"

This is a common question that will likely be asked frequently, but it's also a hard one that you might struggle to come up with answers to! Don't overthink it. Think about keywords that might have been in the job description which can help you better determine what they might be looking for. Include a professional trait, a real authentic trait, and one that is related to your personality – who you really are deep down. Rather than give you an exact answer, here are some keywords that you likely have, but will also help to make you sound great:

Reliable

Trustworthy

Funny

Logical

Positive

Practical

Realistic

Dependable

Brave

Proud

Virtuous

Witty

Artistic

Educated

Flexible

"What did you enjoy most about elementary school? High school? College? Post-grad?"

They've already learned about who you are and what your background is, but they still want to get to know who you really are. We all have experiences that helped to identify us, but it is our emotions, feelings, and reactions that really help to make up the person that we are. They will likely ask what you liked most about school, so be honest!

"When I was in school, I used to love science classes. I was always curious about the way the world worked. As I made my way into high school, I focused more on arts and expressing myself. When I entered college, I started to really be more interested in the community that surrounded me and how I could actually affect the people in the community."

"What do you remember most about your childhood?"

When you are asked to reflect back and look on your childhood, you will want to focus on positive and happy memories. Sadly, some of us have been through more challenging situations in our lives that we wish to not remember, but now is not the time to share them. Instead, bring up something that you remember that has become a part of your character, even if it was challenging.

"I remember always being interested in learning more and finding out as much new information as I possibly could. I also remember having a single mother who worked two jobs. This curiosity of the world along with the hard work that my mother exemplified helped me to become the dedicated person that I am today. Even when things were more challenging, my Mom had a positive attitude and that has stuck with me to this day."

"Let's say you are in a position where you have been given several tasks to complete by a certain deadline. You realize that even if you worked non-stop as hard as you could, it's still an unrealistic deadline. How would you handle this situation?"

This is a common thing that you might run into in real life. Sometimes we have a ton of work to do, and we want to do it, but we just don't have the time to actually complete the tasks reasonably. Even if we try as hard as we can, there is still always the chance that we might exhaust ourselves in the process. Your employer doesn't want to hear that "this wouldn't be a problem for me," because that's unrealistic. Answer honestly! Say something like this:

"I would start by making a list of what I had to do and prioritize things that are the most important. I would make sure that I am taking care of those first. After working for a little bit and getting a better sense of what I can and cannot realistically complete, that is when I would consider talking to my supervisor. I would express to them what my issue was, and what I would need from them. I would still focus on getting as much work done as possible because making incremental progress is better than doing nothing at all."

"Are you more concerned with the overall big picture, or do you care about every tiny detail?"

Many people will categorize themselves as someone that either looks at the overall idea of something, or the type of person that hangs onto every last detail. For most of the questions we've gone over already and others that we'll be touching on, remember that you don't always have to be one or the other. You could find a way to describe yourself as someone in the middle.

"I think this is situational for me. I usually create a plan based around the small details with the bigger goal in mind. As I work, I pay attention to as much as I can. However, I check in with myself and make sure that I remember the big picture. If I don't, it becomes easy to hang onto the very smallest issues, which could waste time."

"What did you want to be when you "grew up"?"

This is a question that will be directly related to your personality. It is something that will help them discover if this position is something that you have wanted all of your life, or if you have only recently become interested in this field. Be honest, and don't try and pretend that you've wanted to be an accountant since you were five years old. If you did, all the more power to you! However, your interviewer will likely know that you are being inauthentic if you make up a lie just to look better in this situation.

"When I was little, I always wanted to be a teacher and a dancer. I love dancing and expressing myself, but I also admired the many teachers that I had growing up. Since then I've outgrown these dreams, but I still have that same passion and compassion that I admired as a child."

"If you had to pick a career completely unrelated to this field, what would it be?"

This is a fun question that many employers will want to hear from you. If you weren't doing what you are doing, what would you be doing in a nutshell? If you are working a retail job to help you get through college while you are studying to become a nurse, then you would probably tell them that you want to be a nurse since that's your eventual goal. However, take this opportunity to be creative if you want and share what you would consider completely unrelated to anything that you are a part of. Here's what you might say:

"Being a financial advisor is what I want to do now, but I always had dreams of being a veterinarian. I would have considered this field, but blood and surgery makes me queasy so I don't think I would have lasted long! I still love animals, but I understand now that my true talents lie within this field."

Chapter 5: Questions about your former workplace.

How do you fit in with a new company's culture?

Every company has its own unique culture and it always takes some getting used to when you change jobs. There may even be some nuances of different cultures between departments. The interviewer wants to know that you'll go with the flow –not expect the culture to change to your standards, but that you'll adapt to the company's culture. I find just talking with people helps clarify and solidify expectations for behavior and norms. I'm pretty good at reading people, but if I make a misstep, I apologize immediately and profusely. Then I change whatever I did wrong so that I'm conforming to the company's norms. There's usually at least one friendly person who'll help a new person navigate their way through the company's culture and I've always been fortunate to be able to find such people.

How have you personally impacted employee safety?

Safety is everyone's business, and if everyone's not watching out for everyone else, accidents can happen. I strongly believe it's each of our jobs to ensure employee safety, and to look out for one another, stopping or preventing accidents from happening. Just a few weeks ago, I was walking through the shop and I noticed that an employee was preparing to pour a clear liquid into a 55-gallon drum that was labeled 'Acetone'. The container the employee was pouring from wasn't marked with the contents, so I asked her. She said it was Alcohol. I pointed out that the barrel into which she planned to pour the Alcohol was labeled Acetone, and it probably wasn't a good idea to mix two chemicals.

We laughed about it, but it could have been serious. She and I then went to her supervisor together and suggested that all the 'interim' containers for used chemicals be labeled for specific chemicals only. BONUS POINTS: The other employee and I made it our project to make labels for all the interim containers and show all the employees what we'd done so two chemicals didn't accidentally get mixed.

Tell me something you would have done differently at work, if you could have a 'Do-Over'.

The employer is checking to make sure you understand the importance of Continuous Improvement and the only way to do that is to constantly be on the look-out for newer, better, faster, cheaper ways of doing things. If you simply imply the identification of improvements is someone else's job, it won't look particularly favorable for you. **This is another area that is everyone's responsibility. If we see something that could easily be tweaked to improve the way it works, we should suggest it or just tackle it ourselves.**

What can you do better for us than our other candidates for the job? The employer wants you to identify your strengths for them. I'm sure your other candidates have their own strengths, but I do know that one of my strengths is not to accept the status quo. If I recognize a better way of doing something, I'll speak up, or if it's part of my own job, I'll just change the process. It makes no sense to just keep doing something the same way it's always been done, just because it's always been done that way.

I think another differentiator for me is my Positive Attitude. Rather than seeing the worst in a person or situation, I look for the good. There's good to be had in everyone and everything, and we're all here for the same reason. I work hard to build on the good, making sure my own work is top-notch and others' work is the very best it can be.

Have you ever had difficulty working with any manager?

Employers will want to know whether you have problems taking direction from ANY manager, not just those younger than yourself. Are you the type that can't stand to have anyone tell you how to do something? Like to figure things out for yourself? Then start your own business. Otherwise, learn how to take direction gracefully and gratefully from others. Not at all. I'll take direction from anyone who knows more than I do – and that's everyone! I love to learn new things and of course I want to perform my job correctly and to my manager's highest standards, so of course I'd take direction from him or her on how to do the job. Some managers can be a little more difficult to deal with than others, but it just takes a little more work to develop a relationship with them.

Can you give an example of a time when you've gotten called out for a misstep?

The employer wants to make sure you're not just saying what sounds good at the time, but that you truly understand how to manage around different cultures. Sure – at one company, I was the last one leaving the office for the day, so I went into the kitchen area, made sure the dishwasher was loaded, put soap powder in it, and turned it on to run. The following morning, I was confronted by a co-worker who demanded to know why I'd run the dishwasher when she'd already run it that afternoon? I explained I didn't know she'd already run it, that it appeared perhaps people had added dirty dishes after she ran it, so I just ran it again.

I apologized and said I wouldn't do it again. I said if it was the standard practice for that particular person to run the dishwasher at a particular time each day, it was good information to have and I certainly didn't want to complicate her life. I was always careful after that, though, not to use any of the dishes in the kitchen area unless I washed them myself by hand.

Why have you been out of work so long? You were laid off from your position at Jones Company in August of last year, and it's been about 9 months now. Are you finding it difficult to find something comparable to your previous job? Again, the interviewer here is concerned that, if they hire you, you'll only stick around as long as it takes to find a job that's more like your old job, that pays better, that has more promotion potential. You need to convince the interviewer that this blip is just that – a blip. I'm really just very picky. I don't want to accept just any job – I want to make sure whatever role I take on next, I'm able to contribute valuable expertise and knowledge. There are probably plenty of "comparable jobs" out there that I could do – but I need to know that my efforts are benefiting the company's mission and moving it forward. From what I know about Nobel and Associates, the culture is very much like I experienced at Jones, and the position you advertised closely matches my qualifications and what I'm looking for in my next role. I don't want to just be with an employer for a few months or years – I'm in it for the long-term and hope to find the right spot I'll still be able to contribute to 5 or 10 years from now.

You've been in a management role for a number of years. Why are you now interested in taking a lower level job with – obviously – a lower pay rate?

This type of move is a hard sell. Employers are always going to be suspicious of someone's desire to take a step back. After all, you're "supposed" to continue to move up to more and more responsible positions, with higher rates of pay.

If you do accept a new position without management responsibility, how will you make that transition smoothly? Employers fear hiring someone who's just looking for a way out of a bad current situation who will latch onto anything to get out.

You'll need to convince an employer your decision to step back is intentional, carefully considered and that you're committed to the change long-term. With the right reasons for making such a deliberate decision, an employer's doubts can be overcome. A year ago, my wife had a serious health scare. I thought we'd lose her. Luckily, it was a case of some medical tests being interpreted incorrectly. It became clear to me that we all only have so much time together and I wanted to make the most of my time with my family. So after a great deal of soul-searching and family discussion, I decided the time was right for me to scale back my work responsibilities and be home more. I'd been traveling three or four days a week for years, and I just didn't want to be away from my family for that long anymore. Believe me, it was not a decision I came to easily, but having made the decision, I felt a great deal of stress lifted off my shoulders. My current boss tried to find ways to reduce my workload and my travel responsibilities, but it became too easy to fall back on old habits when some crisis or other came up at work. I realized I was going to have to step completely away from my current employer in order to get the balance I needed. I know it's the right decision for me. The best part is that my new employer benefits from all my knowledge and know-how without having to pay for it.

I see that, four years ago, you made a total change in your career. What led to that decision and are you happy with the choice you made? The Interviewer wants to know a couple of things: 1) that this was a deliberate decision, not the result of being out of work; 2) that this is a direction you'll continue to follow, because they don't want to hire someone who now has 4 years of experience in a new field, only to have that person decide they liked what they were doing previously better. Yes, I did and I'm so happy I did! For the previous 6 years, I'd been taking night classes to get an Associate's degree in Electrical Engineering Technology. I had been working as a production worker in an electrical wiring factory and I saw the work the Electrical Techs and Engineers did, and knew it was something I'd be very good at. I was encouraged by the Techs and Engineers with whom I worked – they convinced me to pursue my education.

So I looked into schools and programs, settled on the one that fit me best, and dove in. I don't regret it for a minute.

My supervisor supported my pursuit of a degree throughout, and when I received my degree, I was promoted from Production Worker to Electrical Tech, with a nice bump in pay. I've spent 4 years as an Electrical Tech, and eventually I'd like to be an Engineer. I've already registered for night classes at the local University to earn a Bachelor's degree. I'll be back in school this fall.

I'd like you to know, though, that my continuing education won't have any negative impact on my ability to work a full-time job here. If anything, I become more focused and organized when I have more on my plate.

Well, since you asked, I couldn't help noticing that the tool room seems to be in disarray. I'm sure the folks who use the tools all the time know exactly where each tool belongs, but it's a little disconcerting to an outside observer. I'd totally 5S that work area, taping off areas for work benches, trash cans, and tools.

The best 5S layout I've seen is a company that photocopied the individual tools, laminated the images, cut them out and glued them in the exact space the tool should be returned to. It's the visual factory idea – it's much easier to see what's missing, and where a missing tool needs to be returned to.

Why did you leave your last job?

Short and sweet is fine – if the interviewer wants to dig deeper, s/he will continue questioning you about the reasons. <u>Unfortunately, I was terminated along with a co-worker. (or ... along with several other co-workers.)</u>

The interviewer is concerned your problems will follow you to any new job – that perhaps you don't have the skills needed for this job either. They don't want to hire someone who seems like a good fit for the job but who can't get along with others – or whatever the reason for your termination happened to be. Depending on the circumstances, you can turn this into a positive. Be honest: **"The company was going through a major reorganization and my position – along with 35 of my fellow co-workers' positions – was eliminated."**

Chapter 6: Questions on the Organization

Questions on the prospective employer are usually of significant interest to organizations during job interviews. Good answers to questions in this category have the tendency of giving an interviewee an edge over others because most people who attend job interviews are usually not prepared for them. It is imperative to remark that the best answers to questions in this category cannot come through reasoning or speculation. An interviewee easily confirms before the interviewer that he does not know the answers to the questions if he attempts them, needless to say that not attempting them does not increase the interviewee's probability of getting the job. The best answers to job interview questions in this category are usually found through an intensive research on the organization prior to the interview. This is why job seekers are advised to conduct a research on their prospective employers and their activities prior to attending a job interview. Giving the right answers to questions in this category will unarguably give a job seeker an edge over his fellow job seekers because they are usually unprepared for them.

Why do you want to work with us?

Sample Answer

Your company is unarguably the leading telecommunication company in the country. I am confident that this organization earned this wealth of enviable reputation in the highly competitive telecommunication industry because it is focused and has diligent staff. I always have passion for working with such organization, and I know that getting this job will afford me the opportunity to achieve that.

What do you know about our organization?

It is impossible to offer an impressive response to this question if you do not have prior information about the organization, especially through a research you conducted before the interview. You should not try to fabricate an answer to this question if you did not conduct a research on the organization before the job interview. Otherwise, you may end up confirming that you are merely guessing.

Sample Answer

This television house is among the earliest private television stations to be licensed in the country, but it is not among the top 10 television stations, even in the state because of the quality of the programmes it airs. One of the consequences of this is that there is low patronage from advertisers, and this is the major source of income of television houses. If I am offered appointment as the Director of Programmes in the television house, with the support of the management, I will use my wealth of experience in the media industry to revolutionise this organization.

How can you assess our organization?

Part of your research on the organization should include their major challenges, especially the advantages their competitors have over them. You may have a higher probability of being employed if you are able to comment on some of the challenges of the organization and make recommendations on how they can be addressed.

Sample Answer

Your company is one of the oldest manufacturers of powdered milk in the country. One of my observations in the attitudes of consumers is that there has been increased preference of low-price sachet powdered milk, especially among the masses who constitute the largest percentage of the consumers. But your company is yet to start packaging its products in this way. I think this is why your products are available only in the cities, but not in the rural areas because the masses there cannot afford them. I think this is an area the organization should apply an urgent change.

Do you know any of our employees?

This question may be asked because the policy of some organizations does not permit the employment of relations of their employees. In an organization that honours such policy, the probability of being employed will be low, if it is known that a relation of yours is one of their employees.

Sample Answer

To the best of my knowledge, I do not know of any relation of mine who is an employee of your organization.

How did you know about this vacancy?

If the vacancy was not advertised to the outside world, it may be difficult to know of it if you do not know any of the employees of the organization. If you allege that you do not know any of their employees, you may have to justify how you knew about the advertisement without the help of an insider.

Sample Answer

I heard of the vacancy from a friend, who is not an employee of your organization. I really do not know how he got to know about the vacancy, but I just decided to give it a trial by applying.

Can you subordinate your personal interest to that of our organization if you are employed?

This is one of the requisites for working with any organization because there will be time employees will not be able to perform official assignments without sacrificing their personal comfort and interests. You are not expected to answer this question after a second thought. Otherwise, it may be difficult for the interviewer to accept that your response is sincere (if it is in the affirmative). However, you should forget about the job if your answer is not in the affirmative. Answer the question with courage, conviction and confidence.

Sample Answer

I will always be willing to subordinate my personal interests to that of the organization because it will be practically impossible for an organization to achieve meaningful success if the employees subordinate the interest of the organization to theirs.

Do you think that you will be happy working with us?

Sample Answer

Happiness is one of the most reliable standards for measuring success. It would be irrational to apply for a job that will not increase my happiness.

Would you prefer to work with a big or small firm?

There are some merits and demerits of working with either of these organizations. If you express preference to working with a small organization while you are being interviewed by a multinational corporation, your application may be rejected. If you also express preference to working with a big organization while you are being interviewed by a small organization, it may be concluded that you will not be at home (or happy) working with the organization. You should adjust your answer to the size of the organization that is interviewing you if you truly want the job.

Sample Answers

My earliest jobs were with small organizations. I prefer working with a big organization this time because I need to advance my career by having greater challenges in an organization like yours.

I prefer working with a big organization because it offers an employee the opportunity of being exposed to global standards.

I prefer working with a small organization because it affords employees the opportunity of having a detailed knowledge of the activities of the company, unlike in big organizations where division of labour is so high that employees may not understand the inter-relationship of the activities of the various departments.

What do you love most in an Organization?

Sample Answers

I enjoy working in an organization in which the management and the employees work as a team.

I like working in an organization that does not treat some employees as sacred cows. Employees feel at home in an organization when there is no discrimination in the way the management relates with them.

 How will you be an asset to our organization if you are hired?

It may be difficult to answer this question correctly if you did not conduct a prior research on the company. Emphasise how your education, experiences and professional accomplishments will guarantee an enviable success in the position you applied for.

Chapter 7: Team Success Questions

Describe a time when you had to convince a fellow student or peer to use a particular approach to an assignment. What did you say?

Why do they ask this question?

Not all of your team members will know the best approach to a particular project. You need to be able to convince them of the right approach. They might also lack the knowledge of how to do it the right way. Therefore, you have to be willing to show them the right way without making them look like fools. There might also be situations where both your approaches are right, but your approach will get the team there faster and more efficiently. Efficiency is the key to success in the big four accounting firms.

Bad Answer

I had a part-time job at a fast food restaurant one summer after school. That summer I found a way to get my line of customers moving efficiently because of a few tricks I knew on the register. One of my colleagues always had a long line with his customers yelling at him. I raised my voice and told him to learn to be more efficient.

I couldn't understand why he couldn't learn the same tricks on the register that I had. It seemed simple to me.

Why this is a bad answer:

Although this shows how you operated in the team at your restaurant, it doesn't show how you contributed to team success. It just shows how you were successful yet your coworker was not. You didn't seem interested in taking the time to help him learn. You need to show how you worked in a team and ultimately achieved success through an approach that you initiated.

Good Answer

An example of a good answer to this question would be:

In college I once had a computer science class. In that class, we were given a group project where we had to code a project. During that group project, we were having a lot of difficulty coming up with a solution. Therefore, I suggested that we break up pieces of the project for each of us to solve.

One of my group members disagreed with this approach. They thought it was better if we all worked on the solution together all at one time. I didn't necessarily disagree with this approach, but I knew we would finish the project on time if we took this approach.

I told my group member that we would not finish the project by the deadline if we all worked on it at the same time. I told them that in order for all of us to be successful we had to break the project up. The group member ultimately ended up seeing my side of the argument. We split the project up, then we ended up finishing it by the deadline.

Why this is a good answer:

This is a good answer because it shows how you disagreed with a group member, but you still came to a compromise. It also shows the steps you took to get to that compromise which shows your thoughtfulness.

Describe a time when you had to work with a team to complete a project. What role did you play? What actions did you take to influence the outcome of your assignment?

Why do they ask this question?

They want to see if you are an active participant or just a follower. They also want to see if you step into the leader role. If you do take a leadership role, are you overbearing. Do you take on too much responsibility?

Bad Answer

An example of a bad answer to this question would be:
I once did a science project in high school. My group wasn't filled with the brightest people, so I just took the

project over. We ended getting an A because I took over and dominated the project.

Why this is a bad answer:
This just shows that you aren't willing to trust group members and that you are judgmental. You need to show the ability to work with people of all different types of skill-sets. You can't say that you only work with the best and brightest. That makes you seem judgmental and cocky.

Good Answer

An example of a good answer to this question would be:
I once had a very big group project in my advanced accounting class. There were multiple parts that had to be tackled. I was co-leader with another classmate, and we both assessed everyone's likes and dislikes and doled out responsibilities based on that. We assigned someone to research who liked to research. We assigned someone to lead the oral presentation who loved communicating. We delegated the remaining responsibilities in a similar manner. The group got along well and our final presentation was a great success. Our presentation was the most popular in the whole classroom.

Why this is a good answer:
This really shows how you work well in a team environment. You immediately jumped into the lead role

and used that to help the team as a whole and not yourself.

You assessed everyone's strengths and weaknesses and delegated workloads based on that.

Describe a situation when you had to influence another student or peer to cooperate. What did you say?

Bad Answer

An example of a bad answer to this question would be: I once had an uncooperative group member in my intermediate accounting class. In order to get him to cooperate told him to improve his attitude or else. He said that he didn't want to cooperate. Then I told him that I was going to tell the professor if you cooperate. We ended up switching group members to address the issue.

Why this is a bad answer:
This is a bad answer because it shows that you used threats to get what you want. Instead you want to show how you can work with almost any person. You want to show how late you convince someone to come to your side. You don't want to show how you always result to threats. That's what children do.

Good Answer

An example of a good answer to this question would be:

I once had a roommate in college who was very noisy. I asked him multiple times to turn down his music. When that didn't work, I had come up with a different solution.

I ended up sitting down with him and telling him how difficult it was to deal with his noise. I told them how I would really appreciate it if you could keep the noise level to a minimum so that I could study. I was willing to work with him so that he could still listen to his music. I worked out a schedule of when he could play his music so that I could maximize my study time. He would listen to his music while I was at class. This worked out really well for us and we avoided future conflict

Why this is a good answer:
This is a good answer because it shows how you avoid a conflict. You could have yelled at your roommate or threatened him but you didn't. Instead you came up with the common solution. You didn't lose your temper. It shows that you are really interested in coming to compromise as opposed to just looking out for yourself.

Interview Question 25

What techniques have you used to gain acceptance of ideas or plans? Give me an example of a time when you used one of these techniques.

Why do they ask this question?

The big four ask this question to understand how you convince other people of your ideas and plans. That is they try to see if you even convince people at all. Maybe you don't do a lot of convincing, and you have a weakness in this area. That's what they're trying to figure out.

Bad Answer

An example of a bad answer to this question would be:
I normally just mention my ideas as they come to me, and I truly hope that people adopt my idea after the first time I mention it. I might bring up the idea one more time, but I don't really push anything. I try being nice and calm and that's how I try to convince people.

Why this is a bad answer:
Even though this might be how most people communicate, it doesn't make for good answer to this question. The best candidate that the big four want to see should have multiple skill sets to convince people of their ideas and plans. Now is that how people actually are? I don't think so, but you're going to want to make yourself seem that way to the big four.

Good Answer

An example of a good answer to this question would be:

I use multiple techniques to get people to implement my plans and ideas. I try to see things from their viewpoint before speaking to them. That way I don't offend them which will allow them to see things from my viewpoint.I also take people out for coffee, drinks, or even a meal. When you buy people things and listen to them, they are much more willing to support you.

I'm also an active listener. I listen very attentively when people speak to me and my responses are measured and to the point. I only speak when I feel I have something to contribute and whatever I say tends to be a positive response to what the person just said.

Another technique that I use, is that if I disagree with somebody's opinion is asking questions. I ask pointed questions to where I think the weaknesses in their argument are. The questions that I ask are not offensive though. By asking questions, I hopefully get the person to see the weaknesses in their argument.

Why this is a good answer:
You detailed all your techniques that you use to get your peers to cooperate. This is also a good answer because none of the techniques are negative. You want to have at least a couple positive techniques ready. If you have only one, it will make your interviewer doubt that you really have techniques for cooperation at all.

Chapter 8: Questions to Ask

It is now your turn. As the interview draws to an end, it is almost certain that the hiring authority will ask you, "Do you have any questions for me?"

They will expect you to have some inquiries, lest you appear uninterested or unprepared.

Having queries also illuminates on your skills, qualities, and experience and will show your employer that you are the best match for the role.

As you prepare for your interview, have some questions to ask the interviewer. Remember that you are not just trying to get this position as the employers require, but forming a mutually beneficial relationship where you also assess the employer to see whether the position and the company fits you.

General tips for answering the interviewer questions include:

- Avoid focusing on "me" questions, which include those to do with salary and benefits. Remember that you are trying to showcase how you will benefit the company and not the other way around.

- Ask questions one by one to avoid overwhelming the interviewer.

- Avoid the YES or NO questions that can simply be answered by going through the company's website.

- Do not dwell on one point but instead ask a variety of questions to show that you are interested in learning about all aspects of the organization and the role for which you are interviewing.

- Do not ask anything too personal no matter how much you are trying to establish rapport with the person interviewing you.

- Avoid questions such as "What does this firm do?" as you are supposed to have researched that prior to the interview, or "Am I getting the job?" as you will look impatient.

- Ideally, there are three types of questions you ask the hiring manager during an interview. You ought to show your interest in the position, interest in the company, and show more about yourself.

Although you do not have to ask all questions in your list, it is advisable that you have a comprehensive list since some questions may be covered in the process of the conversation.

Questions about Position

- "How does this role contribute to larger organizational goals?"

Employers can easily find an individual to execute a role, but it is often difficult to find one that will not only carry out their role but also understand how their work connects to larger organizational goals. Such an employee is able to set standards and goals and also prioritize how to achieve and maintain valuable performance aligning with a company's growth.

This question offers you an opportunity to learn about some crucial information that may not be availed to you, especially if the company you are interviewing for is not very transparent or forthcoming. Hence, this question aims at giving you a framework to guide you if you land the role.

- "What performance metrics would you use for this role?"

Asking this question indicates that you are goal-oriented and you are ready to account for any goals concerning your work. It shows your accountability skills, which gives the employer confidence that you are out to work, not joke around.

This question helps you get the employer on their toes to figure out the actual importance of your role and communicate it to you. There are many employees out there who only have a vague picture of what their role is and yet do not exactly know what their employer wants from them.

- "What does a typical day for this position look like?"

Asking this question shows the interviewer that you want to understand the norms of your job and the daily routine to ascertain that you can manage tasks effectively and what approach you need to have if you are hired. It shows them that you are interested in knowing your schedules, planning your time, and using the day efficiently.

This question helps you align your most productive moments with your job and how to overcome challenges or handle emerging issues in the course of your work.

- "Who does this position report to?"

It goes without saying that your prospective boss will have a major impact on your career and will highly determine how productive your work is at the company.

Therefore, this question shows the employers that you are keen in getting to know your immediate boss and that you look forward to establishing a proper working relationship with them.

The question helps you to gain an outlook into how the position is regarded in the company, and it will give you impressions about the management style of your job and the approach you are to give to your job if offered.

- "What are some of the challenges and roadblocks that come up in this role?"

This question shows the hiring manager your interest in the job as you have already envisioned yourself in it. It is a good sign to them that you are ready to get armed up for any stumbling blocks along the course of your work.

Asking the question helps you understand the less-appealing aspects of the job, including internal politics or difficult workmates. This information can be used to evaluate if the role is really good for you or if you are okay with the challenge.

- "Why are you hiring for this role?"

This question sends the image that you are interested in knowing the problem being solved by filling this position. It shows them that you are not a person who just indulges into a deal without knowing its source.

The question will help you if it is a new or a replacement role. A new role can indicate that the organization is growing and a replacement role would prompt some explanation as to why the previous employee left. This question will offer insight into whether there are internal promotion opportunities and even foresee any pitfalls.

- "How has this position changed over time?"

Asking this question shows that you are aware it might not be a first-time position. Someone else might have held the role, and it might have evolved. It shows them that you are interested about the future of the organization.

It is crucial to ask this question to know how it might have looked in aspects such as responsibilities. You may even get a sense of where the hiring authority feels it is going in the future. The answer can give you an unbiased insight into your role and department.

- "What is the typical career path here for a person hired into this role?"

This question shows the employer that you are not solely about reporting to work without a goal, but that you are focused and ready to be committed to your career journey. It makes them understand that you are an enlightened person who thinks about the future.

This question will provide light into how the position may advance your career and the direction it will take. It will inform your goal setting and decision making by letting you see how the employer regards career growth.

Questions about the Company

- "What do the most successful newbies do in their first thirty days here?"

This question shows the employer that you are one of a kind; you are a person who wants to get things going as soon as they hit the ground. It is also a good indicator that you are interested in the patterns of success and that you are willing to replicate a successful performer.

This question helps you gauge the unspoken expectations of the company and the specific environment. In case you land the job, this question would prevent you from suffering the case of "I wish I knew then what I know now" six months down the line.

- "What biggest challenge has the team faced in the past year?"

Most often interviewers will paint a pleasant picture of what joining the workforce looks like, some of which you will have to face and help to address once you join. This question shows the interviewer that you are organized and like to prepare for handling challenges.

This question also helps you to know if you will take the job if the offer comes or not. It also opens up your mind into some of the techniques used by the workers to overcome challenges.

- "Why did you decide to work at this organization?"

This question is a chance for the interviewer to talk about themselves and also sell the organization.

It offers insight into what motivated your prospective workmate and what would most probably be good for you if their motivators align with what interests you in a job.

- "What keeps you motivated working in this company in the time you have stayed here?"

First, this is an indicator that you have already studied your interviewer and you know they have been in the company for a while. Showing that you are interested in knowing the taste of the people who work in the company is impressive.

This question helps you learn about your prospective company's workplace flexibility, career growth opportunities, and leadership opportunities.

- "Where do the staff members take lunch?"

This is a relaxed question that you can ask to break the hard atmosphere and create a conversation about shared interests.

It would not hurt knowing a little about the company's culture and lunch suggestions for the future in case you get the job. You would learn if the staff take time to go out, if people eat in groups, or whether they eat at their desks because they are too busy to socialize.

- "What is this company's customer service attitude?"

This question is impressive as it shows your interest in making a connection between how the customer service is delivered with the ultimate result. Typically, how customers or clients are treated daily indicates how productivity is attained.

This question helps you to hear in a better way some information you could have attained an idea about from the company's website. It also helps you in making the decision about accepting the job if offered a chance or to decline, especially if your prospective position is that in which you will be communicating with customers directly.

- "How would you describe this company's values?"

This question shows the employer that you want to know the fundamental value framework that guides the operations of the company. It shows them that you like to prepare in advance to conduct yourself in line with the basic guidelines of behavior.

This question allows you to know the basic standards of conduct expected in the company.

- "Could you please tell me some of the tangible traits of successful people among the staff?"

This question shows that you are interested in attaining an outlook of what success is in the company. It pushes the hiring authority to think about their top performer.

The response to this question gives you an idea of what it takes to be a star candidate and generally how to impress your employer.

- "Which manners do the people who struggle most on the job display?"

This question shows the hiring authority that you are a straightforward individual who is trying to attain a concrete idea of what to do and what not to do if you get hired. It is impressive because it portrays you as a candidate who is confident about asking tough questions.

This question response offers you an idea of what poor performance looks like, which will inform your decision making and standards setting. You will also see how your employer handles such a tough question.

25. "How is negative feedback delivered?"

This tough question is important as it showcases your confidence levels and shows that you are interested in learning how the team works. It also tells them that you are a mature person who expects some negative feedback if things go wrong.

It helps you know how people react to negative feedback differently and how your employer is likely to give negative feedback. You will learn if the negative feedback is given differently depending on who is asking or whether feedback is a two-way approach. Therefore, you will know if you are able to work with them.

Questions about Yourself

- "Do you have any queries about my qualifications?"

This question sends a positive light of you to your interviewer since it shows that you welcome feedback. It shows that you understand yourself and would be willing to work and improve on yourself. It gives the hiring authority a chance to ask you about anything you might have mentioned in your résumé and was not portrayed in your conversation, and which may be holding them back from hiring you.

This question offers you a chance to make clarifications about concerns face to face without confrontations.

- "What should I expect to wear on the first day to work?"

Dress code is among the touchy subjects of an interview since you want to show that you are concerned about following the company culture but you do not want to show you might have wardrobe malfunctions. It is important to ask this question, especially if business wear has not been your thing.

This question helps you get the firsthand information from the human resources manager about the company culture.

- "How much travel is expected?"

It is important to know if regular travel is expected for a prospective job and to establish if you are able to travel as much as the job requires. It shows the employer that you like being organized, clarifying that even though you like to travel, you would like to know how often and where you have to travel.

Asking your employer this question helps to inform your decision on whether to accept the job if offered or whether to decline. It will help you relate the obligations at hand and how flexible you are to travel.

- "Is relocation a possibility?"

This question shows the employer that you are mindful of the job posting process to avoid inconveniencing both your family if you have one and the organization too.

Response to this question gives you an idea of the location you are being posted to and to determine whether you will relocate or not. The employer will also give you an outlook of the relocating process and expenses for you to plan ahead if you are extended the offer.

- "If I am extended a job offer, how soon would you like me to start?"

This is one of the most important questions to ask at a job interview. It shows the employers that you do not just assume things, especially issues that might affect your schedule and make you fail in fulfilling a commitment.

Response to this question will give you a glimpse into how essential the position you are applying for is to the operations of the company. Even if you have not gotten the job offer yet, it is good to think about a tentative time frame for hitting the ground if you get the job.

- "When should I expect to get a response from you?"

Asking this question reaffirms your interest in talking to employers after your interview. It also indicates that you are confident about being a good match for the role.

Response to this question helps you to assess the level of importance this role has to the organization, and also whether it is most likely good news or bad news that you will be receiving. Although you may not get a definite answer, you will get an idea of how long the employer takes to respond to job candidates.

- "Are there any other questions I can answer for you?"

This question shows your recruiter that you are keen to explain all details they may want to clarify. It shows them that you accord them their status by giving them a chance to ask you any other remaining issue of concern.

The question also gives you a chance to reaffirm your interests in the position, reiterate your skills and abilities, and to show the interviewer why you are worth the position. It also helps you gauge the interviewer's final thoughts as the interview comes to an end.

Chapter 9: Questions You Should Not Ask at the Interview

The following are examples of some questions that you should never ask during your interview:

1. Can I do this job at home?

If you are interviewing for a job that is a freelance position, then the job advertisement would have mentioned it. If you ask the interviewer about working from home, then you imply that you don't like to work with other people. You also don't like to be supervised and have a difficult work schedule. Sometimes, the option is given to work from home, but you should never assume that the same opportunity will be given to you.

2. What does your company do?

You should never ask the company about what they do if there is information readily available on the web about it. We should emphasize that you need to do your research on the company beforehand and gather as much information as possible. If you have not done your homework beforehand, the interviewer will assume that you are not actually interested in the job.

3. How much vacation time do we have?

If you ask about vacation, then you're going to imply that you are a lazy employee who is not committed to the job and that you will not be an effective worker. This could be a red flag for the company that is interviewing you.

4. Did I get the position?

When you ask this question, you put the employer in an uncomfortable situation, and it makes you look like you are impatient. Instead of asking this question, you should ask when you are likely to hear back about the position. Ask a question such as the following: *Do you have multiple rounds of interviews? When will I likely hear back about the position?*

5. How many hours do you have to work for this job? Will I need to be available to work on the weekend?

If you talk about the hours of work, you show that you want to work as little as possible. Instead of asking about the amount of work hours, you should ask a question like, "What is the typical workday like?" This will talk about what kind of commitment you will give to the job.

6. How long would I need to wait before getting a promotion?

If you ask this question, you imply that you are not actually interested in this position, but would rather like to move on to the next level. Instead of asking about this, you should ask for the opportunities for professional development and growth within a company.

7. What kinds of benefits are offered to employees?

Questions about benefits, such as health insurance, should wait until after you have received a firm job offer from the company. If you need to have a certain benefit, then you should talk to an HR person rather than the interviewer.

8. How long is lunch?

You should not ask how long lunch is, because then you are implying that you don't want to work a lot and that you would rather play than be an ideal employee.

9. How late can I arrive to work before getting sacked?

You don't want to ever talk about arriving late to work. It is simply unprofessional. Arriving late to work shows you don't care about your job or the consequences of it. You should try to be on time every day.

10. Does this company monitor internet usage?

If you ask this question, you are implying you have something to hide in your Internet usage, which could be a red flag for the interviewer. It is important that you steer clear of this question at all costs.

11. What warnings do you receive before getting fired?

This question is also a red flag, because it shows that you might go all the way with something or try to get away with whatever it is before getting fired. Don't ask this question ever.

12. Do you check references? Do you conduct background checks?

If you ask this question, you will reveal that you have something to hide. So, you should not ask.

13. Do you have security cameras watching all that I do?

This question assumes that you may not be trustworthy and therefore would not be a good candidate for the company.

14. Will the company monitor my activities on Facebook?

You should assume that your online profile is public and that information revealed on it will be available to your employer. Try to refrain from posting any racy material on the web because it could end up getting you fired from a job.

15. Is it always noisy in this place?

This question would give a bad impression, because it would show that the working environment is not suitable for you. Try not to ask this question.

16. How soon can I get a raise?

This shows that you are more interested in money rather than the job itself. You should not ask questions related to money or salary at the interview, especially the first one.

Conclusion

It is clear that there are some questions that are just best not to ask as they indicate red flags that could make the interviewer question your ability to join the team. Even if you cruise through the rest of the interview and answer the questions thrown at you, it is still possible to mess everything up if you ask the wrong interview questions, so don't blow your chances by asking unacceptable things.

Chapter 10: Behavior-Based Questions

Preparation

Many of the behavioral questions aim to find out how you respond to negative situations. You should have a number of examples that show how you faced some negative situation and had a positive outcome.

Identify seven or eight examples of situations from your previous jobs where you exhibited the skills that employers usually seek in a candidate. Think of examples that bring forth your best skills and behaviors.

Half of the examples you choose should be positive and show your accomplishments and situations where you met your goals.

Half of them should be examples of situations that were initially negative but ended positively.

Your examples should be from different areas of life.

Use examples that are quite recent.

Techniques

There are various techniques that you can use for answering behavioral questions. They are:

STAR: This is mostly for interviews where you are asked questions related to your competencies, skills, interests, values, and personality. You are expected to support the answers with some sort of evidence. You can use the STAR method to answer questions based on competency and to provide that evidence.

Situation: You should briefly describe the who, where, and when.

Task: You can give an outline of the task and the objective.

Action: Describe your actions. You must focus on the role you played and your contribution.

Result: Explain the result or outcome and the skills it helped you to develop.

Use this format to create a wide variety of examples. Take these examples from various situations in your career.

CAR: "C" stands for context or challenge, "a" stands for action, and "r" stands for result. First, describe the problem or the task that had to be dealt with. Next talk about how you responded. Finally, explain the outcome of your response.

OKEYO: This technique involves: giving an overview, explaining the key events, describing your role, and detailing the outcome or result.

PAR: First, talk about the problem, then describe the action you took, and finally, explain the Result.

Sample Questions

Here are some sample behavior-based questions that are asked in interviews. They are related to various areas such as leadership, problem solving, communication, and teamwork.

Leadership

- Describe an occasion where your achievements were vital to the success of a project.

- Tell us about an occasion where you took charge of a situation, sought out support, and achieved positive results.

- Tell us about an occasion where you disciplined or fired a friend.

- Describe an occasion where you had to help leaders grow under your guidance.

- Describe an occasion where you were disappointed in your behavior.

Initiative

- Tell us about some situation where you had to overcome obstacles to accomplish your objectives.

- Describe one of your goals that you are trying to achieve now.

- Give an example of an important contract that you won or lost.

- Describe a situation where you helped implement a new program.

- Tell us about a scenario where your actions played a significant role in the success of a goal.

Problem Solving

- Give an example of a situation where it was necessary to analyze the facts quickly, state the key issues clearly, and either respond instantly or make a plan for the future.

- If you had to perform that task once again, how would you respond differently?

- Describe a situation where you missed the obvious solution for a problem.

- Tell us about a scenario where you were able to anticipate the problems and take preventive measures.

- Give an example of a situation where you overcome a big obstacle.

Communication

- Tell us about an occasion when you successfully presented one proposal to a person of authority.

- Give an example of a situation where you persuaded someone to use your idea.

- Describe a situation where you persuaded the members of your team to listen to your ideas. What was the effect?

- Tell us about an occasion where you showed tolerance toward some opinion that differed from your own.

Work in an Effective Manner with Others

- Tell us about an occasion where you motivated others to get the desired result.

- Give an example to show that you have been successful in maintaining a productive relationship with others despite having different views.

- Describe how you handled a tough situation with your coworker.

- Tell us about a situation in where you helped to get your work group or team back on track.

Work Quality

- Give an example of a situation where a report that you had written was positively received. Why do you think that was?

- Tell us about an occasion where a report you had written was not received well. What do you think was the problem?

- Describe a specific program or project you worked on that brought about an improvement in an important area of work.

- Tell us about an occasion where you fixed some objectives that were too high.

Innovation and Creativity

- Give an example of an occasion where you found a new and better way to do something.

- Describe a situation where you solved a problem creatively.

- Tell us about an occasion where you came up with novel ideas that proved to be helpful to the successful implementation of a project.

- Give an example of a situation where it was necessary for you to make the others use their creativity.

Priority Setting

- Give an example of a situation where you successfully maintained a balance between competing priorities.

- Tell us about an occasion where you were expected to choose the most vital aspects of an activity and ensure that they were completed.

- Describe a scenario where you successfully prioritized the various elements of some complicated project.

- Give an example of an occasion where you became caught up in the various details of some project.

Decision Making

- Tell us about an occasion where you were required to make an important decision but had very few facts.

- Give an example of a situation where you had to make an unpopular decision.

- Describe an occasion where you had to adjust to a difficult situation. How did you handle it?

- Explain a time where you made the wrong decision.

- Tell us about an occasion where you fired or hired a wrong person.

Work in Various Conditions

- Describe a situation where you worked well under pressure.

- Give an example of a project that you could not complete in time.

- Give an example of an occasion when it was necessary for you to change the work midway because of a change in organizational priorities.

- Describe how you deal with stressful situations.

Delegation of Work

- Tell us about an occasion where you effectively delegated a project.

- Give an example of an occasion where you did not delegate work properly.

- Describe a situation where you had delegate work to someone who already had a big workload. How did you handle it?

Customer Service

- Give an example of a time where you had to deal with an irate client.

- What programs related to customer service that you have participated in are you proudest of?

- Have you ever made a lasting impression on a customer? When?

STAR Method Sample Answers

Question: Describe a time when you were under pressure but successfully completed the job.

Step 1: Situation

When I was working on my previous job, my coworker suddenly left for personal reasons. He had been taking care of a very important project. Now there was no manager for it.

Step 2: Task

The task was handed over to me by my supervisor. There was no concession regarding the deadline. The project, which required several weeks time to be completed, had to be done in a few days time.

Step 3: Action

I asked that my weekly workload be reduced so that I could focus on this task. I delegated these weekly goals to my teammates.

Step 4: Result

I dedicated more time for the project and completed it accurately and on time. My efforts and attitude were appreciated by my supervisor. After that, my responsibilities were increased. Eventually, I got a promotion and my salary was raised.

Question: Give an example of a situation where you were the team leader.

Step 1: Situation

I was working as the software developer for a company. There were six members on my team. We were developing a novel finance module that would be used for the core accounting products of our company.

Step 2: Task

It was a critical project, and the launch dates were fixed. Quite a large sum of money had been invested in advertising the products. The work on this project was very slow and very little time was left when the leader fell sick and had to take time off work.

Step 3: Action

When I was in school, I was the captain of the sports team. I enjoyed the challenges and responsibilities involved in leadership. Therefore, I offered to take the responsibility for the project. Using my skills for technical analysis, I spotted some minor mistakes in the basic coding. I saw that the mistakes caused sporadic errors that slowed down the work.

I negotiated with my product director and arranged for a bonus incentive. We decided to give pizzas to the team members who worked in the evenings to make corrections in the coding. In this way I was able to speed up the work.

Step 4: Result

Although the cost of the project went up slightly because of this bonus, we reached the target in time. The additional cost was negligible in comparison to the loss we would have incurred if there was a delay in launching the product. Besides this, it would have a negative impact on the product branding. Moreover, the team members were delighted to get the bonus. As a consequence, I have been promoted and have become the official team leader.

CAR Method Sample Answers

Question: Tell us about an occasion when you solved some major problem in your company.

Step 1: Context

A major event was going to be held in the company, and a colleague of mine had arranged with for an overseas supplier to provide the materials. He had chosen the shipping date as the same date of the event. He did not consider the time that would be needed to clear customs and get the things transported to the event location. It was obvious that it would not be possible to get the supplies in time for the event. He was very upset and asked me to help.

Step 2: Action

I found out that similar materials were available in another city and could be transported by train. I asked him to cancel the shipping order and contacted another supplier who agreed to send the materials to the local railway station two days ahead of the event. After the materials arrived at the railway, we used trucks to transport them to the event location.

Step 3: Result

The materials arrived on time, and the event was successful.

Question: Give an example of a situation where you had to demonstrate initiative.

Step 1: Context

When I started at my previous job, the phone was used to handle all of the requests related to customer service. This took up the staff's valuable time. In addition, errors occurred in the quotes and documentation that caused further delays and customer satisfaction, among other issues.

Step 2: Action

I wanted to rectify this, so I took the initiative to develop an automate workflow system. The customers had to fill in a form and make the service request online. They would provide all the information required. This minimized the documentation errors. The service requests were reviewed daily, and the details were automatically added to the database.

Step 3: Result

The staff did not have to spend time taking calls. This reduced the labor costs and improved the productivity by 20%. Additionally, the turnaround time and customer satisfaction rates improved. The system helped to save time as well as resources, and it was so successful that it was used in the company locations.

Question: Tell us about an occasion where you organized a large event.

Step 1: Context

While working as a personal assistant in my previous job, I was given the responsibility to organize a seminar for the management team. Plenty of planning and attention to details were needed for this task. I had to find a venue; make arrangements for speakers, catering, and accommodations; take care of the finances; and communicate with the stakeholders.

Step 2: Action

I wrote down all of the things that needed to be done and then made checklists. I recorded the names of the people involved and their contact details. I sent daily reminders to them through email and phone regarding specific tasks. By following this detailed and strict schedule, I ensured everything was on the right track. I was able to see how much work had been completed and make sure nothing was forgotten.

Step 3: Result

The seminar went on very smoothly. All the attendees were highly satisfied, and I received positive feedback. Since I had been successful in organizing this function, I was given the responsibility to plan other events for the company. This expanded my role as an organizer.

Question: Describe an occasion where you had to overcome some challenging situation.

Step 1: Context

While working at my previous job, the company went through a difficult situation. I was given the responsibility to reduce expenditure and save money in a short time span.

Step 2: Action

To fulfil this task, I looked at various options that would help reduce the costs. I considered reducing the headcount, cutting departmental budgets, freezing wages, changing the company's accounts policies, and examining capital structure. I analyzed the cost-benefit for each alternative and evaluated the long- and short-term consequences, as well as the risks.

Step 3: Result

It was not easy to lay off the staff, but it was necessary. I made a number of changes to the company's expenditures and allowed a few of the employees to work part-time. In this way, I managed to save money without negatively impacting the company's operations or staff morale.

Question: Tell us about an occasion where you demonstrated adaptability.

Step 1: Context

I worked as the project leader for my company's marketing campaign. By coincidence, a week before launch one of our competitors launched a similar campaign. If we continued with our initial plans and launched our campaign the following week, it would look as if we had copied them even though we had worked on the project for weeks before they launched theirs.

Step 2: Action

I understood that it was necessary to make some changes to maintain our originality. I called all of the team members for a meeting and a brainstorming session. We had already done all of the research, so we only needed to come up with fresh ideas to make the content look different without changing our goals.

I quickly modified the old plan and delegated the work to the different team members create new content. I also engaged a freelancer to produce high quality content. All of us worked long hours that week and completed the project on time.

Step 3: Result

Our campaign was very successful. The new content was much better than the original plan. We were happy that we could quickly modify the plan and deliver a great campaign.

Chapter 11: Describe how you work.

You might have heard something about work style. This is a really common kind of question, but there are many people that just don't know how to answer effectively. When it comes to this question, you'll want to avoid talking about your personality in this question. They just want to know how you get through the day.

You might feel tempted to say that you're laid back when it comes to work, but this answer will really just work against you. Being laid back is really a personality trait, and it's not a necessarily desirable trait when it comes to work. No one wants an employee that just kind of meanders around at work. They want to make sure that you're going to give them the most for their money.

You'll also want to avoid saying that you're not a fan of conflict. This doesn't really have a lot to do with your work style. This answer doesn't really tell the interviewer anything about your work style.

For a good answer, there are a couple things you will want to do. You will want the answer that you give to mesh with the job that you're applying for. If you've got a very straight forward, data-driven position, then you won't want to spend time talking about the creative solutions that you're able to come up with. It isn't a necessary trait for your job.

You'll want to address whether you like to work in groups or by yourself. You might have an actual preference, but you'll also want to address what this particular job requires of you. Being able to work both alone and with someone else can be a great bonus for most companies. Talk about how comfortable with both.

You'll also want to tell them about how much instruction you need on jobs. This is something that you should be upfront with, especially if you tend to only function well with a lot of instruction or very little instruction. This can help see if this job will be a good fit for you. The boss might be on the other side of the spectrum from you. Without being upfront, you could be stuck in a job where you aren't able to function at your most effective.

With this kind of question, you'll want to touch on the strengths you have that fit well with this job. You might talk about organization, planning, performance, and more. These are just ideas to get you thinking. Regardless of the exact answer, you will want to approach these questions with a prepared, strategic answer that will not only address the question, but that will touch on other parts of your personality and work style that make you a good fit for the job.

1 In one word, describe yourself.

When you get to this kind of question, you have to understand what the interviewer is trying to do: get inside your head. Hiring is a gamble. Companies always worry about who they're hiring. The person that hires you also has an interest in how well you go because they can be blamed if you aren't a good hire.

So you'll want to refer to the four basic questions to help inform your answer: Are you capable of doing the job? Do you have an understanding of the job? Will you be able to do the job? Do you pose a risk to this person's continued employment?

If you don't do well in this position, you'll find yourself posing quite a huge risk to another person. So in order to get an idea of how well you will do, they ask some odd questions like this one.

There are a lot of words to pick from. There's dynamic, motivated, successful, responsible, strategic, dedicated, creative, flexible, reliable, dependable, fair, helpful, valuable, enthusiastic, organized, steady, focused, honest, and many more words that you could use to describe yourself. This is a really hard question to pin down.

Personally, I use 'dynamic.' This word works because I'm adaptive and do whatever is necessary to succeed. It's an all-purpose word that applies to many different jobs. However, I want you to avoid just picking a word for yourself. You'll need to think about your job and the kind of words that might fit well with this job.

Every answer that you give is hopefully leading you to a job offer. So you will need to be aware at every point. Don't think about this question as just about who you and what you are like, but focus on how you can relate that back to the job. You might pick a trait that will help you stand out from the rest of the applicants. You might want to use 'bright' because you're quite smart, but 'successful' will probably be a better fit for the employer.

Other good words include responsible, dependable, creative, flexible, strategic, dedicated, motivated, valuable, enthusiastic, organized, steady, focused, honest, fair, helpful, and reliable. Regardless of what you want to pick, think about the job and what kinds of traits are good for someone in this particular position. Be aware that this question can also be followed by a request for an explanation or example that shows off this trait, so you'll want to be prepared with at least one story that can show off the word that you have chosen.

2   **Do you like working alone or with a time?**

This question is fairly common, but that doesn't mean that it isn't a tricky one to deal with. While they are asking about your preference, there are few jobs that you will find that don't have you working both in a team and alone at some point. That's where the tricky nature of this question comes into play. You might actually prefer one, but saying so will cause you more problems. Being comfortable with both work styles is really important for many jobs.

There are some standard answers, such as, "I work well both ways. I do great when I work as a team, but I'm also comfortable when working alone." However, you'll really want to see if you can improve this answer. In order to improve it, you will need to know a little bit about the job that you are trying to get into. You'll need to know what is typically part of the job. This might be research that you complete ahead of the interview or things that you might know from working similar jobs.

So after looking at the job, you might be able to use an answer like, "I typically prefer working alone; however, working with a team can help creatively because we can bounce ideas around and it helps us learn from each other" or "I usually prefer to work in a group, but having a part of a project that is my own is also nice at times."

Both of these answers get at your preference without being outright negative about the other side of the situation. This positivity is extremely important. A hiring manager will feel much more confident hiring someone that is confident and positive. Flexibility is a desirable attribute in people.

However, we suggest that you don't just stop at answering the question. Ask them a question back about the situation like, "Roughly how much time is spent working with a time versus time I will spend working on my own?" You can ask about the kind of environment that the business encourages. This allows you to not only learn more about the situation but also keeps the conversation going.

3   **Have you had to conform to a policy that you did not agree with? Tell me about that time.**

We have discussed behavioral interview questions already. The key to the answer is usually the STAR (situation or task, action, result) structure for the story, but this question is one that you don't want to have a good story about. This question is possibly worse than asking you about a difficult situation that you handled. This one prevents you from looking like you overcame something. Instead, it's showing you in possibly one of your lowest moments. You're not going to look good during this question.

You'll want to think carefully about your answer to this kind of question. What made you not conform at first with the policy? What made you conform in the end?

You may think of yourself as some sort of martyr in the situation, but someone else might not see that. In fact, if the policy was bad enough, you might come out looking pretty bad.

You might have known something that your previous boss didn't know, but that doesn't make you look good either. That's getting close to badmouthing your former employer. That's something you should definitely avoid. In fact, that kind of answer might get you in trouble with your new boss or even prevent you from getting into this new job.

When you get to the heart of the matter, most people can't really affect the policies at their work. All of those rules are set up by someone else and you can't do much to influence them. Even if you bring information to the table, you might not be able to change anything or get a message across. If you don't comply, you could lose your job.

With this answer, you'll have to be careful. This question is hard, but it's also giving the potential employer a lot of good information. They're wanting to know how you communicated, whether or not you confronted your boss, and if you managed to avoid the situation entirely.

The best answer might simply be, "Sorry, I can't recall that happening in my previous jobs." Of course, this might not be enough to stop the interviewer. If they press, you can follow up with, "If this happened, I would probably ask questions or express my concern. It is part of my job to support the rest of the team. That included bringing potential issues into the light so they can be dealt with before they actually become problems. However, the decision belongs to my supervisor in the end." You are showing that you think critically, work with the team, and respect authority. This kind of answer can be really attractive to potential employers.

4   Describe a time where you believe you went beyond the call of duty.

This is the best kind of question to get. It's a behavioral interview question, but this kind of question really gives you a chance to shine. This is the kind of story that you should always have on hand. Exceeding expectations is always a good thing to talk about. This shows that you bring quite a bit of value when you work.

You should always have a story prepared before you go into the interview. Try to pick one that will speak to the job that you are applying for, not just the job that you have had in the past. Speaking of what you can offer in the future is always a good choice. You can focus on particular skills or tasks that might be in your future with this job. The situation should be a little bit difficult.

Conflict and resolution are always part of a good narrative.

The general story should follow this outline, "We needed (blank) done. There were some specific tasks that we needed to do. I did X, Y, and Z. These were the results of the situation."

This is just following the STAR method. It will really help you get the most out of your story. Don't feel like you have to hold back or not brag. This is a situation where you are meant to brag. This will help you show off your best qualities and also show you communicate well. You can even provide a 'brag book' which will be a physical representation of what you did and show all of the proof of what you did. Combine a good story with the book and you'll have major points in this interview.

5   If you were made to choose to become any animal in the planet, what would your choice be, and why would you pick it?

While a job interview tends to be a formal affair, there are some interviewers who are fond of throwing the prospective applicants a few curveballs. Their reasoning behind this can vary. Some think that your answer to such an odd question would reveal much about you. Others may just want to find out your reaction when confronted with an unexpected situation, like being asked such a question out of the blue. Whatever reason the interviewer has for asking, these questions do offer a hint into how you think, and these questions can be seen as opportunities to display your wit and quick thinking. After all, when you head into an interview, you should be prepared for anything they may throw your way. One of the better methods to get in the right mindset for an interview is to think about what qualities and attributes are most suited to the job you're seeking. If you're able to identify this, you'll have a much easier time answering any type of question appropriately. You can use this insight to prepare answers on how who you are as a person, your personality, your skills, or even your hobbies make you well-suited for the job.

For this specific type of question, picking a specific animal isn't really important, but rather, making sure that you can link your choice and the attributes needed for the job is. Of course, it would be best to avoid picking animals that already have negative attributes associated with them, like bugs, snakes, or even chickens. Once you've made your choice, you have to start explaining the reasoning behind it. You should link yourself to the animal, explaining the similarities that you find. Some examples would be liking yourself to an eagle, at least if you're going for a higher position, but that comparison may be unfavorable for jobs that need lots of cooperation.

Horses are also a good choice, as they are strong and hard workers, who function just as well solo or as part of a bigger group. Ants are diligent and known as tenacious and hard workers, as well as being one of the best team players in the animal kingdom. Dogs are known for their loyalty and friendliness, which may suit certain roles. Many other animals may prove to be good choices to display your chosen attributes, just make sure you are able to link them properly. If the interview is going well, you may even be able to end it on a light note by asking your interviewer what he would choose if the question was posed to him.

6   If you could rewind the clock, repeating the last ten years, how would you choose to do things?

This is a question that invites much thought. After all, we tend to have many regrets, big and small. We may regret speeding that one time on a country road, investing in a bad portfolio, buying a bad outfit, or any number of other things we wish we didn't do. However, when it comes to this question being posed during an interview, the interviewer is most likely thinking of something else. This question is in fact designed to make you reveal what you feel your weaknesses are. This question tends to draw out your flaws, as they can see that based on what you regret. This question may be a good opportunity to address any possible issues you had in your past work history, and in fact, this question may be triggered by their knowledge of such issues. For example, if they see that you have had a previous employment that lasted for a suspiciously short time before you left, this may pique their interest enough to ask the question. You can explain this in a diplomatic manner, perhaps saying that you regret quitting your job to take another, saying that it didn't turn out to be a good move, but when it happened, it was the best decision you felt you could make with the information you had available. You can follow that up saying that regardless, you learned much from it, but if you knew what would happen, you wouldn't have done it. Try to frame issues as positively as you can, but do not lie. If you lie, you're out of the running for sure.

If your career has been on the smooth side, and there are no incidents to really explain, then you may be able to answer this with a lighter note. If you want to be more serious when answering however, you can say that while everyone has regrets, decisions and choices that they wish they could reverse, you are happy with the general direction and trajectory of your life, both career-wise and personal. That answer is fairly neutral, while showing the interviewer that you have not really made any major mistakes that you truly wish you could reverse, and that answer will most likely do its job in most situations.

Chapter 12: Salary Questions

Getting the amount of money you deserve is truly an art, because of two conflicting agendas: Employers want to hire you as cheaply as they can, while you want to get as much as you can. Timing is oh so important, so delay discussing salary until you receive a job offer, when you're in the strongest bargaining position (even if you're chomping at the bit to find out what it pays). The interviewer will never want you more than he or she does at that moment.

Whoever mentions a number first loses in this game, and both the interviewer and job-hunter can jostle to get the other to show their hand. Be strategic and dance around a bit with your responses, ask for more information, display thoughtful silence, and utter the immortal words: "Is that the best you can do?" Often interviewers have "wiggle room" with salaries, and can pay more if you convince them you deserve it. Learning how to use classic negotiation techniques is invaluable in upping your ante in obtaining the best salary.

What are your expectations regarding promotions and
   salary increases? How much do you expect if we
   offer this position to you? Or: What salary are

you looking for? Or: What is your salary requirement?

I want to understand the job duties and responsibilities completely, so I don't know at the moment. What do similar jobs at the company pay?

What the interviewer is asking/looking for: If the interviewer asks this in your first interview, he or she may hope you give a figure outlandishly high or ludicrously low, which either way will knock you out of serious consideration. Or a figure that will steer the interviewer toward an end of the range the employer is willing to pay, or set a figure if the amount has not yet been decided. If asked much later in the interview process—perhaps after three interviews—the interviewer may be ready to offer you the job.

Good answer: Avoid giving a number as long as you can. Say you want to make sure you understand the job duties and responsibilities completely, and tick off what you know one by one. Then try to counter with your own question, like the salary range the interviewer is allowed to consider for the job, what similar jobs at the company pay, or what he or she thinks someone with your qualifications and skills will command. Stall by saying that without knowing all the details about benefits, it's hard to cite a figure.

If throwing the ball back into the interviewer's court doesn't work and you are pressed to give a number, offer a salary range that reflects your research about this type of job before the interview. ("Help wanted" ads, employees in this job type, trade associations, and salary information websites can be helpful.) The low end should be the minimum you want to accept. Of course, you may already know the salary being offered from an ad or the recruiter who told you about this job.

Bad answer: Blurting out a figure that may knock you out of the running for being too high or too low, or box you into a figure, instead of seeing the question as the negotiating gambit it is. Or saying salary doesn't matter, you just need a job. Never show an interviewer you're desperate—your value will go down in his or her eyes.

How much are you worth?

I feel I deserve at least $xxx pa due to my qualifications and career accomplishments.

What the interviewer is asking/looking for: The interviewer wants you to make a case for the salary you want and match up your qualifications with the job requirements.

Research what you're worth online. Salary, com shows salary ranges for jobs in many industries by years of experience, metro area, and zip code. Career Journal, com, a Wall Street Journal site, shows median salaries by job title, industry, and city. Jobstar.org links to over 300 salary surveys in many different industries.

Good answer: Be aware of the market rate for this job from your research in the salary range you name, and confident you meet all of the job qualifications, which you list, if not more.

Bad answer: An answer that shows you are operating in the dark, with little or no knowledge about what the going rate for this job is. A naive job-hunter is usually an underpaid job-hunter.

What are you making now? Or: What was your salary in your last job?

My last job was totally different so it does not matter.

What the interviewer is asking/looking for: Sadly, many interviewers are unduly influenced by your last salary, and use it as a guide to offering you a similar salary, or a bit more.

Good answer: Say that you feel your current (or last) salary shouldn't be relevant to the salary for this job, since they are different. Perhaps you are coming from the public or nonprofit sector, which often pay less, started the job at a low base, or there were budget cuts, **etc.** If pressed, and you know you were underpaid, you can include the dollar value of benefits like health insurance, profit sharing, stock options, and salary instead of vacation in your figure. Just be able to justify it if asked why it doesn't match your pay stub.

Bad answer: A flat figure, with no explanation if it's underpaid, which tempts the interviewer to tie a salary offer to your last salary.

Sometimes interviewers ask to see payroll stubs or W-2 tax forms when you are hired, or condition the job offer on salary verification with your employer or an outside agency. Your signature on a job application with the tiny print gives them permission. So don't invent a figure you can't justify.

What is your salary history?

I don't know, I need some time to figure out.

What the interviewer is asking/looking for: He or she wants to know how often you received raises and promotions, and how much, for clues to how well you did on the job to decide on the salary to offer you.

Good answer: Frequent and sizable jumps in salary look good, obviously, so why not admit it if this is the case? If not, or if you don't want your salary history to influence the salary offer, dodge it by saying it will require some time to figure out. If the interviewer expects you to do so, respond that you will do it as soon as you go home. If pressed to do it on the spot, okay.

Bad answer: Lack of steady, upward progress, which makes the interviewer willing to lowball the salary offer or gives him or her second thoughts about you.

Don't ask what salary the job pays. This pegs you as someone too interested in money and not enough in the job. Wait for the interviewer to bring up salary.

You've been stuck at the same salary in the same job for the past few years: How come? Or: Why aren't you making more money at your age?

Unfortunately, the advancement opportunities were severely limited at my employer due to budget constraints, so that is why I am here.

What the interviewer is asking/looking for: The interviewer shouldn't know this—hopefully, you didn't volunteer this, or perhaps the ad, application, or interviewer insisted nobody would be considered without a complete salary history. He or she is wondering if your lack of steady upward progress signals something sinister about your job performance, like laziness or lack of motivation.

Good answer: Note that advancement opportunities were severely limited at your employer, due to budget constraints or employees with more seniority. Segue quickly to this is why you are job-hunting, and eager to apply your skills and expertise to this particular job.

Bad answer: Shame, defensiveness, or anything that shows you are not a desirable commodity this employer should snap up.

That's too high for us. Can you come down a little?

Yes, I can. No problem.

What the interviewer is asking/looking for: He or she is interested, but wants you at a somewhat lower price.

Good answer: Cite a lower range that you are willing to accept. While negotiating up can be hard (because lowballing your salary can trap you), negotiating down is much easier. You should always ask for more money than you expect to get, because you have a better chance of ending up with the amount you expect even if you lower your demand. You can also ask for the benefits or perquisites to be sweetened if you do well in a few months, instead of money up front—for example, a performance review with a raise and/or promotion, a bonus, more vacation or comp time, **etc.**

Bad answer: You are not willing to budge, because the figure or range you cited was your absolute minimum.

Never mention a fixed number. It will box you in, perhaps knock you out of the running if it's too high, or peg you as a cheap hire if too low. Cite a salary range instead, if pressed. If job applications ask for desired salary, write "open" or "competitive."

How about a salary of (fill in the blank)?

Is that the best you can do?...

What the interviewer is asking/looking for: The interviewer hopes you will grab this amount without ever learning he or she was prepared to pay $5,000 to $10,000 more.

Good answer: Repeat the amount offered in a reflective tone, and then be silent—or say "hmmm" and be silent. Silence seems to unnerve interviewers, who often rush in to fill the vacuum with a higher amount. Try it—it often works like a charm.

Or say you're very close, since the range you were considering was X to Y—with your low end a bit lower than the high end (or fixed amount) the interviewer offered. For example, he or she offers $35,000; counter by saying you're pretty close, since you had a $34,000 to $40,000 range in mind.

Bad answer: You grab the amount offered without negotiation, so they get you at a bargain rate. Or you say no because you want X and he or she said Y—and don't realize there may be "wiggle room" to go up from Y.

Summary

You've learned the importance of timing: how to stall on salary questions, how to wait for the interviewer to throw out the first number, and how prudent silence may buy thousands of dollars in a salary offer. You know to avoid fixed numbers, and stay on your current salary as long as possible. You'll never go into an interview blind again, but be armed with valuable information about how much your qualifications are worth and how to prove you deserve a certain salary.

But you've been interrogated enough.

• Postpone discussing salary until you get a job offer.

• Wait for the interviewer to reveal a salary figure.

• Avoid revealing your past salaries if you can.

• Don't mention fixed numbers, only ranges.

• Research salaries in classified ads, on websites, and by talking to employees and/or trade associations.

Chapter 13: Saying Thank You

When you are invited to an interview, it is crucial that you know how to say thank you, because this shows gratitude, humility, and a sense of grace toward the interviewer and the HR team. It is likely that HR has looked at many different candidates. They have spent a lot of time reviewing applications and therefore have done a lot of work to weed out candidates and find people who are qualified to do the job. They chose you for a reason, but clearly, it took them some time to sift through all the applications to reach yours. Therefore, you should feel thankful that you got the interview in the first place.

To demonstrate that you are thankful, you should say thank you immediately when you walk into the room and do the interview. This is a step that many people forego and do not remember, but when you do it, you demonstrate a level that is above the average candidate. So, you should say something to the interviewer like the following: *Thank you for inviting me to have this interview. I appreciate the time that you have committed to talk to me about this available position.* You don't have to fluff up your words or try to make it into something fancy. Instead, keep it simple and to the point, because then you can show your gratitude to the interviewer.

In addition to expressing thanks to the interviewer at the beginning, you should also say thank you at the end of the interview. It is important to begin and end with gratitude, because even if you don't get the job or the interview doesn't go well, you can still thank the interviewer for his or her time, because they will likely be seeing a lot of candidates and have to make decisions based on the interview results. It can be an inconvenience for them to take time out of their busy schedule to do these interviews. You must be mindful of the time, money, and investment in these interviews, because it is a costly affair to replace or hire a new person for a job. It is not something that is easy for a workplace to do. At the end of the interview, you should say something like this: *Thank you again for your time and consideration. I appreciated the chance to talk to you about this position. Have a great day.*

7   The Thank You Note

Another step that goes above and beyond what is expected is writing a thank you note. This is something that the majority of candidates will not do, but it will result in you becoming an outstanding candidate if you do it. Many people forget to say thank you at the end of the interview. Usually, it doesn't guarantee that you can snag a job offer. Don't think automatically that sending a thank you note is going to get you the job, but it is something that helps remind the interviewer of you and your experience with interviewing them. This is especially important when they are considering a handful of candidates and have to distinguish between them in the results. When you have an interview thank you note, then you can set yourself apart from the other candidates and show that you are sincere and really want the job. Express yourself in writing and share your experience of the interview. Here are some tips for writing a thank you note.

Begin with gratitude

The first thing you should say is something such as this:
> Thank you for taking the time to speak with me about this opportunity. I appreciated the chance to learn about the job and how I could fit into this company.

You should share how much you appreciated the time that the interviewer took to be with you and talk about what your interview experience was like.

Share about how the company aligns with your goals

Next, you should share how the company's values align with your goals for the future. Talk about your skills and relevant experience and how those would help you succeed in this role. Mention the types of job responsibilities you would be expected to carry out and talk about how your experience will help you do everything that you must do. Talk about how the company has values that align with your personal career objectives. This will assist in showing that you are a good fit for the company.

Mention something you were unable to discuss at the interview

Additionally, you should mention something that you were unable to express during the interview, because there was not enough time or you forgot to include it in your answers. This will show that you remembered something important and wanted to bring it to the attention of the interviewer. Then, the interviewer will also know that you are a good fit for the job.

Talk about how you're the best candidate

Finally, you should leave a strong impression in regards to how you are the strongest candidate for this position. Here, you need to reiterate your skills and experience and talk about how those provide you with the best qualifications for this position. Don't shy away from talking about your professional achievements, and highlight the important parts of your career that make you an excellent candidate for this position.

8   Example of a Thank You Note

Applicant: John Smith

Richard Tate

Assistant Professor and Native English Teacher Coordinator,

_____ University in Japan

17 November 2017

Dear Richard,

Thank you very much for giving me the chance to come to Tokyo to interview with you. I loved my visit to _____University. It felt nice to be there in the natural surrounding with the mountains in the background. I appreciated hearing about the English program at _____, and I feel that the teaching environment is very conducive to developing as a teacher and having the potential to do some research on the side within the education department.

From what we talked about, teaching English conversation within the context of the General English program and other departments would be a task that I am ready to carry out, having had the experience in Spain as a conversational English teacher for two years. I believe my skills and experience will match the requirements of this position. In addition, I want to take on an active role in the campus community while doing outreach with English tutoring one-on-one and participating in extracurricular activities, all to help the students' English language level. I also want to help prepare students for overseas study and assignments with Business English lessons and interview preparation.

What I wanted to emphasize that I didn't feel I was able to articulate at the interview was that I would choose _____ because of its emphasis on educating the whole person and providing a liberal education to all students. Its concept of instilling creativity in the next generation of leaders is something I really wanted to be part of. I want to teach at the _____ University to equip students to be global communicators, and that is why I am an educator. I want to use my experience as a teacher to inform the best research practices and have the chance to share my ideas with other teachers. This is why I hope to work within the College of Education to inform and inspire the new generation of teachers.

Lastly, I wanted to thank you for taking me around campus at the end of the interview. I was not expecting it, and I'm glad that I could become more acquainted with the campus. It was a wonderful way to show the entire circle of the campus.

I'm still in the process of applying to other schools at the moment, but I think that _____ is a top choice for working as an English teacher.

Thank you for your time and consideration. Have a great rest of your week.

Best regards,

John

Conclusion

It is vital that you include a thank you note in your application to the company. Usually, this will be a final impression that you can make on them prior to either getting a job offer or rejection letter. It is crucial that you emphasize your strengths and potential contributions to the company, because that will be what the interviewer is looking for in your application. Highlight your achievements and the mission of the institution where you are applying. Then, talk about how you would be a good fit for the company. Write using persuasive language that will convince your interviewer to hire you. You could be successful in landing the job.

Conclusion

In summary,

• Write an excellent application cover letter. No spelling or grammatical mistakes. Address the email to the person by name. Don't use mobile text language, like "c u soon." People really do! Follow the instructions in the job advertisement if you are responding to a job ad.

• If you are applying for a job where the company has not advertised, keep your cover letter brief.

• Always tell them what you can add to the business, only if you really can. I have had applicants stating that they can do all sorts of things when by their resume I can see that they can do nothing of the sort.

• Be honest

• Be eager, persistent, positive and passionate

• Follow up

• Learn from your mistakes. If you were not hired, ask why and learn from this.

• Arrive on time for your interview

• Be neatly dressed, have a good posture and a firm handshake.

• Be yourself

• Have questions prepared about what you want to ask the company. This is very important

• Most important of all, do your research on the company, go to their website, google them, research the industry, learn, learn, prepare and prepare.

• Go with a list of good questions. Often the questions you ask the interviewer are the most important part of the interview process. After doing good research, you will have a list of good questions. Make sure that they are good and that the information is not freely available on the internet and the company website.

• Make sure that your CV has no mistakes, is short and to the point, no spelling errors, no grammatical errors, that you give the dates of your employment, starting and ending.

• You could prepare a piece of work that will benefit the company to show them the quality of your work and bring it to the interview. Or something that shows the type of work you can do.

• If you are giving references, make sure you have the permission of the person whose name you are giving to use them as a reference and let them know that they might be expecting a call. If someone does not want to give you a reference, then better that they are not on the list. In some countries there is regulation on what a person can and can't say about an ex employee. I was once given someone's name as a reference and when I phoned her, she was not able to give me much of a reference at all.

• Google the founder of the company, or the HR person interviewing you. You will find a huge amount of information on this person and be able to quickly build up a feeling of what type of person they are. This will give you a good indication of the type of person interviewing you. When you meet with them you will then be able to connect with them on a personal level. This is important to do if you can.

• Social media profile. You can be sure many interviewers have done their research on you, so keep certain social media profiles private if you have any photo of wild parties that you would rather they not see!

• Remember that employers and HR department have a problem, they need a new staff member and need to fill it with the right person. You need to make their job easier, hold of your hand, say that you can do the job, want to do the job and will be an asset to their business. Of course all this needs to be true.

• When offered the job, consider the offer carefully and remember you can negotiate what you want. If you want more pay or more leave, ask for it, you never know. My much younger cousin is a great negotiator, she is great at what she does, but has no hesitation in asking for exactly what she wants when offered a new job. She knows her worth and can do an excellent quality of work to justify this. In my younger days, I was so old school, that when I was offered a job, I was very grateful and took it. I had 4 jobs before starting my business.

• Once you start your job, chances are you will be given a trial period, so work like a rock star. Attitude is key, willingness to do the little things that others don't want to do, greet everyone in the morning with a cheerful smile, if your boss enters the office after you, go and find them and say good morning. This is just a basic courtesy. Follow instructions and remember to report back. Often I will ask staff to do something and they might do it, but not send me an email saying it is done. Confirm that you have followed instructions. Communication with colleagues, your boss and customers is always important.

Okay, so in signing off, just in case you missed something . . . remember preparation is key. I cannot overemphasize this enough. Research on the company and the person interviewing you, will give you such confidence in the interview. I sometimes hear people talking about their employers and it just sounds like want, want, want, want more money, want more leave **etc.** How about give, what do I give to you to deserve an increase or more leave? As an employer the happiness of my staff is paramount to me in every way. I want a happy team and will do all I can to motivate, inspire and help my staff grow. I also want to pay them as much as the business can afford and above the industry norm. Employers do make mistakes and one of the worst is employing someone who is wrong for your company in terms of culture, work ethic and ability to do the job. I have made this mistake before more than once. So the hiring of new staff is extremely serious and I am always delighted to hire someone fantastic as my team is. But it really is a problem to find great new staff and many businesses feel this way, it is a long and tedious process, so if you can make it any easier for us, then you will stand out from the crowd of applicants.

I really do hope that this book has been of benefit to you. So in ending, preparation is key, check your cover letter and cv for spelling and grammatical errors, follow up, be keen and just so don't forget, preparation is key.

Made in the USA
Coppell, TX
30 September 2020